Uphill Walkers

ALSO BY MADELEINE BLAIS:

The Heart Is an Instrument: Portraits in Journalism
In These Girls, Hope Is a Muscle

Uphill Walkers

Memoir of
a Family

Madeleine Blais

ATLANTIC MONTHLY PRESS
New York

Published simultaneously in Canada
Printed in the United States of America

FIRST EDITION

Library of Congress Cataloging-in-Publication Data

Blais, Madeleine.
Uphill walkers : memoir of a family / Madeleine Blais.
p. cm.
ISBN 0-87113-792-5
1. Single-parent families—Massachusetts—Holyoke. 2. Fatherless families—Massachusetts—Holyoke. 3. Irish American Catholics—Massachusetts—Holyoke. I. Title.
HQ759.915 .B55 2001
305.85'6'0974426—dc21   00-065059

DESIGN BY LAURA HAMMOND HOUGH

Atlantic Monthly Press
841 Broadway
New York, NY 1003

01 02 03 04   10 9 8 7 6 5 4 3 2 1

For Nicholas and Justine, Rob and Drew,
Christopher and Gregory

Our beginnings never know our ends.
—T. S. ELIOT

In the first place, you should know that Cranford was ruled almost enitrely by women.
—ELIZABETH GASKELL

Chapter One

The World of My Father

MY FATHER DIED WHEN I WAS FIVE, AND ALL MY LIFE, I HAVE WONDERED if he ever thought about how it would all turn out.

What I know of him is skimpy and cobbled together from the obituary in the local paper, his yearbook from college, a few letters sent to my mother during the war. After he died we had no contact with his side of the family. My mother explained that both his parents were dead, which was not entirely true: his mother was alive, though hospitalized, incapacitated in some mysterious, unspoken way. We had a blurry hunch that there had been some kind of friction between my mother and his only sister. There were other Blaises in Holyoke. It was a common name, like Shea in Chicopee. When we were asked, as we sometimes were, if Leo or Clement or Roland Blais was any relation, we were schooled by our mother to answer no, emphatically, and to offer no further explanation, though chances are we weren't telling the truth and we were part of an intense cousinry that my mother, for some reason, wished to deny. We dodged discussions of the cause of death, and if people assumed, as they often did, that our father died of a heart attack, we were to nod in agreement. Cancer was in those days even more frightening because it was shameful, a judgment. My mother believed in euphemisms. We were taught to say he was "deceased," because it sounded more genteel, but which, in our agony to get it right, as often as not came out "diseased," adding to the confusion and prolonging the discussion.

Of course our mother mentioned him from time to time, but what she offered were scraps of memories, drained of any real substance. Your father liked pea soup, or, he enjoyed a round of cards. One time he brought home a hand-crafted pine chair from the Eastern States Exposition. He liked golf and football and fishing. Once, in an expansive mood, he brought home four Easter dresses for his four little girls. He and a couple of his pals sponsored a middleweight boxer who had done well in a couple of appearances at the Valley Arena. He was a man's man and even the men cried at his funeral.

One time I talked to someone who'd gone to dental school with him at the University of Maryland, and he said that when they car-pooled home, they had a favorite Italian restaurant they stopped at somewhere in Delaware. When I must have betrayed in my expression an eagerness for something of greater substance, he added, "The guy who took over your father's office on Maple Street wasn't nearly as good. He ended up," and here he paused, as if to hammer home just how low my father's successor had sunk, "at the mall." A friend of my father's has told me that every November on the anniversary of his death he arranges for a mass to be said in his memory in Fort Lauderdale.

Holidays were always a big deal in our house, a marker against the march of days, but we were not always sure what they meant. "Happy Ash Wednesday," we would say, or "Merry Armistice Day."

At Christmas the year that my father died we had an unbelievable bounty, an avalanche of dolls and wagons and nurse's kits. Grief and greed commingled in my mind, mutual parasites. The more you lose, the more you want. My toy of choice was not found under the tree. Instead, it was a paper bag filled with the cards that came to our house after my father died. I could not read, but I liked their glossy feel, the big letters, the indisputable importance that attached to any envelope with a two-cent stamp. One day, the bag disappeared. So, instead of playing with the cards, I looked for them. Had Lizzie, our housekeeper, stored them in the pantry? The laundry hamper? Had my mother put them in the linen chest in the back hallway upstairs, the same hallway that would later contain her moldering collection of unused gowns and rarely worn suits? There were so many places to check. Maybe my older brother Raymond had hidden them in the cellar, that musty series of rooms made of stone, one of which had a Dutch oven in which occupants of the house had probably cooked meals in the summer a century earlier.

The search became a game and occupied me for hours. I prayed to Saint Anthony, patron saint of lost objects, for a reunion with those cards. Over the years, I have had the impression we abused his goodwill, praying to him at the slightest hint of something's being missing, even the most humble object, someone's misplaced hairbrush or pogo stick or Halloween candy. To this day missing objects rattle me: when for some reason the scissors fail to materialize in the scissors drawer, I can feel a rage and despair totally at odds with the loss. Before any major trip or vacation, I enter a state of high distractibility in which I become convinced that my good watch or my favorite earrings have disappeared for all of time. When I find something I really like at a store, I am often tempted by an impulse to make a duplicate purchase. Once, during a reconstruction, a window was boarded up in a house where I lived, and for a long time afterward it recurred to me as an image in my dreams, restored and gleaming. In another dream, the house I live in has a whole extra house inside it but no one will acknowledge it.

"You were five when he died," people always say. "Five," as if involved in some complex computation. And then they ask the question I have come to loathe, "Do you remember him?" I experience it as an impertinence—what right does someone have to ask something so personal?—and at the same time it stirs up a feeling of inadequacy.

What little I may have known about my father once upon a time has been both overexposed and undernourished. Long ago, my father began to fade in the way a desert plant, rinsed by too much sun, denied its share of rain, eventually grows vague and dry.

Do I remember him?

The answer is yes and no.

Yes, maybe.

No, probably.

His obituary appeared on the front page above the fold in the *Springfield Union* on Monday morning, November 17, 1952:

Dr. R. E. Blais, Granby Dentist, Dies in Holyoke
Had Practiced in Paper City for 12 Years;
Served in Navy.

Holyoke, Nov. 16 — Dr. Raymond E. Blais of Center St., Granby, practicing dentist in this city for about 12 years and well known in professional circles, died today at the Holyoke Hospital after an illness of about two weeks. He was a veteran of World War II and served in the Navy.

Born in this city he was the son of Mrs. Annie (Nolin) Blais and the late Phileas Blais. He was educated in the local schools and received his Bachelor of Arts degree from Holy Cross College in Worcester in the class of 1934. Dr. Blais entered the University of Maryland Dental School from which he graduated in 1937. He took a postgraduate course at New York University and interned for one year at the Jersey City Medical Center.

During the war, he served in the Navy and was commissioned lieutenant, senior grade. After his discharge from the service, Dr. Blais resumed his practice here and had offices in the Medical Arts building.

Dr. Blais was a member of the Holyoke Lodge of the Elks; Holyoke Council No. 90, Knights of Columbus; the Kiwanis Club; the Beavers Club; the Holyoke Dental Association and the Holy Name Society of the Immaculate Heart of Mary Church in Granby. He also had memberships in the state and national dental organizations.

His leaves his wife, the former Maureen Shea of Chicopee Falls, a son, Raymond, four daughters, Madeleine, Jacqueline, Christina, and Maureen, all at home; his mother, Mrs. Annie Blais and a sister, Viola Kettell, both of Holyoke.

The funeral will take place at the John B. Shea funeral home Wednesday at 9 with a solemn high mass of requiem in the Immaculate Heart of Mary Church, Granby, at 10. Burial will be in St. Patrick's Cemetery, Chicopee Falls.

Throughout my childhood, this flaking document was stored in the drawer of yet another piece of furniture that we had to be careful not to dent or damage because it, like so many other artifacts of dubious objective value in the house, might be Worth Something Someday. I treasured this record in part because it relieved me of the misleading burden of dead-end fantasies. We had not lost our father to a bitter divorce, to abandonment, to prison, all of which would have been far more desirable. No, he was gone for good, gone for all of time, and here, for what it was worth, was proof. On the left ear by the masthead the paper advertised itself as costing "three cents everywhere." I have always liked that ambitious everywhere, the implied conviction that this paper had a worldwide web of potential readers. On the right ear, the weather was predicted as "partly cloudy today and tomorrow." There was a weight to the paper beyond the mere ounces of space it occupied in the universe, a kind of gravity that linked my father's death with all the other events of that day on the crowded front page with its eight columns of news.

The United States government acknowledged it had been testing the H-bomb in the Pacific.

Korean truce talks bogged down at the United Nations.

Other people had died, including a woman from Bennington, Vermont, who left a daughter named Edith, and a fifteen-year-old boy from Granby whose car rolled over on a country road.

The paper is filled with incidental sociology.

In the world my father left behind, race was as highly charged a subject as it is today. Black people received two mentions. Under the headline "White Drummer to Wed Negress" we learned that Louis Bellson, Jr., a musician in Duke Ellington's band, planned to wed jazz singer Pearl Bailey. A photo shows the good-looking couple, heads resting cheek to cheek, with a caption in which Bellson "denied a New York report he had jilted a white show girl, Iris Burton, of Brooklyn" in order to run off to London to marry the singer. What the paper doesn't say is that Bellson was Bailey's fifth husband, and it also doesn't say—how could it? the fullness of time had yet to unfold—the marriage to Bellson lasted thirty-seven years, until her death at the age of seventy-two.

The other black man who received attention on that day was Paul Robeson, the son of a slave, who sang a signature version of "Old Man River." He had visited Hartford for a concert and drew an audience of seven hundred along with two hundred and fifty policemen. His inflammatory message on that evening was that in his opinion the "white ruling class" in the United States sought to keep "Negroes in their place" and he refused to "go along with that."

In the world my father left, want ads were divided by gender. Women could become clerks and typists or an undraped artist's model for museum classes at Smith College. They could be a seamstress or a nurse. They could work as a waitress at the Arcade luncheonette on State Street in Springfield or as a dining room maid at the Clarke School for the Deaf in Northampton. They could be the housekeeper for two motherless boys. They could be a feeder, a folder, or a shaker at the Wells Laundry on Franklin Street.

There were at least four times as many ads for men, who could be mechanics of cars or air conditioners or furnaces or airplanes, assistant foremen, chauffeurs, grocery store managers, gauge makers, plaster molders, TV repairmen, newspaper printers, chemists, draftsmen, druggists, wood workers, tire and car salesmen, elevator operators, circulation managers, haberdashery salesmen, bellmen, porters, short-order cooks, shoe salesmen, shipping clerks, tool makers, truck drivers, time-study men. If a man had a way with words and a college degree, he could work at an advertising agency. A "jolly man" was needed for about four hours a day from November 28 to December 24 at the Forbes & Wallace department store.

In sports, among the schoolboys, Chicopee and Westfield both had good football seasons, and someone named Pete Pippone of Greenfield was said to be a "slick kicker."

For amusement readers could go to the all-new 1953 Ice Capades and see *Brigadoon* at the coliseum in West Springfield.

Or, they could tune into the new flickering hearth with its black-and-white fuzzy flames. They could watch television. Three channels were available, with shows such as *Guiding Light*, *Howdy Doody*, *Gabby Hayes*, *Musical Mom*, *Owl Theater*, *Daily Prayer*, and *Nightcap News*.

In the world my father left behind, readers could plan ahead and get a ticket to a flute recital by Miss Margaret Hanford, who would be accompanied by a string quartet on the following Monday evening at the Women's Club House on Spring Street. Selections from her upcoming program included Mozart's Quartet in D, reported to be a favorite of Albert Einstein's, and the seldom performed "Goldfinch Concerta" by Vivaldi, which, when executed with just the right combination of deft touches and well-timed trills, at least according to the *Springfield Union* on November 17, 1952, results in a kind of celestial warbling that might fool even a bird.

Chapter Two

5 Center Street

THE HOUSE WHERE I GREW UP SITS TOO CLOSE TO THE ROAD FOR SOME tastes, as old New England houses so often do, but it has a certain shopworn grace. It is across from the library and looks out on a small patch of grass in which a large rock with a plaque memorializes the town's veterans. This knoll was the annual destination of the Memorial Day parade, all those Scouts and trumpeters and aging men in hard-to-button uniforms, a spectacle made all the more endearing because the marchers always outnumbered the audience. When we were children, we felt honored in some morbid way that the house had a front row seat on a pivotal American ceremony in which the living salute the dead.

There were ghosts even before we moved in, though naturally we added some of our own. These invisible intruders were accepted as only normal in a house built (if the records are right) in the late eighteenth century. Their noises, the unexpected rustling sound in a remote hallway or the odd guttural half laugh from behind a curtain plumped by the wind, joined the noises of children at play, as we fought one another in mock battle, armed with all kinds of weapons, especially cap guns and feathered arrows aimed at each other's heartbeats.

The purchase price of twenty-two thousand postwar dollars was a pretty and an optimistic penny in 1950. The heavily mortgaged deal included a red barn and a grape arbor and a private well, more fetching in concept than in actuality because of the skittishness of the pump. The four acres divided themselves into a front yard, side yard, backyard, and garden yard, and beyond all that, a wild unkempt field demarcated by the fierce, sweat-filled, labor-intensive barrier of an old stone wall. The house had five thousand five hundred square feet. By the cramped urban standards of my father, born as he was in the most depleted part of Holyoke with the sense sometimes that everything is rationed, even clean air and sunlight, this was opulence indeed.

My parents met at a New Year's Eve party during the depression. My mother had finished her four years at a state teachers' college and was living at home with her parents. They met because someone told a joke and when my mother threw back her head to laugh, my father asked, "Who is that lovely woman?" The joke and the punchline are of course long forgotten, but from that fleeting laughter flowed a dense series of repercussions: marriage, children, a Maytag dishwasher, the freezer from Sears, Lincoln Logs and Tinkertoys and Betsy Wetsy and Tiny Tears dolls, velveteen dresses with lace collars, Pontiacs, Ramblers, and Chevelles. There would be loss and sorrow and even a few more laughs. But what if on that day he hadn't been moved by her bounce, by the unusual lightness of being, the long neck thrown back, the cascade of dark hair tossed without thought? That lovely woman, wishing even then for a life with more expansive borders, told a wishful lie about her circumstances and said that she was pursuing a graduate degree in English at Columbia, thus postponing their courtship while he waited for her to finish this mythical spring semester before calling on her that following June.

To be of Canadian ancestry, as he was, and to be all-Irish as she was, made them fiercely ethnic in their time. It was my father who married up. He was the son of a factory foreman from Holyoke, though for years I had the vague notion that his father was a bricklayer—hard, even boring, facts were sometimes difficult to come by in my childhood. My father was born in the flats of Holyoke, the established landing place for the lowliest of the newcomers in that traditionally divided town, the French having replaced the Irish who have currently been replaced by Puerto Ricans. In that low-lying warren, filled to this day with grim buildings and clotheslines dangling ever weary garments, he grew up speaking Canadish, which is what we children came to call the spotty French you used to hear more commonly in the Connecticut River Valley. His bride-to-be was the daughter of a doctor in Chicopee who had gone to Georgetown and spent a postgraduate summer in Vienna. Only a few letters from him to her survive their courtship, containing the trivia of his schoolwork and their logistics intermingled with avowals of undying love:

> I've got to give my first injection for anesthesia this week.
> I don't know how it will be, but I'll be hoping and
> praying. It should be a lot of fun though.
>
> The dance is definitely set for April 23, and after the
> initiation next week, I shall be able to give you every
> detail.
>
> You know what I would like to do right now. Just
> hold you and squeeze the breath right out of you. Really,

I can think of nothing better. Darling, I think you better
get working on a trip to Baltimore this fall. Anytime
would be fine, and the sooner the better, so get going,
honey, and we'll be together again.

   I think that is all for now, my sweet, and I'll write
more soon. I love you (if I were a poet or a romanticist, I
might be able to put it in a more delightful manner.)
However, it still goes.

Love, Ray

They married in October of 1941 to the strains of "Panis
Angelicus." Maureen Shea wore a gown of duchess slipper satin
made in classic princess lines; Irish lace edged the sleeves and
the sweetheart neckline. Her veil was fastened in a scalloped
Tudor bonnet, and she carried a cascade of bouvardia, roses, and
orchids. The ceremony was followed by a wedding breakfast, and
the couple left later on a motor trip, the bride traveling in a brown
wool suit with Persian lamb trimming, headed for a honeymoon
at Crocker Lake Camps in Jackman, Maine, where they stayed
for a fee of four dollars per day per person. A brochure that
survives says, "This is an excellent camp for ladies, also a good
place to send your family during the summer months. Meals are
served in a clean and pleasant dining-room, overlooking the lake,
with fresh eggs, milk and cream, berries, and fruit, and vegetables
from our garden." The drinking water was from a high mountain stream. Fishing and hunting (partridge, deer, bear) licenses
were available.

   Their first child arrived in the spring in 1944, during a war,
marking him as a child of hope. Our father was stationed at a
land facility, the U.S. Naval Training Center USS *Burston*. Tele-
grams were sent: "SHIP RAYMOND JUNIOR LAUNCHED
SMOOTH SAILING AHEAD" and "MOTHER AND SON

DOING WELL." But within days my mother was worried. The baby had been born premature, weighing only five and one quarter pounds, and he kept spitting up the milk he was given to drink. At three months he was only eleven pounds. For several months, he lost weight rather than gained it. All her life, she remembered this statistic with a panicked clarity. Was he suffering from a case of what they now call failure to thrive? Why wouldn't the doctors help find something that would satisfy those colicky outbursts? It was an image that would not leave her consciousness: the robust fat-legged newborn she had envisioned was small and puny, shrinking before her eyes into a pale and listless creature. Finally, a formula was found. The baby began to prosper. (She never stopped searching for an explanation. In 1987, the *Springfield Union* ran a *Washington Post* wire-service story entitled: "Infant Psychiatry: Birth of a New Specialty," which she saved and pored over.)

After the war, my father chose to move to Granby because it had been a summer retreat when he was a child, deep country where you could ride horses and be paid to pick corn and beans and tomatoes as well as to bale hay. In those days the chief product was meadowland; later, after the war, it would seem to be quickie houses, or perhaps children. It was such a quiet sort of place that when the Public Works Department decided to stencil the words, "Stop, Look, Listen," at several intersections, a photographer was dispatched from the local paper.

The family home on 5 Center Street was once visited by a columnist from one of the local papers for one of those "At Home with . . ." feature stories:

> Last Sunday we stopped at Dr. Blais' lovely Granby home
> to accept a long-standing invitation to view his collection
> of Currier prints and found that the Blais home not only

contains many unusual relics of prints but a wonderful assortment of other items of early Americana as well.

The house was originally a colonial house of the late
1700's which has been skillfully expanded with wings and
additions which faithfully preserve the beauty of the original old homestead. Its cheerful red window shutters and
spotless white clapboards proclaim it as a house where happiness and comfort abound.

The first change my parents made was to the goldfish pond
in the garden yard. My mother thought goldfish were fascinating: their fat gleaming bodies, urgent with allegory, growing as
big as their environment permits. But she could not shake the
vision of one of us—at the time of the move she already had
four—toddling off to see the fishes and being discovered, hours
later, face down. And so the pond was drained and filled with
soft sand, a large dry square, with a row of pines lining the far
end.

The front door opened onto an unusual center staircase so
that on either side was a full living room, like the right ventricle
and left ventricle of the heart. One was formal with a fieldstone
fireplace whose embers predictably launched my mother into
one of her brooding moods. The other was less formal, the even-
tual roost of that great miracle of the fifties, the TV. When you
turned it on, it emitted a strange white light that I thought might
be, if not the Holy Ghost himself, then his first cousin, an un-
mistakable and eerie whoosh. We were the first family in our
neighborhood to get a TV. On Sunday nights we had root beer
and ice cream. This made us rich, sort of. I remember visiting
my father's office in Holyoke, in which there was a long table
where presumably he fashioned crowns or dentures but where I
thought, since he said that at work he made money, he drew

dollars. Our TV attracted kids from all the other houses—the
Brooks kids, the McCools, the O'Sullivans, the Kosciuskos—all
stopping by to watch *The Gene Autry Show* or *You Are There* or
I Remember Mama.

Off the formal living room was the Green Room, a winter-
ized sunroom, which contained the piano and the hi-fi. The dining room looked out on the garden yard, where the neutered
pond offered its pool of dirt. The house had red shutters and a
red front door, above which, like an eyebrow, was a half-moon
window.

Most houses of its vintage have wide uneven hardwood floors
filled with an implied history of a grand lineage as the tallest,
oldest pine in a former life. But this house had stone flooring
from Italy that was cold and unappealing, colorless slabs soon
covered with rugs. Magazines of the time heavily promoted fancy
ovens as the executive desks of a good cook, so modern appli-
ances, top of the line, were added to the large country kitchen
with its view of the big yard and the barn and three or four
apple trees whose yield was always, unfortunately, wormy.
Over my mother's not too strenuous objections, my father had
someone demolish the graceful octagonal porch off the kitchen
and replace it with a mega-porch, four times as big and not
nearly as beckoning. The day the concrete was poured we got
to carve our initials in the soft belly of the steps before it turned
to stone.

My father died unexpectedly, if one can say any death by cancer is unexpected. Some cancers are quicker than others are, and
he had one of the quickest kinds, attacking the body at its hidden center, the pancreas. He became ill enough to acknowledge
that something was wrong in September, right around the time
that Rocky Marciano knocked out "Jersey Joe" Walcott for a heavy-

weight boxing title in thirteen rounds. He died two month later, during deer hunting season, just before the big snows.

I found out about his death in a haphazard way from my older brother. I can still hear his voice, its unsettling singsong, bringing the news.

"Daddy's dead."

We were sitting in the living room with the TV. He was eight, and I was five and one quarter years old. I called my brother Rayboy to distinguish him from my father, Raymond, which I heard as Rayman. Already I knew that Rayboy was not the most trustworthy of big brothers. He made fun of my Buster Brown shoes, thick leather contraptions, saying they were for old ladies. He lied about the Davy Crockett song, saying he wrote the words himself. He was disloyal in public and liked to lead other kids in a chant meant to humiliate me:

> Matt, the brat
> The skunk
> In the rat.

It worked perfectly.

I was left to wonder: why would my brother be moved to tell the truth about anything, even the death of a parent? Yet, I was tuned in. For weeks, I had to concede, since September, something unusual had been happening in the house. Whispers, whispers, whispers. One day Daddy took a trip to Boston to a clinic. When he came home, he said maybe he had something called dyed beets. He used to be strong and he could pick us all up at one time, one huge scoop, and then he was doubled over, stricken with pain. His skin was yellow like the silky stuff at the top of corn. It turned out he didn't have dyed beets, so he went to a different place for more tests. Maybe he would get better if he had what we children called "those vacation shots," like they gave you for the measles, which left a white splash on the skin, playful as ocean foam.

"Daddy's dead," my brother kept saying. I remember looking at his wide-open mouth. Rayboy was lucky. He had out teeth and in teeth. I only had in teeth.

As much as I wanted this to be another of my brother's horrible tricks, I had a strong feeling it wasn't.

I looked outside the large window at the once green, now brown and rusting yard of late November and could see more and more grown-ups pouring into the house, big black cars filled with friends of the family, men who'd gone to Holy Cross with my father, my mother's sister from New York, the minister from the parsonage next door. They were pale and silent. Now and again you could hear the sharp strike of a match and soon smell the smoke from their Pall Malls and L&Ms. I could not read but I could identify letters, and I knew the joke.

Do you know why L&M got kicked out of the alphabet?
They got caught smoking.

The grown-ups appeared paralyzed, especially my mother with her dark hair and red lips smeared with color so they always looked like crushed petals, her eyes blank. The men radiated tweed and rectitude. There was no use running to Nana, my mother's mother. A blur of wrinkles and spectacles and nervous gestures, she was usually fixed in her chair, distant and frail, sucking on peppermint Life Savers and reading historical fiction and, somewhat surprisingly, given her reserved nature, westerns.

I began a frantic search for Lizzie, who could usually be counted on: Elizabeth Cavanaugh, the Shea family housekeeper, who came to this country from the Dingle Peninsula at the age of seventeen, following her older sisters in a chain migration. When she first arrived, she found herself weeping nonstop tears. Then someone gave her a banana and she brightened, basically for the rest of her life, figuring that any country with fresh fruit couldn't be all bad. She began taking care of my mother as a newborn. In age, Lizzie's hair was still red, if faded. All she ever did, and her energy for it never flagged, was radiate goodwill. Usually she was in the kitchen, but on this day the Sunday morning odor of homemade bread, the friendly greeting of flour and butter wrapping itself around the house, was missing.

Was something wrong with Lizzie, too?

"Daddy's dead," my brother said again.

He was trying not to cry. He kept turning his back, fiddling with the television set, a massive contraption even bigger and uglier than my shoes. Because it was a Sunday morning when Ray informed me of our father's death, there was nothing to watch except bishops in beanies. The transmission was fuzzy. We both kept poking at the TV, slapping it on the top and sides, until my brother said, with manly authority, "I bet it's on the blink."

Do I really remember someone saying, "It's been decided. Maureen is adamant. None of the children is going to the funeral," or is it that the words have somehow become encoded over the course of time? She refused to attend her husband's funeral with all those children tugging at her. My main reaction, other than the empty feeling that goes along with grief, was complete confusion. What did it mean, any of it? My mother is adamant; my mother is a damn mint. I had never been to a funeral, but I knew it was one of those ceremonies you had to be quiet at and where men had to remove their hats, yet one more puzzling detail. Why? Were hats noisy?

"Madeleine will go to Holyoke to the Mahoneys. Ray Junior is going to the Murrays."

Nothing could have proved the point more dramatically than this precipitous farming out of the older children. It must be true. He must be dead. But I wondered about the meaning of the word. "What's 'dead'?" I kept asking everyone.

Either they didn't hear me or the enormousness of the question, its boggling philosophical grandiosity, managed to keep the silence afloat. My inquiry was so naked, it seems to me now to contain a kind of pornography.

"Lizzie," I heard someone say, "can stay home with the younger children." People nodded and glanced at my three baby sisters: Jacqueline at three, Christina at two, Maureen at one. *They're the lucky ones*, went the common refrain. *They're too young to remember, and you can't miss what you never knew.*

Within weeks after my father's death there were more whispers in the house, less sad than the ones we heard in November. My mother kept getting bigger and bigger while her face grew more and more white and pale and narrow. And I knew that a baby was coming. My reaction was mixed. I pretended to be excited, but deep down I thought: *Oh, no, not another one.* My sisters still seemed useless to me: whiny, malodorous appendages who relied on me to tie their delinquent shoelaces and to tell them which hand was right and which was left. It was my job to keep them from darting across Route 202 with its surprisingly heavy traffic and to prevent coins from being stuck in their ears during magic tricks. I helped them pick out their clothes in the morning. Clashing was the chief fashion sin with which I was familiar, and I saw my job as a matter of keeping plaids and stripes, pinks and oranges, Belfast and Dublin, apart. I taught them the joy of licorice: "See, it makes your spit black."

Everyone said they hoped this final baby would be another boy, as if this would be a blessing: a male to replace a male, a sign that our luck was changing. Girls in our family were, by our very commonality, devalued coinage. When my mother left for the hospital, I told her I hoped she would bring me back something, as if she were off on a shopping jaunt to downtown Holyoke, to Steiger's or Forbes & Wallace. "And," I added, "something good." My mother remembers the formal way I phrased it: "Let it not be a ribbon."

When my younger brother was born on June 1, 1953, he was given the name Michael, and two middle names, Francis and Anthony, so two saints could watch over him. Saint Francis is the patron saint of nature, the saint who loved birds and got them to sit in his hand. It is a truism that a child born after a major death is often turned into a symbol of hope. Eager eyes chart his progress, grasping at proof not only that life goes on, but that it can be just as stupid with happiness as it had been before. To honor Michael's birth, a statue of Saint Francis was placed in the garden yard, his thick-featured plaster gaze overlooking the extinct pond. The air of wonder that accompanied Michael's arrival fed into the excitement that greeted two other events from around the world. His birth coincided with the coronation of Queen Elizabeth and the first successful expedition up Mt. Everest. Whenever in the late fifties I saw a puzzle map that breathlessly exclaimed, "Hawaii and Alaska included!" I thought of Michael with his distended little boy belly and his friendly face framed by light curls, curls our mother often touched with maternal hunger, with hands that lingered. The Blais kids: Raymond, Madeleine, Jacqueline, Christina, Maureen, and "Michael included!"

The summer of Michael's birth, Raymond got to go away to camp. It was assumed that a certain antsiness on his part, a vague disgruntlement, might be squelched if he had the wholesome experience of time away with other boys and with male counselors in the fresh air. My father's friend Tim Collins, the one who ensures the annual mass, sent my mother a note. She saved it, along with so much else, as consolation, and as proof of something about my father and about the past, its hold on her, on all of us.

Dear Maureen,

A week ago or so I wrote to Mr. L.W. Francis at New Haven and told him that I would like to assume the expense of Ray's stay at Camp Leo this July, as I know if the tables were turned Ray would have been the first one to have done something like this for my child.

Today I received a reply from Mr. Francis stating that the fee had already been paid by you. He suggested that Ray might stay for two months. You can use your own judgment. Meantime, in memory of my best pal I am enclosing a check to help underwrite the expense of Ray's stay at Leo this summer.

One phrase leapt out, the unsolicited tribute in it:

If the tables were turned Ray would have been the first one to have done something like this.

Others of my father's friends followed Tim Collins's suit with actions of their own, including doctors like Tim Murray, Eddie Welch, and Ed Mahoney. They saw us throughout our childhood at a moment's notice, checking Christina's knee when she got water on it, removing from Michael's nostril a fat purple crayon, prescribing hydrocortisone cream for me when my face broke out in mysterious blotches, never once sending a bill.

I watched with envy as Raymond's trunk was being packed, while he paraded about with his new canteen and pre-stamped postcards for writing home.

There was no kindergarten in town the year I was five, so as I awaited the beginning of first grade, I was in a fever to learn, the kind of child that would be instantly clasped by teachers. I think of that time after my father's death, before the start of school, as the loneliest time of my life. Despite all the people in the house it had been bereft, marked by a sad hush, except at night, when I thought I could hear soft weeping noises. For a big house, it never seemed to have enough bedrooms or enough privacy. My mother had a room; Jacqueline and I shared another, which we decorated with lipstick flowers, using the deep red shade that was in favor in the early fifties. There was one for Raymond and Michael, one for Lizzie and Christina and Maureen, one for Nana.

In first grade, I recognized in the way my teacher, Mrs. Knightly (whose very name possessed a perfect balance of chivalry and darkness), looked at me—the slightly longer gazes, an undisguised curiosity—that as a half orphan I was one of the lesser but still real wonders of the world, a child who had been dealt a difficult hand. Our town didn't have any divorce then, and it didn't seem to have any other dead fathers. Yet we were hardly the worst off, not by a long shot.

The kids who were the worst off were the state kids, who were always unscrubbed and several years behind in their schooling. The state paid people to let them live on their farms, and the children were expected to sweeten the ransom with their labor. More often than not, one would have a mangled leg or a hand with parts of the fingers missing because he'd operated a thresher or a tractor before he was really old enough. It was understood that their futures were as bleak as their present and their pasts. The teachers put them in the back row and never called on them. I learned early the paradox of public schools, theoretically the fairest places in the world, welcoming one and all, but in practice often guilty of a callous triage.

My father had left very little insurance: he had not planned to die. But there was enough to pay off the mortgage, and there was a little telephone stock, which meant that for a few years we subscribed to the *Wall Street Journal* as well as the *Transcript-Telegram*, the *Springfield Union*, and the *Springfield Daily News*.

We had the big house, the TV, and an overlay of grown-ups including my mother, my grandmother, Lizzie, and from time to time, my mother's brother, Uncle Dermot. We had parties and studio portraits from Grenier-Ducharme of ourselves in dresses with sashes and ruffles. We had toys and of course, when we got old enough, a series of infernal lessons, which took up less time than one might imagine because, except for elocution with Mrs. Guild, they always fizzled for one reason or another. It was too much work to get to class. The ballet teacher went suddenly and disastrously modern, specializing in a bizarre jungle dance that required us to crouch as we crossed the stage in leopard-skin leotards with our toes pointed inward. The piano lady dyed her hair blond, went back to college, and left her husband.

But most of all we had airs and aspirations. At her most determined, our mother saw us as part of an overarching narrative, a kind of pioneering, live sitcom in which *so what if the father wasn't around to know best?* The weekly plot would not vary. Widow carries on! One-parent family beats odds! Kids have six-for-six success rate! Everything stays the same! For her own part, she seemed to fare best when she pictured herself as a character playing a role, a fey combination of Scarlett O'Hara and Lucille Ball, turning draperies into gowns, pratfalls into soft-shoe. We would attract a prestigious corporate sponsor such as Monsanto ("Better Living through Chemistry") or Maxwell House coffee

("Good to the Last Drop"). For a theme song there were any number of maudlin Irish ballads to choose from. We wanted to be part of the nationwide sweep of progress, the coming together of ingenuity and imagination resulting in one breakthrough or invention after another. Every day, it seemed, there was something new to be grateful for: a vaccine or a harvester, commercial jet service to Europe, the first kidney transplant, power steering, artificial heart valves, even nonstick saucepans.

On the playground in Granby in the 1950s we jumped rope to the time-tested chants. We had word games that involved going through the alphabet and naming kinds of cars and their manufacturers: "American Motors, Buick, Chevrolet, Dodge, Edsel, Ford. . . ." We sometimes switched to cigarette brands or movie stars.

We were racists, of the most unthinking variety.

"Eenie meanie minee mo," we said when picking someone to be "it." "Catch a nigger by the toe."

World War II and the Holocaust barely grazed our consciousness. We thought Hitler and his followers walked funny, and for some reason we often repeated the joke, "What did Hitler's mother say when she had a baby?" "Hotsy totsy, another Nazi."

The most disturbing game, day in, day out, morning recess, lunch recess, and afternoon recess, was one in which you could spread a disease that was worse than cooties. You got it from a girl whose name I have changed, but consider that it might have been something like Beverly Kaye, a quiet grayish sort of girl who never fought back. She stood there like a box of oatmeal on a shelf while people tagged her and then sought to contaminate others with this terrible virus that afflicted its victims with oily hair and a dirty, ill-fitting coat.

Tag.

"You've got Kabies."

Tag.

"Pass it on."

Tag.

"Oh, no, it's the bell."

Teasing is the basic discourse of people caught in certain kinds of childhoods. Diminished people are the first to diminish others.

"Uphill walkers, are you ready?"

There was a self-conscious boom in the voice of Maureen McCool, our patrol leader when she was in the eighth grade and I was in the first. Across her chest was a white sash, attached to a belt around her waist. We stood at attention, the girls in their plaid dresses, the boys in their striped shirts. In our small ink-stained hands we held black metal boxes with thermoses clanging inside along with the gnawed apple cores and crumpled waxed paper containing the residue of our deviled ham sandwiches, which for some reason we always saved to throw away at home. It wasn't until I was in the fourth grade in 1956, one year before Sputnik, that Granby, Massachusetts, entered the Modern Age and we got a cafeteria that served hot lunch, in which the offerings were like object lessons in a color chart: red Sloppy Joes, orange canned peaches, green Jell-O.

"All present," we would reply, "aye, aye, ma'am." How eager we were to turn everything into a parliamentary procedure or a military operation.

"Well, then," she would say, "let's go," to which we replied, "Forward march."

And so we would head home toward the center of town, leaving behind our classrooms filled with thirty or forty students, overseen by a single teacher who invariably claimed to have eyes in the back of her head, leaving behind the smell of peanut butter on nearly everyone's post-lunch breath, the graininess of the dust from the chalk used to draw a hopscotch grid, the cold metal bars of the jungle gym, off limits for most girls in their skirts, except for the more daring or thoughtless. Everyone, even the most backward child, knew how to pronounce, if not spell, the word *antidisestablishmentarianism*. "I like Ike" buttons in flag colors brightened many corduroy jackets and wool sweaters, though not ours. In 1956 I had my first, and last, fistfight, defending Adlai Stevenson.

The children who lived close enough to walk to and from school were divided into two groups, the uphill patrol and the downhill patrol. Despite the more challenging nature of our journey, we uphill walkers thought of ourselves as lucky not to have to take a bus, and lucky also in our direction. "Up" was the anthem of the fifties. It meant progress, prestige. It implied hard work and inevitable rewards. Vance Packard's book *The Status Seekers* caused people all over America to try to figure out whether they were middle middle class, lower middle class, upper middle class, or the category most coveted by my mother, lower upper class. We were the kids on the common; our houses were considered if not better, at least older and bigger. The downhill walkers lived in the kind of housing I admired, convenience-laden postwar ranches in which the picture window in the front and the garage on the side were given equal architectural weight. Some defect in my nature had turned me into a person who would gladly trade charm for efficiency. A bit beyond the ranches was the trailer park, which occupied a huge field and was always the subject of controversy as to whether it possessed the requisite toniness for a town such as ours, a somewhat comic concern given our big calling cards, which included a place called Dinoland, in which the owner advertised dinosaur tracks *and* the cure for leukemia; more than one turkey farm, their slippery landscapes composed of feathers, mud, and manure; and, at the edge of town, a motel never once referred to by a grown-up without a nudge, a sneer, or a guffaw.

Moving up West Street, we stopped first at a low-slung white farmhouse on the left to drop off daydreamy Eileen O'Sullivan, who married young and moved to Ohio, and her younger brother, Brian, who became a doctor specializing in pediatric pulmonary disease. We shaved Brian's eyebrows when he was a toddler because younger siblings invited that kind of experimentation in the same way that basements invite flooding. Eileen and Brian lived with their buttoned-down Yankee mother and their dashing Irish father, P. Pearse O'Sullivan. Mrs. O'Sullivan went to the Congregational Church on the hill across from our house: its leaves blew onto our lawn every autumn. Mr. O'Sullivan was Catholic, and he went to the Immaculate Heart of Mary, also in the center of town, along with our family. In our town the divisions were simple: you could be young or old, male or female, Catholic or Protestant. Mr. O'Sullivan would leave his house late on a January afternoon in 1964, just as the light thinned into dusk, and after traveling a short distance on Route 202, be hit head-on and flung against his windshield. There were no seat belts in those days, and although he lived for years, he never in fact recovered.

The Protestants were different from us in that they did not kneel in church and they sang more during their services. We sang haunting robust songs in a foreign language, "Stabat Mater" and "Ave Maria," while their hymns were pale and plain with wispy little rhymes, like hills and rills: scraps of sound, word tendrils. The inside of their church was also plain, with none of the garish colors of our stained glass, the gilt and pomp of our altar, the smell of incense, foreign and molecular, and candles, waxy and hopeful. Protestants, from what I understood, had firm and positive feelings about Christ the King, but they did not revere Mary with our special ardor. Our mother, who had, after all, given birth six times, sometimes thought Mary had had it pretty easy. Yet she thought the Church was right to fuss over her. "The Protestants are wrong," she often said, "not to give the Blessed Mother her due."

Next, we would pass the common on the left and cross Route 202, a main thoroughfare famous not only because it cut through our town but also because it kept on going to faraway foreign places like Delaware. In front of us at this point would be John's Center Pharmacy, decorated with a mortar and pestle. The Brooks kids detached at this juncture, turned left and headed home. They were Mormons, an obscure form of Protestant—or so we wrongly assumed—and although they liked to dance, they did not believe in coffee, tea, cigarettes, whiskey, or gambling, which Catholics, more or less, did believe in. Just beyond their house on the same side of the street was the Immaculate Heart of Mary Church. During the fifties, it expanded, sprung an addition, as did the whole known world, Big Y Supermarkets sprouting up in empty fields, highways slathering tar where once the green trees grew, new restaurants with signs bragging about how many hamburgers they had sold. My family had the opportunity to subsidize two stained-glass windows in the newly renovated church in honor of my father and my grandmother, who died in 1957. We children could not easily embrace the excitement the grown-ups felt at these memorials, which we saw as rubbles of color and weak substitutes for the living, breathing humans. We had our own ideas about what was worth jumping up and down about: snow, Tastee-Freez, the first dip of the summer—certainly not the unveiling of ecclesiastical tributes.

* * *

Bless me, Father, for I have sinned.

Over and over we practiced the words for our first Communion. We were shown a picture of a bottle filled with black milk: an image of our soul at birth. Then we were shown a picture of an all-white bottle: what our soul would look like after baptism and after every confession, provided we had made an honest Examination of Conscience. It was important that when the priest deposited the Host on your tongue, your teeth did not actually champ down on it. The way to practice was to take Wonder Bread, flatten it into chunks the shape and width of a quarter, and swallow it in one gulp, an activity easily accomplished while also watching *Hopalong Cassidy*. The nuns who taught us our catechism were imported to Granby on Sundays, having already put in long hours during the week as teachers in parochial schools. With their huge wimples, heavy crucifixes, and pale hands gripping black beads, the nuns had the power of their peculiarity and their easy anger. They offered a compelling invitation into the world of horror and redemption, stigmata, and the Beatific Vision.

We tried to distract them from the rote drills. "Tell us about Maria Goretti," we would shout. "Fatima, please." Certain saint stories infested our imagination more than others, because either the gore factor or the spook content was especially high. We liked Fatima because we wanted to be like those lucky foreign children chosen for some mysterious reason to be witnesses to a divine apparition.

As for Maria Goretti, the nuns always began her story the same way, referring to a book called *Lives of the Saints:* "On a hot afternoon in July 1902 Mary, as Maria was sometimes called, was sitting on the top of the stairs in a cottage, mending a humble shirt. She was not yet twelve years old, and it must be remembered that in Italy girls mature earlier than in more northern countries. A devout but cheerful girl, Maria repelled a bullying farmhand who tried to rape her, but he killed her anyway. The man who killed her was released from prison, having repented, and lived to see her canonized in 1950."

We heard about heaven, hell, purgatory (our likely stopover spot), and limbo, the refuge of unbaptized babies and good-hearted heathens who through no fault of their own missed out on the Word of God.

Death, the nuns declared, consisted of a process in which the room goes white and fills with angels. This principle would someday be proven with scientific accuracy, just as soon as those smarty-pants physicists who had figured out how to split the atom learned how to do something really complicated, such as weighing an angel.

Holy Communion was special because you got to dress like a bride and you were given a scapular, a scratchy cloth necklace that protected you from evil and clued ambulance drivers to the fact of your Catholicity, should there arise a need for Extreme Unction, the sacrament of the sick and dying.

Over and over, we recited our rote drill:

"Who made you?"

"God made me."

"Why did God make you?"

"God made me to know, love, and serve Him in this life so as to be happy with Him forever in the next world."

Simply seeing the church reminds me of the argument my mother and I had on my first Holy Communion day, when I wanted more than anything to go to the Hilltop Nook, a greasy spoon that catered to truck drivers hauling loads through our town to all the other places that were lucky enough to have Route 202 slicing them down the middle. Girlie calendars enlightened patrons as to the exact day and month of the year.

The jukebox played "The Yellow Rose of Texas" constantly. The smell of flesh being grilled, fifteen-cent burgers and ten-cent dogs, was thick and insistent. These things, and especially the tendency of the truck drivers to graze a heavy hand against a slender young back and to let it linger there, made it obvious this was not a place to visit except in a group. The owner had said that if I showed up in my dress (spousal and radiant, veiled and holy) with my First Communion certificate, I would get four free candy bars.

"That's four," I said to my mother when she refused to let me cash in. "Not one, but four."

"If your father were alive," she said, "he would never permit it."

I came to loathe her propensity for reading my father's posthumous thoughts. The very words *if your father were alive* guaranteed in me a knee-jerk reaction of impatience and frustration. He wasn't, so her hypothesizing was an exercise in futility. "Besides," she added, "weren't you pleased with all the presents from your brother?"

In honor of the sacramental milestone, I had gone with Raymond and his friend Bob and Bob's sisters Pauline and Pee-wee, who were celebrating the same milestone, to a double bill of horror films, one about a she-devil and the other about a large insect who crushed skyscrapers and juggled cars. Raymond also gave me a Tarzan book, which he took back for himself, and a box of pennies covered with turpentine. The sticky goo stained my hands and was supposed to trick me into thinking I was turning into a colored person, just like the ones I had seen in Springfield.

Raymond commanded my respect because he could remember our father, in the way that a child remembers, with a vivid, sense-filled memory, uncontaminated by fact. Daddy was the smell of automobiles and cut grass and fried potatoes. He was big hands and the sound of coins jingling in pockets and a deep voice at the end of the day. Beyond that, Raymond was older, and the simple arithmetic of his seniority gave him the mystique of wisdom and power. Yet it was already obvious, though not acknowledged, that something was off-kilter about him. His very presence created a commotion in the house. When he was around, the noise was always noisier. Since my earliest memories, he appeared to me to lack a certain protective membrane. He had a vulnerability that left him open to assault, and given to it as well. He was the pond that invited the skimming rock, the branch that could be twisted off a tree, a weed waiting to be trampled. Sometimes the boys who teased him would include me in their insults. "Hey," I remember them saying, "there goes Razor Blades' kid sister."

"He's my brother," I would answer, telling the truth, "and I'm proud of it," I would add, lying. My relationship with him was more complicated than mere pride. Early on I recognized that I was his protector rather than the other way around.

Bless me, Father, for I have sinned.

I realized as I prepared for my first confession that the words were affording me a secret delight. Was it possible that behind the grid of the confessional my real father lurked? Or would the parish priest turn into him, the way the bread and wine transforms into the body and blood of Christ? Was this fantasy a potential sacrilege, a sin far worse than the standard fare of talking back to one's elders or plain old bad thoughts? And, if I failed to acknowledge the flight of fancy, would I then be guilty of making a faulty confession? Congratulating myself for a moment at the quality of my moral thicket, I soon quivered with the knowledge that perhaps I had committed yet another sin, the sin of pride. I could sense, in some dim way, even at the age of seven, almost eight, how a life of wrongdoing builds on itself, how turpitude begets turpitude begets turpitude. I began to despair of ever feeling pure enough to accept, with a totally clean slate, the Communion wafer into my mouth, the presence of God into my soul.

During the cold war, the skies above Granby boasted B52s, sleek bombers that bragged their way across the sky, cocksure and light, reminding us, as someone put it, of prom kings and class presidents on their way to heroic touchdowns. We were on our guard against the appearance of similar aircraft from either the Union of Soviet Socialist Republics or Red China. As school-children, we computed that we were better than the USSR because they had gray weather all the time and we had watermelon, sunshine, and fireworks, culminating in the Fourth of July. And we were definitely better than Red China because, in one of those conundrums that can create a headache if you think about it too hard, we got tomorrow after they did, meaning we could savor it longer, like hoarding the inside of an Oreo.

At school we began each day with the Lord's Prayer as well as a salute to the flag and to the "Republic for Whichistans." School days were punctuated by frequent air raid drills, in which we would quickly file out into the corridors and crouch, our elbows cradling our ears, waiting for the big bang. We were especially vulnerable because Westover Air Force Base, which borders Granby, was a force to reckon with in the world of international defense, a SAC (Strategic Air Command) base. We were right up there with a base in Texas as a prime target. It made all of us, even the state kids, who usually reacted to everything with a dull shrug, shiver to learn that the Soviets kept atlases of places they wanted to destroy, including Granby. For all we knew, the Hilltop Nook or the Town Common was at the top of their list.

To be part of the world stage, even at its annihilating worst, created a borrowed pride.

With flickering clarity, as through heat waves on a highway, I remember us lumbering in a slow procession down 202, angling our way onto Center Street, walking past the rectory, and finally arriving home. Time moved as slowly as we did. For my mother, the dailiness of life was as massive and unyielding as the fieldstone fireplace. There were sometimes moments of passing gladness, not the least of which was the sorority of other mothers.

They shared domestic secrets:

Peanut butter removes gum from hair.

The perfect menu at a child's birthday party is lemonade and Lady Baltimore vanilla cake from the Fannie Farmer Cookbook.

Birthday presents should be simple and predictable: pencils, hankies, Golden Books.

Except for Mrs. Ila Brooks, the Mormon, they all smoked. For a long time in our house, every flat surface seemed to contain an ashtray, the standard arts-and-crafts gift from children, but they were more than mere decoration. Form married function: those ashtrays got used. When I envision my mother and her friends of that era, I picture the innocence with which they smoked and how exciting it was to watch the at first absentminded, then slightly panicked search for the pack of tobacco, the patting of one pocket after another, and when it was found, to see the fingers graze the top, preparing for the smooth extraction of one, and only one, cigarette. To an onlooking child the suspense built, so that this gesture, which took but a second in real time, seemed to go on and on. Finally, when the cigarette was out of the pack and in hand, it was rapped against a flat palm or a hard surface, tap, tap, tap, so as to batten the interior, to fatten the virgin, and then, at last, time for the pyre, the actual ignition, always preceded, maddeningly, by a pause to find a match, more pat, pat, pat of the pockets, and when one was finally found, at long last came the sound of inhalation and its opposite, a process conducted not in today's skulking atmosphere of apology, but out in the open with a spirit of ecstasy.

The women reveled in the unspoken recognition that women all shared the same boat, which is to say the boat of their bodies. The human womb was the perpetual motion machine that scientists kept trying to invent. Good news was meant to be overheard: "Someone on the common, not me, is pregnant," a woman would crow, and the guesswork created hoots and hollers, making all the women appear rejuvenated and less burdened for a brief moment. They saved their mumbled confidences for the bad news. They mumbled when they discussed the "mistakes" within a marriage, or worse, the mistakes outside one, especially if a young single girl, someone's forever-labeled daughter, had become pregnant. They spoke in hushed asides about each other's early hysterectomies, routinely offered in a paternalistic way as a form of birth control by doctors who counseled their patients that if they got rid of all the "yuck down there," life would be a lot simpler. But the kinship with other women and our yelps and giggles and antics were not enough to guard against the conflation of one moment with the next.

Our mother used to say, with a weary sigh, as she struggled to get us grown up, "Day by day, we chip away." She had a private stash of doleful quotes, which she dipped into and trotted out whenever sufficiently dismal circumstances presented themselves. One of the top ten was adapted from Yeats: "The years go by like great dark cattle driven by the master herdsman, God."

From François Villon:

> *Time goes, you say*
> *Alas, ah no*
> *Times stays, you see*
> *It's we who go.*

From John Millington Synge's *Riders to the Sea*, she appeared, with her usual appreciation for the morose, to revel in the last line, in which a character laments the drowning of yet another fisherman: "No man can be left living forever and we must be satisfied."

And another, anonymous as far as I knew, featured one day above the masthead of the Holyoke paper, prophetic as well as terse: "It's not the first tragedy, but the second, that breaks a man."

There was always a moment of profound quiet before our return, before the clunk of shoes being scuffed off, the thud of *Dick and Jane* and other books dropping on the floor, the banging of the door of the fridge as we lunged for the peanut butter and jelly, the shout of "first dibs" on the cold milk in the glass container with its thick ridge of cream on top. One of my mother's favorite poems was by a woman with the truly unfortunate name of Adelaide Crapsey, the mention of which would launch us into the same spate of giggles with which we used to greet the information that we had some distant Irish cousins with the last name of Hoar. Yet the words my mother liked to quote had a kind of dreadful beauty:

> *These be*
> *Three silent things:*

The falling snow . . . the hour
Before the dawn . . . the mouth of one
Just dead.

To which my mother sometimes added a soft fourth: the house at 5 Center on a school day shortly before three in the afternoon. Her first major decision as a widow was not to sell the old white colonial, so that even though my father became less real to me over time, the house, which was his monument, became more real, almost like a member of the family, a breathing, sometimes tyrannical, sometimes enveloping presence filled with nooks and crannies, history and eccentricity.

Chapter Three

Bread and Hope

LIKE ANY MOTHER, OURS ON OCCASION HAS AN URGE TO CITE THE VARI-
ous ways in which she not only went to bat for us as children,
but also walked the extra mile and managed somehow to get
water from stones as well as blood from turnips. This tendency
has only deepened due to her status as a "single mom" long before that phrase, with its pop sociology peppiness, came into
being.

In their marriage, my father got the premature berth at
St. Patrick's Cemetery across from the Moose Club in Chicopee.

He got the pickled adulation of a passel of children.

He got our prayers.

My mother got the house in Granby.

She got all the doctors' appointments, the calls from concerned teachers, the bills from various colleges. She also got the
challenge not to make his death her death too.

Being fierce, from New England, she took the words of Robert Frost personally when he wrote, "Provide, provide." On the
other hand, being Irish by heritage, she took Frost's meaning in

the most unlikely light, not so much concerning herself with the homely task of supplying the basics in a cold climate, firewood and flannel, as dedicating herself to giving us what she thought our lives would have been like had our father lived: a swirl of lessons and opportunities and symbolic offerings, such as red meat and equestrian training at Mt. Holyoke College. Sometimes she still cannot resist the urge to name all the ways in which she sought to enrich our lives.

"It wasn't easy, you know."

No, it wasn't, we readily agree.

"I felt inadequate. Who wouldn't? All of you so different, the one from the other, such distinct individuals. And so needy. I used to think wouldn't it be great if on Sunday I could just fill you up with stew and milk and then not have to feed you again all week. I was younger than I thought when your father died. I didn't appreciate how young. I didn't have much to fall back on, just the hope of a teaching job if I was lucky. And then time went on and you got so tall and bold and definite, you threw me for a loop. Besides, what resources did I have?"

We know our cue, answering interchangeably, the same response no matter which child is speaking. We had to be careful to answer with just the right pitch of sincerity. Our mother had a gift for detecting the clammy and counterfeit.

You did have the Waterford glass pitcher.

"That would have been worth?" she nudges us along.

A thousand dollars . . .

"If it weren't cracked."

Our mother could see the lost promise in anything, including a cracked pitcher. The vaunted value of a thousand dollars is a willful inflation, typical of her impulse to fictionalize reality, to take what is true and reshape it, so there is not only a better ending, but also a better beginning and a better middle.

We rush to reassure her.

You did your best.

Our mother nods in agreement: "I did feed you steak."

Yes, you did. Sirloin.

"And I didn't run away and join a commune back in the sixties when it was popular for housewives to be, well, skittish."

No commune for our mom.

"I arranged for you girls to study with the smart nuns."

Yes, you did. The Ursulines. The female equivalent of the Jesuits.

"You took piano."

And learned one song: "The Londonderry Air." But at least it was a good song.

"You joined the Scouts and got all those badges."

That proved so useful in adult life.

"I exposed you to Irish Step."

Way before anyone heard of those River Dancers.

"And don't forget. I also arranged for you to take elocution with a famous thespian, Mrs. Jean Guild of the Valley Players."

By the time the four Blais girls came under Mrs. Guild's influence, she had faded gently from empire, and what early stardom she had experienced and ambition she had once entertained had been downsized to playing bosomy busybodies in summer stock standbys like *Arsenic and Old Lace* and to passing on her skills and secrets to unappreciative pupils, such as me and my sisters. She was a commanding alto and was capable of a convincing emotive quiver should the right stimulus present itself.

We met once a week in the city of Holyoke in a building named Wisteriahurst, arranging ourselves in a semicircle under the high ceiling in hard-backed chairs, legs crossed at the ankles, hands folded in our laps. We began with tongue twisters: "The ragged rascal ran around the rugged rock." Then we had flash cards with words like "hoi polloi" that the hoi polloi would be likely to mispronounce: "The car is called a coupe," Mrs. Guild would say, "Not kuPAY. It's Theodore Ruse-a-velt, not ROSE-a-velt. And now this word, so liquid and lovely, how do we say it?"

"Lapis lazuli," we would reply, dragging our voices.

These exercises tested our tolerance: what possible utility was there in learning the correct way to say words that we could not envision using ever? Mrs. Guild told us this last word referred to a mineral famous for its blue color, but try as we might, we could not imagine the circumstances under which we might ever employ it, ever compliment some boy of our dreams on his lapis lazuli eyes.

Finally, our larynxes warmed, we graduated to the recitation of poetry, as always encouraged to stress each syllable and flag every emotion, a kind of overcooking that managed to remove all the healthy nutrients.

"My dears," she would sometimes say with girlish glee, as if about to suggest we spend the rest of the lesson writing our names as "Mrs. Pat Boone." A big wink followed by a crafty grin: "Let's do Lord Alfred Tennyson's 'The Lady of Shalott.'"

"Oh, boy," we used to say when she turned her back, sticking a finger down our throats. "Tennyson." Our delivery was accompanied by sweeping gestures, huge strides, the ceremonial hoisting of hand to forehead as we scoured an imagined landscape.

> *She left the web, she left the loom,*
> *She made three paces thro' the room,*
> *She saw the water lily bloom,*
> *She saw the helmet and the plume,*
> *She looked down to Camelot.*

The most important line was the last: we were both to lower
the register of our voices and to raise the volume on the word
"down," so that the final line had a big boom in the middle:
"She looked DOWN to Camelot."

We must have disheartened her, but she never let on, perhaps the truest measure of her acting talent. Week after week,
she labored over our delivery so that we too could enter a room
armored with confidence and crisp diction. We were ashamed
to be taking voice lessons, embarrassed to be pursuing something
so old-fashioned and out of it, longing instead to take accordion,
or tap, or best of all, baton. "You're taking what kind of lessons?"
our friends would ask. "Electrocution?"

But nothing, absolutely nothing, impressed our mother so
much as what she came to think of as her most stunning entry
in the good mother sweepstakes. It surprises her more and more
with each passing year, the daring of it, the glamour, the sudden heedlessness of expense. She took us, one or two at time,
never the whole lot, naturally (you'd need to be a saint for that),
to New York City.

These excursions stood out. We were not the Grand Can-
yon type, not temperamentally suited to long car trips and
lengthy pilgrimages, leading to caverns with stalactites or empty
battlefields or roadside stands that sell shells and beaded
moccasins.

Mostly, we just stayed put in the Bay State, which held its
own amusements, such as maple syrup and melting snow. If
our mother ever writes her autobiography, her chosen title is
Me, Maureen, from Massachusetts. Never a confident driver, she
avoided all major arteries and took side streets whenever possible. Sometimes to create a false impression of an accelerated pace
as we inched down narrow byways, she would sing, "Zoomie,
zoomie, zoomie, zoomie, zoom." She despised the Massachusetts

Turnpike from the moment it opened in 1957 and spoke of it as if it embodied some unnamed evil, as if its soft shoulders were lined with gambling casinos and thousands of dancing girls clad only in sheets. I remember at times being so desperate for a change in scenery that when our mother used to get in the car simply to drive the mile or so to Dressel's Service Station for gasoline, we lay in wait for the roar of the engine and then flew out of our rooms, propelling ourselves out of the front door, diving into the two-toned blue Nash Rambler, which had the strange distinction of being both stodgy and salacious. Before we became teenagers, the Rambler's most prized attribute, the way the front seats reclined to a horizontal plane, the object of the same kind of snickering that attached to certain otherwise normal words, like *miscarriage* and *queer* and *balls*, when pronounced in a low, knowing way, was lost on the Blais girls.

We didn't go to Boston, we didn't go to the Cape, we hardly went anywhere at all, but for reasons that had more to do with the kind of life my mother wished to live than with the life she was leading, she energized herself, with an unnatural fury, for her visits to New York City, which entailed a four-hour train ride and two nights in a hotel.

Once there, our routine did not vary.

First stop: Tall Gals, which specialized in shoes for tall gals with narrow feet. She wanted something strappy that suited her quadruple A (or was it quintuple A?) heels. We visited the public library to admire the stone lions. We went to Lord & Taylor, where our mother sashayed into Better Dresses to inquire about the latest Anne Fogarty, rattling off the name of the designer with a kind of bored aplomb, the purpose of which was to establish once and for all that she knew Something about Something. Lunch followed, at the Birdcage Restaurant, which served sherbet and miniature sandwiches. Then, on to more of the usual tourist hoopla: the Empire State Building, the Oyster Bar beneath Grand Central, the Met to see the pictures of the fat naked ladies and blurry landscapes, the Rainbow Room for peanuts plus a view. We ate dinner at Horn & Hardart's Automat, mesmerized by what passed for high tech at the time. After we deposited a series of nickels into a slot, a fresh sandwich would slide into view in a small metal compartment. This apparition of bread and hope in a germ-free cubicle had the air of a certain kind of low-level miracle such as you might hear about in New Jersey or the Philippines when people claim they can see Jesus's face in the folds of a cinnamon bun or in the arrangement of seeds in a pomegranate: the Immaculate Conception of Cold Cuts.

While we were there, she tried to instruct us in some of her random convictions.

Ladies do not swing their arms when they walk.

No one should butter his or her bread in the air.

Diamonds, ideally, come from Tiffany's.

The most pleasing serving platters are oval, and black and brown can be a very smart combination.

I remember trooping behind our mother as she sailed the streets, borne forward by a private breeze. The exhaust was a kind of perfume, the honking an aria, the jostling crowd an appreciative claque.

One time we took a sightseeing bus. In the Bowery, we saw the bums, as we called them, men warming their hands and stubbled faces in the heat of barrels rosy with lighted trash. This scene served to launch our mother into her standard Great Depression reverie, a familiar spiel about how people wrapped up butter and put it under the Christmas tree and how men she knew, proud men from proud families, were forced to leave their neighborhoods and go to places like Hartford, pronounced as if Hartford were the end of the world, and sell pencils and apples on street corners. She knew women who were so traumatized by those lean, frightening years that they practiced thrift for the rest of their days to a deranged degree, even hanging used tea bags on the clothesline. From a distance it would look as if someone were lynching mice.

"You cannot understand how hard it was unless you lived through it . . . ," she said, her voice trailing off, her gaze devouring the horizon. "You don't understand."

On that particular day, as we made our way past the gauntlet of fumes and beggars, one of the men eyed the bus and, assuring himself, falsely, that no one was watching, took an empty bottle and smashed it on the pavement. Then he stowed it, shards and all, as future weaponry, inside his coat pocket. Who were these men, unattached and slovenly and full of menace? What combination of bad luck, bad judgment, and bad dice led them to these shadowy concrete corners, huddled and grubby and neglected? Later, we went to Chinatown, where our mother got what looked like chopsticks to put in her hair and where the drinks had umbrellas and the cookies had mottoes.

She changed in the city, with each inhalation of pavement and commotion.

In New York, trailed by one child or another, dressed in a suit, Maureen Shea Blais would transform, become a different, lighter person. Though well into her forties, she was pleased to realize she was making an impression, creating a tableau. When she returned home, she would sigh and say how much she missed it.

"In New York," she always said, "the men still whistle."

The mother we were used to simply vanished in New York. She was gone, the creature who loosened her bun at night, removed the switch she used to fatten it and the wire pins that kept it tamed and cowering by day. Out would spill the long dark hair, down to her shoulders and beyond. Often in the evening she delivered herself for hours to her daily stack of newspapers, entering the den of information in black and white with an addict's wish to obliterate the present: this was her gin and her bingo. She picked it over, reading not only the news and the political columns in which men of swagger opined and fulminated, but also "Today's Chuckle" and the advice columns and the ads, the letters to the editor, the crossword puzzles, even, fruitlessly, the household hints, disappearing into the world of facts and figures, irony and despair. She would skim the ads for mink stoles and consider just how much of a bargain it would be to eat a dinner of pot roast and all the fixin's for seventy-five cents at Waldorf's Self-Service Restaurant, or fried scallops for ninety, skipping only the agate describing scores from games all over the country as well as in local high school gyms, pausing to shake her head at whatever commotion had been caused by Furculo or Peabody or Bellotti or by those silly Red Sox who were always discovering whole new ways to shoot themselves in the foot.

"Now, doesn't this take the cake," she would say, whenever something offended her sensibilities. One time there was a story in the paper about a lady who had triplets and how she felt thrice blessed. The triplets were already six months old, and if you looked at the lady's picture, you saw someone who looked plumb tired out, certainly not someone you'd care about one way or another. The lady's husband was out of work, but somehow things would take care of themselves. Maureen Blais's dislike could not have been more swift or more profound; she could take the tiniest grit and massage it into a pearl of pure pique.

"Just listen to this nincompoop," she said, "as if talking about the mortgage is the same as paying it, nattering on and on about how the three in her arms aren't anywhere near enough. All that palaver, acting as if she's the first woman ever to have a baby when any cow can have a calf. *Oh*, she says, *I want a dozen more.*" And then, building to her worst slur. "Just who does she think she is?" Pause. Then again, "Just who does she think she is? You know, I have the urge to track her down and ask if I can speak to her for just one minute. I could tell her a thing or two about the heartbreak that's in store for her. Oh, I hate to be the kind of person who discourages someone from setting out with full sails in such an obvious high wind of, well, personal optimism. But I feel honor-bound, woman to woman, to tell her she should stop now while she's feeling so positive. The thing people don't understand is that babies are more than just coos and big eyes. Babies are work."

Years later, I heard babies described as soil-depleting crops, and I think that's what my mother was driving at, the contradiction at the heart of human generation, the way, as they say in the South, children sharpen their teeth on their parents' bones. We were what kept her up and we were what kept her down.

But certainly we were not soil-depleting all the time. We conspired to find ways to make our mother smile. Our plan was to get her to live forever. Having lost one parent, there was always a sense of impending doom, a question of when the next shoe would drop. We proceeded slowly, wary of change, fearful of leaps and falls, cautious and elderly at a tender age. No black diamond trails for us: just getting through the day was an extreme sport. We soon learned that good report cards lifted her spirits, as did drawings, especially of her. We would guess what kind of flower she would be if she could be a flower: a rose on the days she was acting stern and official, a peony when she

seemed rugged and exuberant, or a daisy when she was acting
humble as a smile. Putting on kerchiefs and proceeding to douse
everything with disinfectant, singing songs we'd heard on commercials, "There's less toil with Lestoil," we would organize
ourselves to clean the house when she was at the Food Mart or
the S&H Green Stamps Redemption Center so she could return
home to a big surprise. We brought her breakfast in bed. The
toast might be burned, the marmalade gummy, the orange juice
weak as water, but it revived her to see us carrying the tray into
the room. She would draw us into bed with her, cradle our heads.
Sometimes on the table next to the bed would be a book, tossed
aside in the night, or a jar of cold cream that accidentally served
as an ashtray, signs that she had been up late. When our mother
was angry or distracted, we were a nameless blur: *this one*, *that
one*, *his nibs*, *her nibs*, *yooouuu*. Or she would go through the list
of our names and get the wrong one. When corrected, she would
say, "You know who I mean." On the good days, the breakfast-
in-bed days, it didn't matter whether she remembered our names
or not: we were little lost lambs, pumpkins, even princesses. We
were grand, we were brilliant, her pride and joy, her little lovies,
her old stars.

Our mother was above all a connoisseur of obituaries, otherwise known as the Irish sports pages. She remarked the calling
hours at the wakes for people she'd never even heard of, let alone
met, monsignors and teachers and politicians, professors, lawyers,
and doctors, as well as all those Lucky Joes whose chief claim to
fame was that they'd survived the Cocoanut Grove fire in Boston
in 1942, only to be felled at a later date by more mundane causes.
She had a particular regard for the obituaries that made nuns sound
interesting: "It's a real gift to describe a life that's both contem-
plative and altruistic with any kind of drama, unless of course she's
the kind of nun with a secret specialty, like a great pitching arm

that she uses at recess to win favor with the boys, or she can play an instrument at one of those singalongs."

With a splash of sherry in a glass at her side, just a cheerful little splash, a cigarette aglow in the nearby ashtray, ignored, consuming itself, she would sometimes compose her own obituary, taking pleasure in reviewing her entire life, losing herself in a haze of smoke and sentiment. The past called out to her the same way cotton candy and fake tomahawks called out to me at the annual Columbus Day Fair in nearby Belchertown.

For a woman whose tongue could be sharper than the lid of a freshly opened can of tuna, she found herself overcome by shyness when it came to putting words on paper. She would sit in the living room in the house in Granby, decorated in the style of the fifties with turquoise walls and gold drapes. We had American eagle everything, especially lamps. Over the mantel of the fireplace two crossed swords were mounted. Such a patriarchal flourish had a zany effect in a house dominated by women. At Christmas these instruments of war were laced with garlands of tinsel.

"Born in Chicopee," she would begin, though the exact date was usually withheld for reasons of vanity. One of her father's many sisters wrote a tribute on the day of her birth:

> *Fair is the unfolding of a flower*
> *The gentle sprouting of the springtime sod*
> *And fair the bright white burst of morning's glory*
> *But fairer still thy birth, oh flower of God.*

As morbid as the composition of her own death notice might seem to someone outside the family, it was hardly noteworthy inside it. After reading all those obituaries night after night, she could not help but speculate where she fit in. What kind of last-ditch spotlight would her life merit? The answer was bleak but obvious: unhailed in life, she would be in all likelihood unhailed in death. "Who'll print this anyway?" she would say, in a fit of despair, rattling the piece of paper with her proposed obituary. "Probably not even the weekly shopper."

But still she labored over it, piling up detail upon detail.

"Born in Chicopee," she would start it again, and again the year 1913 eluded print. She misled us about her age, lopping off fifteen years, liposuctioning time itself, by revising a camp song from when she was young. She'd gone to Bonnie Brae in 1927. She sang,

> 1-9-4-2 at Bonnie Brae
> No other year the same
> Every scout a camper true
> No matter her name or fame.

We weren't yet cunning about math or chronology, so we accepted her numbers: if the song had been accurate, she would have been a girl at camp in 1942 and two years later, a grown woman with her first baby.

"Daughter," she would write, "of Dr. Michael I. Shea, former mayor of Chicopee, and Madeleine Mahony Shea."

My mother had the preposition problem that undermines the sense of personal identity of so many women: daughter *of*, sister *of*, wife *of*, mother *of*. Her father's tenure as mayor, which lasted all of two years, was presented to us as a landmark event in the nation's political history: you could sign the Constitution, you could be president, you could be mayor of Chicopee.

She never heard the unintended comic effect of the word Chicopee, seeing in it only her pleasurable beginnings. It was an old mill town, and the Irish and the Polish and the French Canadians lived there at the beginning of the twentieth century in easy harmony. In fact, her father learned Polish in order to do his job and was sometimes paid in pirogi or kielbasa for a new baby or a cured cough.

"Graduate of Chicopee High School."

During the commencement ceremony she was asked to stand up four separate times: for having perfect attendance all four years, for being a member of the Pro Merito Society, for composing an original graduation march (she can't remember how it goes anymore), and of course for the awarding of the diplomas. All her memories of the high school are positive except for one mean English teacher who allegedly never gave anyone Irish more than a B plus. "Her name was Ruth Stone. And there was one very unusual thing about her. For some reason that no one could figure out . . ."

If you had not heard this story before, you immediately prepared yourself for a major confidence. At the very least, my mother's tone promised that one would learn that Ruth Stone had an extra finger or a morphine addiction or fancied other women. My mother would then whisper, "Everyone called her Peggy."

"A graduate of Bridgewater State Teachers' College."

One of her favorite memories from college was how on Saturday afternoons she and her friends used to go to the nearby prison and entertain the female inmates, most of whom were prostitutes caught selling listless, broken-down bodies during the depression.

She accompanied a girl with a beautiful voice on the piano. Our mother would pause again in the midst of her composition to serve tea to the memory: "The girl sang, come to think of it, what was probably not the most sensitive choice given the prospects of the audience, 'Look Down That Lonesome Road,' and my friend Miggie danced, wearing red shoes. Whenever we showed up, the male inmates would lean out the windows, to ask, 'Is Red Shoes here?' and if Miggie was with us, they would all applaud."

"Member of the Granby Library Board of Trustees for twenty-two years. Head for six."

It was my mother who introduced writers such as Seán O'Faoláin and Frank O'Connor to the town, over the objections of other board members who found her nearly exclusive allegiance to Irish and Irish-American writers a bit lopsided. For her part, she felt that anyone who objected was, to put it simply, a bigot, just like that Ruth/Peggy.

She had that peculiar relationship to Ireland so common among Irish Americans, people who were not born there and perhaps never even visit, but who cultivate a sentimental tie that expresses itself in wearing green on St. Patrick's Day and keeping a bottle of crème de menthe in the pantry, knowing the words to the Irish national anthem or to Robert Emmet's dock speech, and seasoning conversation with expressions like "streelish" and "we ourselves" (the translation of *Sinn Fein* and the unofficial family motto). A meager individual who threw his weight around was filled with his "wee self." In the twenties, her parents supported the American Commission on Irish Independence, sending contributions, saving the receipts: "This certificate will be your record that when Ireland appealed to you in the name of *Liberty*, you responded to the acid test of sincerity." They also saved correspondence from the commission urging the support of only those elected officials in America who supported a free and united Ireland:

> The need for your aid is urgent. Because they hold to
> their right of self-determination, the Irish people are at
> this moment tortured most cruelly.

A foreign soldiery swarms over their country. No
Irish patriot's home is safe. His liberty and life even are at
the arbitrary disposal of an irresponsible military cabal
who have not hesitated to add private to public assassina-
tion. Thousands are taken from their homes and deported
or imprisoned without trial or any definite charge being
preferred against them. The women suffer equally with
the men.

For people like my mother, the longing for Ireland takes on
the form of a dream of happiness in some ancestral town: oh, to
spend a week in Cork, to gaze at the cathedral nestled in the hills,
to throw a coin in the roiling river, to smell the turf heating in
hearths all over town. To stroll across St. Stephen's Green in
Dublin, to see the swans in Galway Bay. There is the nagging
thought that everything is better in Ireland: the priests, the tea,
the trout, you name it. To be Irish, we learned, is to feel that no
family gathering is ever complete, because there's always someone missing, usually due to something that begins with the letter
d: death, disease, dementia, or distance. To be Irish is to think too
much about drink and to drink too much without thinking. It is
to profess a naïveté about the meanness in teasing: "Really now,
nothing was meant by that," when something clearly was. To be
Irish is to troll for the crack, the dig, or the insult, and to remember it forever, whether real or imagined. "What's Irish
Alzheimer's?" goes one joke. "You forget everything but the
grudge." And to appreciate talk as long as it is public and noisy—
sermons; speeches; editorials; ornate, vivid, vengeful mono-
logues about what you would do if you had a windfall—but to
eschew the kind of exchange that takes the form of intimacy,
of heartfelt and troubled confidences, mainly because that talk
could be used against you later. My people, humble people;

my people, Humphrey Democrats, who talk all the time about winning the lottery.

We called anything that possessed even the faintest whiff of finality the Last Hurrah.

"Let's see," she continued, laboring over her obituary. "First complete sentence was 'I like lilacs' around age one. Favorite month: May." She was born on May first and often referred to herself as Queen of the May. "Second favorite: June, because you can get peonies at a bargain."

By now the ashtray would be filled with discarded butts, the ends smeared with the red of her ever present lipstick, the one womanly wile that she never abandoned.

"Should I say I loved birds and squirrels? Should I mention an affinity for fog? Should I lie and describe myself as a passionate gardener, a gifted dancer, and a galleried artist? Claim that I traveled extensively, particularly in the tundra? Should I put hobbies?" she asked herself and then answered her own question. "When you come right down to it, what hobbies did I have other than you children?"

Often the hi-fi would be playing a mournful tune, about a boy named Danny lost in sunshine and in shadow or that other one about a pale moon rising above the green mountains. She would quiz us, a Celtic rather than a Roman catechism:

"What year was it that your great-grandfather Patrick was born in Ireland?"

"1839."

"And why did he leave his village?"

"Because the British burned it down so often."

"And when did he come to the United States?"

"As a child, during the Famine."

"What kind of work did he do here?"

"The same sort as his own parents. He trained horses and worked as a blacksmith. Later, he was an undertaker in addition to serving as postmaster for the town of Chicopee from 1886 to 1890 appointed by" (long pause for effect, as if this were a certifiable brush with glory rather than a routine bureaucratic gesture) "President Grover Cleveland."

"And on my mother's side what poet is our relation?"

"Our grandmother's grandfather's cousin Frank Mahony, known by his pen name, Father Prout, was the author of 'The Bells of Shandon.'"

"Which goes?"

> *On this I ponder, whe'er I wander*
> *And thus grow fonder, sweet Cork of thee:*
> *With thy bells of Shandon,*
> *The sound so grand on*
> *The pleasant waters of the river Lee.*

By then the needle of the record would be caught at the end, making that repetitive rasping noise.

She would sigh as she got up to put it back, her full skirt rustling, ashes falling willy-nilly while the singer sang the praises of one Mother Machree and the light in her eyes everlasting. "John McCormack," she would announce to anyone within earshot, "was the most famous Irish tenor who ever lived. He was even better than that Italian scamp, what was his name, Enrico Caruso. This," she would say, as the music poured forth, muffled and ancient, "is your heritage."

Chapter
Four

Kissing the Sky
Good Night

IF OUR MOTHER DID NOT ALWAYS LIKE THE FACTS OF HER LIFE, SHE COULD at least control the interpretation of them. To this end, she maintained a paper trail, a series of a dozen or so scrapbooks that survived as the official documentary narrative of our childhood, our true inheritance. These archives, as haphazard as they sometimes seemed, have always been treasured: big bulging repositories filled with elementary school report cards in which "Maintains Good Posture" and "Courtesy" were separate categories, along with "Takes Pride in Personal Appearance"; Christmas lists in which we asked for "charm bracelets, key necklaces, and blue long-legs"; and frail yellowed newsclips memorializing "the children's horse show set for Sunday at Mt. Holyoke" or this long forgotten social event:

"Mrs. Romeo Grenier was hostess at a supper party at her house on Juniper Hill Saturday in honor of her daughter, Joan, who was observing her fourth birthday. Among those attending were Joan's playmates, Tina Blais, Mary Apgar, Jacqueline Blais, Debbie Sexton, Kevin Brooks and Bobby Grenier."

Record keeping is by most definitions an orderly act, proceeding from an urge to impose limits. As a result these scrapbooks provoked wonder in a household that was topsy-turvy and chaotic with so many children: we were like a kitchen with too many pots and pans, all about to boil over. The surfaces of the tables all sported a multiplicity of rings. The cereal boxes in our house looked as if they had been assaulted rather than opened. Orange juice cartons invariably had fat lips. I thought it was normal for toothpaste to squirt out from the middle. Towels rested in damp lumps on the bathroom floor. The ice trays in the fridge were usually bloated with frost and in order to coax any ice out we often slammed the entire device on the floor. If a coat happened to be hung in a closet, it was usually askew, as if it had made a halfhearted attempt at escape. I once found a sweater belonging to Michael that had survived his childhood; although it possessed the correct number of buttons, each one was different and each had been fastened with a different color thread.

Little Eileen O'Sullivan once told her mother that we seemed like *very* nice people, but our sinks were often clogged and we appeared not to possess a pencil sharpener. I think of us in those days as disorganized, ragtag, ad hoc. During my high school years I remember standing guard with a broomstick over my Latin vocabulary lists at breakfast so as to prevent anyone from inadvertently smearing food on the precious passwords to my future, *pelliculum* and *lacrima* and *gravis*. To me the house itself seemed covered with jelly, so it is amazing that these scrapbooks and their contents survived the general rot of time as well as the specific continual descent from refinement that a house and its objects inevitably face in the vicinity of that many kids.

When I was younger and I looked at the scrapbooks, I experienced their offerings narcissistically; I was more interested in how I came across as an individual than in how the others appeared. In snapshots I occupy the bossy center, wearing a ribbon in a bow the size of a sofa and radiating the most imperial forced smile. The overbearing center is still my spiritual bailiwick, doomed as I am to the role of social leader, hostess, faux mom. Even as a child, I sometimes behaved like a sailboat that had caught a permanent good wind.

What does this crayoned self-portrait done on September 10, 1953 ("Madeleine's first paper from first grade") say about me at that moment in time? At the same age I drew a picture with four round nearly identical heads and labeled them:

Madeleine: prutty.

Jacqueline: hapy.

Christina: not hapy.

Maureen: truble ahead.

Did I really ever think madras patchwork Bermudas were right on me?

Was I getting a fair representation, or was the work of my siblings receiving more space?

How did their drawings compare to mine, their Bermuda shorts?

Only with the passage of time did it occur to me that these books are not the objective accounts I had always assumed. During their gradual page-by-page assembly our mother was more than just some file keeper. She was in fact an author, a shaping intelligence, and we were the characters, the players. The various versions of us had been put through the filter of her hopes and the gauze of her fantasies.

The papers that survived our schooldays were the ones that showed "originality" or that argued in the affirmative about our "promise" and our "imagination." They spoke to our best selves, just as the photographs never showed anyone fighting but instead offer one seamless pose after another of variously grouped happy siblings.

Among my favorite pieces of writing were several biographies, especially one sister's saga about Utensil the Pencil, who traveled east from the great timber forests of the Northwest, and another bit by another sister, composed during the Kennedy years: "I am a chandelier. I am in the White House. I am in the blue room. I can remember when I was worthless sand. Now people admire me very much. I am Irish crystal. . . . Once I remember very clearly when a boy at the age of six almost broke me. I can imagine how his parents felt. But think how I felt . . ."

Raymond wrote an essay entitled "How Do They Dress?" "The Eskimos make their clothes from the skins of animals. Most Eskimos wear jackets and hoods, breeches, and high boots. The women make the clothes. They use bones for needles."

We documented national milestones. From a paper by Raymond, dated January 20, 1953: "Mr. Eisenhower will become our new president shortly after noon today."

We were urged by our mother to write to famous people, such as my delusional message to Grace Kelly, "I am a little girl who looks just like you" and this note from Michael to a right-wing zealot, "Dear Mr. Birch, I would like to draw to your attention that your party is wrecking America" and the plea for help from one of the girls to Dear Abby, "My problem concerns boys. . . ." The mystery of how these people could hear from us and yet not ever write back, not even send an autographed picture with a stamped-on name, was solved when the realization dawned that since these letters were saved intact, they clearly had never been sent.

We were brought up to use language with precision. If, in composing a thank-you note, any of us were fool enough to say something was "nice," we were guaranteed an outburst: "Nice is a nice word. Can't you think of something with more verve, more backbone? With, well, panache?" The new note would read: "Thank you for your panache gift."

Our mother's deepest wish was that we would "enter the field of poetry," and the way she said it, with each word given a dreamy elongation, one envisioned a location with an exact latitude and longitude, overwhelmed by flowers. She organized haiku contests, and she was understanding when we struggled with the syllable count. "It is, I grant you, a difficult form to master," she would say, "like trying to catch a butterfly without a net." She relished the offhand creativity in our casual observations about which is more, sand or stars, and why does the moon always let you be the leader and follow from behind, and is it true that hail is lightning that hits the earth? She perked up at our neologisms: words like *pickery* to describe the peculiar taste of ginger ale, the way it drilled holes into the tongue. If you called the sunset God's birthday cake, you were on your way to a big hug. Better yet, claim that at dusk the mountains stand on tiptoe to kiss the sky good night. She saved even those dreadful holiday poems of mine teeming with seasons and reasons and stars from afar. There is one poem about bees whose handwriting belongs to Michael. I don't know if the work is original or if it was the result of one of those copying lessons that becomes in the course of time a gentle plagiarism:

> *There wouldn't be sunflowers,*
> *wouldn't be peas,*
> *wouldn't be apples*
> *On the apple trees.*
> *If it weren't for fuzzy old,*
> *Busy old bees,*
> *Dusting pollen from off their knees.*

If we weren't destined to be poets, our mother was willing to settle for musicians, artists, or stage performers, and she assiduously squirreled away the documentation that upheld our early proclivities in those pursuits: mimeographed concert programs in which it is noted that I would be performing Peter Tchaikovsky's *Pathétique* Sixth Symphony op. 74, a high school playbill heralding my sister Jacqueline as Monsieur Purjan in *The Imaginary Invalid* by Molière. To be a politician might not be so bad; Michael's biography of Abraham Lincoln was preserved perhaps for its own sake, but perhaps also with a future electorate in mind. We were encouraged to be politically inclined, and as a family we supported any and all candidates as long as they were FDR liberals and preferably Irish.

A more practical sort of woman might have steered at least one of us to pursue a more solid professional goal, to become an electrician or even a plumber, some line of work in which concrete skills result in concrete accomplishments. She might have emphasized facts, physics, charts. She might have actively encouraged us to improve our standardized scores in number facility or spatial reasoning, but these were not our areas of strength and she even saved, as joyful evidence of certain desirable inadequacies, the old printouts from school tests that demonstrate as much.

This constant proof of our cultural attainments, preserved indelibly, was accompanied at times by proof of our alleged high social standing, not just the two-inch account of a child's fourth birthday but also a letter from the Headmasters House at the Choate School signed by a Mrs. Seymour St. John to my mother, dated January 28, 1967:

"We at Choate are all agog as February 17th draws near, and with it the arrival of the fair sex on our campus.

"It gives me great pleasure to welcome Christine" (Wrong, wrong; her real name is Christina; one little vowel, yet a lamentable omission, proof that the chattiness of the note, the *intime* tone is at its center, false) "as the guest of Tom Shorten, and I should like to assure you that we shall take every possible care of her."

The elegance of Mrs. St. John's correspondence runs counter to my memory of a childhood spent much more preponderantly watching shows like *Leave It to Beaver* and snacking whenever possible on a set menu from the Hilltop Nook of twenty-five cents' worth of junk food—which in those days meant one Sky Bar, two Hostess cupcakes of the Snowball variety with marshmallow and coconut flake frosting, and a bag of State Line potato chips—and reading from the Trixie Belden series, wishing for a new life in which I'd been born with a truly terrific first name like Trixie. But when I try to tell our mother that I remember things differently, with a slightly more mundane spin, she thinks I am just showing off or engaging in an irritating tease, a baiting sort of deflation, and she reminds me that this is nothing new; what about the time I came home from my Catholic women's college and announced that although I would concede that Christ was indeed a world historical figure who had captivated the imagination of millions, I could no longer be certain he was divine.

The photos we took were steadfastly black-and-white for a long, long time, almost the entire length of my childhood. Every few years or so we gathered our suited, velveteened selves and posed in front of the fieldstone fireplace for a Christmas photo. In all those years, we sent out only two formal Christmas photos. In the first, taken when I was eight in 1955, my mother sits draped in a lovely dress on one side of an unlit hearth, its black hole too overdetermined to work as a metaphor. Raymond, in a white sports jacket, balances her on the other side. The five younger children are all seated on the floor, with me in the middle. Michael looks as if he is trying to make a fast break, in true toddler tradition. Our hands are clasped together as if in prayer. I can almost hear Uncle Dermot, surely the final element in the photo as the photographer, ordering us to pretend we were in church, not so much to appear pious as to ensure we wouldn't hit each other. Five years later, we also gather in front of a hearth, but the line-up has changed. The players have moved. Chess, family style, is being played as its usual slow place. This time Raymond and my mother are on the right, together, nearly fused. She is seated, her head turned toward the rest of us, smiling. Raymond's expression is flat. I balance them on the other side, my face quiet and steady. I am wearing my mother's gold locket. Jacqueline and I are no longer dressed alike, but the other two girls have on long-sleeved cotton dresses with cross-stitching at the bodice. Michael is wearing some kind of sailor outfit.

There are no real candids; if, as sometimes happened, a spontaneous incident occurred that suggested itself as suitable for a picture, we would have to track down the camera, a laborious process in a house where very little had a definite place, and then we would be forced to engage in its historical re-creation—which explains the picture of everyone in the kitchen doing the limbo. When the Christmas tree toppled, we retoppled it for posterity, just as we jumped in a just raked pile of leaves over and over and took our first bite from our first TV dinner several times in succession. This last was a noteworthy event because convenience food was a huge luxury, not a way of life, and those first frozen suppers were considered fascinating. In fact, the first time we had them, we sat on a sheet in front of the TV, but it was *off*, the better for us to concentrate on the various foods occupying the separate compartments.

Our inaugural meal was Salisbury steak.

"But," said one of my siblings after peeling back the foil in which it had cooked, "this isn't steak, this is hamburger."

"Even if it were just plain burger, and I'm not saying it is, don't you think it's commendable to treat it with such hope? Don't you think it's ennobling the way it has a whole new name?" my mother said. "And just look at these mashed potatoes. If I didn't know better, I would think that pat of butter was more than just butter, it was the sun."

The majority of the photographs were taken outside, the easier to manage the light. Interior shots required the trickery of flashcubes, not easy among a group of people for whom gadgetry always seemed an alien menace. Photographs with no people in them weren't photographs; they were a complete waste of film. In the entire collection of scrapbooks there is just one picture of a scene, a pond with some ducks, and I am sure someone outside the family took it and gave it to us, because there would be no other way to excuse such a grotesque display of conspicuous consumption.

The click of the camera was an event unto itself, nearly as special and celebratory as the circumstances prompting the picture in the first place. As I look back at the photos, studying them for the stories they tell, one of the biggest distortions concerns Easter. Anyone leafing through these albums would be justified in concluding that this was without doubt the premier holiday of the year, dutifully captured annually with endless combinations of us standing at attention on the brown and barren front lawn of our house during spring in New England. In fact, birthdays were a bigger deal, and certainly Christmas was the biggest: those were the days on which the children were allowed to come in by the front door rather than the back and to use the front stairs with its red carpet. The emphasis on Easter occurred because during other special events no one was organized enough to remember the camera, but since the chief purpose of Easter appeared to be its own commemoration, it received far more than its true share of the spotlight.

Not that there wasn't some merit to preserving the moment:

After the doldrums of winter, whether one is pagan or religious (or a touch of both), the heart longs for rebirth, to shed that heavy weighed-down feeling, and what is touching about the photos is the sense of optimism. No matter how scrappy and unpromising the lawn itself, we experienced it as green and lush. No matter how goofy the year's fashions, we thought of ourselves as possessing at that moment a high degree of sophistication. On chilly Easters my mother wore her mink stole or the Persian lamb collar with matching muff or the brown scarf that ended on both sides with a small animal head with shiny eyes. Back then fur was money, not murder.

Over the years the styles we wore varied, from shirtwaists to John Meyer suits to Indian wedding dresses, but one constant was those flower-bedecked extravaganzas on our heads. The Catholic Church used to require that females cover their heads as a sign of respect and of gender mortification. My mother happened to love hats all her life, the result of flyaway hair as well as a face whose bones come to life beneath a brim. Not for her or her daughters those flimsy mantillas or, worse, emergency headgear, paper hankies stuck on the back of the head with a bobby pin. When we were old enough, our hats would be like hers: stately showpieces that moved forward in space with the elegance of a yacht. There are photos of me as a child at Easter wearing the hats of a child, stiff bits of straw not unlike upside-down baskets, but as time went on, we progressed from the pillboxes of the Kennedy years to the last hat I remember, a turban made of pink chiffon. Of all the poems saved by my mother, I always suspected that her favorite was one written by my sister

Jacqueline when she was in the fifth grade and which had as its thematic center that old family passion, Paschal millinery:

> *I think I like the yellow or green*
> *Or the pink one I have seen.*
> *I want one to go with my dress*
> *Oh! picking out hats is just a mess.*
> *I think I like the one with the rose*
> *I like the one with a daisy who knows*
> *After an hour or more*
> *I decided to keep the one that last year I wore.*

Chapter
Five

Queen for a Day

GIVEN HER TEMPERAMENT AND HER STYMIED AMBITION, MY MOTHER never should have been a housewife in the fifties, one of the more diabolical decades ever invented, especially for women, with its combination of self-abnegation coupled with bizarre domestic competitions involving canned soup and dried onions and frozen string beans. In her netherworld state, as A Woman Alone, she couldn't win.

Cooking bored her: dinners at our house were at best sturdy and workmanlike, stout stews to which the addition of salt and pepper was considered a daring intrusion, boiled chicken served with the skin hanging off it in sad puckered folds, and rice topped with canned tomatoes. Our tuna was usually the cheaper, brown variety, dumped, undrained, into a bowl, dressed with a glob or two of mayonnaise, and served on top of recently defrosted Wonder Bread, sometimes sporting freezer burn. The few times we were served milk toast, which is exactly what it sounds like, a piece of toast in a bowl of milk, we rebelled and staged a very short hunger strike. Several times a year we colored outside the lines and got take-out fish and chips from Schmererhorn's in Holyoke, tasty bundles of heat and grease and protein that mocked our normal fare. To us cheese was cheese, orange and bland. Food was food, neither a joy nor an adventure. Every now and then she challenged herself to undertake something new and ambitious, but seemingly bright ideas like Patriot's Pudding Jell-O, which was supposed to appear in distinct layers of red, white, and blue but arrived at our table in one bruised shade, never quite measured up.

Our mother's best dessert was a mixture of oatmeal and shortening and sugar that came out looking brown and mealy.

When we first viewed this concoction, we balked at eating it.

"It looks," we said, "just like dog food."

Our mother did not have to beg us to eat, however. As Lizzie always said, "Grab while the grabbing's good." Eventually, one of us got hungry enough to sample the dessert, and soon enough we were all digging in, even learning how to make it on our own. In one of those not infrequent, somewhat chilling moments reminiscent of *Lord of the Flies*, I recall that in order to get a piece of dog food, the child chef made the others bark first. "Come here, little puppies," one of us would shout, and the rest would all come running.

Dogfood
3½ cups oatmeal
⅔ cup sugar
¼ cup flour
1¼ cups butter
½ teaspoon salt
1 teaspoon vanilla

Work all together in a bowl. Have a 13×9×2-inch pan buttered and floured. Put mixture into pan and press down firmly. Bake in moderate oven, 325 degrees, for about 30 minutes or until lightly browned. Take out and cool about 10 minutes. Cut into squares.

Oh, she tried to learn the vocabulary of thrift and flirtation, to the degree that she subscribed to a couple of women's magazines. But after a few tortured minutes spent reading some article or another, she would look up, hurt and puzzled. She didn't see the thrill of making a romper suit for your toddler out of freshly laundered dish towels for less than a dollar or following recipes for which the secret ingredient was, invariably, marshmallows. It plain exhausted her, just reading the articles about planning meals for a week, even a month ahead of time. Sometimes I am drawn to these magazines simply to see the world through the eyes in which she was forced to see it, for their anthropology and their archaeology, to plumb them for their strange customs, especially as regards mating rituals, and for their buried broken bits of Fiesta ware.

Housewives were urged to prepare special meals for special occasions, the most special being the day your husband brought his boss home for dinner. The suggested menu did not vary from one magazine to another: tenderloin, string beans with canned onion rings, and baked Alaska. These husbands, whose whims were the central engine of a good wife's life, were supposed to be waved off in the morning while the woman wore "a happy face and a clean, crisp robe." When he arrived home, lipstick was recommended along with a fresh ribbon in one's hair, not to mention a trio of daisies clipped to one side. His favorite cocktail should be mixed and waiting. "When you have domestic news of your own, by all means tell it. But keep anecdotes witty, short—and uncomplaining."

The magazines whipped up a constant froth of paranoia about losing your man, including advice on how to hang on to one: "Your husband's physical drive is probably stronger than yours. Both parties in a marriage should acknowledge this, he by showing enough attention to arouse her, she at least by an appearance of interest."

Ladies' Home Journal once ran an ad for the Great Books:

"The women your husband works with . . . are you as interesting as they?

"Can you compete when the talk gets around to ideas? Or do you stop short at diapers, pot roasts, and doctor bills?

"It takes so much these days to be a wife and mother. Love, of course, and devotion. Understanding. Courage. Wisdom.

"The willingness to do the many drugdey [sic] little things that keep a family going.

"But, sometimes—just sometimes, don't you find yourself envying the 'Gals' at the office just a little bit?

"Let's be honest. In the press of everyday affairs, did your mind slip out of gear when you slipped on that plain gold band?"

The ad goes on to pitch 443 masterpieces. A special thrill, it is suggested, would be the opportunity to "check Plato's ideas on motherhood against Karl Marx" as if your basic housewife with a slew of kids couldn't come up with her own scintillating thoughts on the subject of motherhood, Plato and Marx aside.

My mother and her women friends met once a month in a group called the P.M. Club, gathering in the evening for coffee and dessert and guest speakers. So eager was she for the stimulation of adult company that she once ignored winter storm warnings to go hear a man with an impenetrable accent discuss heart disease in the Himalayas.

Our mother's hankering for a life of the mind was honorable and heartfelt. It took the form of incessant reading. But
books can be traitors, creating an even greater sense of restlessness. The impulse to bury yourself in someone else's story pro-
vides a passing pleasure sometimes undercut by a pang. The
problem with books is that they often describe lives you wish
you could lead. Even if the circumstances aren't always the best,
at least they are heightened. In the same way that an amputee
has phantom feeling in the missing limb, books can make you feel
you missed out on a phantom fate. In books you could roll ban-
dages for brave soldiers, you could ride on a raft, you could get
lost at sea, you could fake your own funeral. In books, if you were
orphaned, at least it was in India, by cholera, which has the virtue of a certain exoticism. It was hard to see what was exotic about
being stuck in Granby, in a rapidly deteriorating house, with six
quarrelsome children, forced to economize with powdered milk.

She staved off leaving the house to earn a living for as long
as possible. She had worked before she was married, as a sixth-
grade teacher at the Valentine School in Chicopee, enjoying
the forested smells of the classroom, the calming piney odor of
wooden desks. She resigned from the job after her marriage
because only single women were allowed to teach. For some
reason, probably a twinge of loss and regret about leaving the
children behind at the beginning of the year, she told them a
tall tale about an imagined successor, Miss Orange Brown, a nasty
hag who ran a hideously tight ship: my mother's fictions were
always inspired by mixed feelings. When she left, she was given
a packet of letters, carefully inked on lined paper, from the children, who wished her well as she approached her new life. I was
entranced by these letters, mining them for the glimpse they gave
of the former Miss Shea at the last edge of girlhood when she
was chock-full of glad grace.

Dear Miss Shea,

   I have been dreaming all night of you and Dr. Blais.

   I am very sorry you are leaving us. And I dont no
what I will do with out you. I like you very much.

Yours sincerely,
Alfreda Bielanski

Dear Miss Shea,

   I am having a good time in your room. I am studying
hard because I want to be a avater. I want to fily a
filyingfortess. A filyingfortess is the bigest plane in the
World.

Your friend,
Robert Gaynor

Dear Miss Shea,

   Is it true that Miss Orange Brown said no parties and
is she really an old crab apple with a worm whole in it? I
know you were only fooling.

   I made up a poem about a bride and groom:

> *Here comes the bride*
> *God bless the groom.*
> *If he doesn't behave*
> *She'll hit him with a broom.*

   I hope you have the best wedding anyone ever had,

Lots of love,
Florence Gibson

P.S. Who is this? Five feet six inches, black hair, hazel
eyes, light blue dress, pearl necklace, pearl bracelet, navy-
blue shoes, beautiful face and beautiful temper.

Dear Miss Shea,

I wish you would not leave us. Tell Dr. Blais not to
marry you.

The boys in our room love you why don't you marry
them?

Yours sincerely,
Norma Bauch

Our mother expressed her reluctance to plunge back into
the world of full-time work with excuses ranging from, "If your
father had lived, I would not have to go out and grub for a living" to a genuine desire to be home for all of us, especially
Michael. She was fortunate to have a calling card in the form
of a college degree, but the prospects still were bleak and ill paid.
Extension universities pitched home courses to women in how
to be an accountant, secretary, income tax specialist, or steno-
type operator, one less appealing than the other. The newspapers were filled with free advice: "Before you begin your job
search, you will need to prepare a résumé. A résumé is called a
vita, a data sheet, or a brief. Awards, offices held, volunteer work,
and such should be listed only if they are directly related to the
type of job you are seeking." She waited until Michael was in
the third grade to venture back into the ranks of the employed
by working as a substitute teacher, and before she set forth that
first day, she struggled with how to position her new hat in the
hallway mirror, muttering, "Nothing is sitting right today." We
were appalled that she had mismanaged her life on such a scale
that she had degenerated into that most reviled of creatures, a
sub. How could she make herself the possible target of any scoundrel who happened to have a spitball at his disposal? She thought
about other professions, for instance, being a weather girl, for
which her main qualification was that she had a barometer that

she would bang on with almost sledgehammery vigor to see if a storm was coming on. But most weather girls were young, blond, single, small waisted, and ditzy, so her chances hovered at zero. She couldn't be an airlines stewardess; the ads required that applicants be between the ages of 20 and 26, the heights of 5'2" and 5'8", and single.

"Maybe I could be a hostess at a swank restaurant," she would say, and then she would pretend to be one: "Good evening, come this way, please," while handing out imaginary menus. I knew the kind of establishment she was dreaming of from pictures in magazines in which men are forever placing engagement rings on the hands of sleek, straight-backed women. "Ordering restaurants," we children called them, "restaurants with the lights out." It would have clean, sparkling wine glasses and stiff white linen tablecloths on all the tables, and everyone would talk in whispers and eat slowly. No one would flick peas in someone else's face to get his or her attention, and no one would yell "shortstops" the way we did, meaning that you could fling some food onto your plate from the bowl you were supposed to be passing. The meal would begin with individually owned fruit cups and end with elaborate desserts named after that famous French dictator. But there was no chance of that in Granby, where the highlight of the social season was the Grange Fair, in which we would guess the weight of pigs and give cows citations. Our local eateries included the Granby Cafe, famous for its stuffed cabbage, and that other joint with its one-note-Charley, all-turkey menu (croquettes, soup, pies).

I had the idea that maybe, given her expertise on obituaries and thanks to our great-grandfather, who had perhaps passed on his undertaker genes, our mother could have been a gifted greeter at a funeral home. From her nightly reading of the papers, she already had a store of ready-made patter: "At least it was a heart attack, and not like what happened to that poor man in North Dakota . . ."—her voice sounded thin and stricken. Or: "I always said yo-yos could be dangerous." But that kind of job, she would sigh, usually went to men because they were presumed to possess greater dignity. We wondered if we should say a novena; maybe there was a special saint for getting work, just as there appeared to be a car raffle saint and a saint of perfect pies every time. We believed that good things happened not so much because you lifted yourself up by your bootstraps, the Protestant explanation, but when luck and prayer collided in the heavens.

We girls did have one game plan that we hoped someday to get off the ground. Maybe we could get her to appear on our favorite TV show, *Queen for a Day*.

Nicknamed the Cinderella Show because of the way it churned out rags-to-riches reversals on a daily basis, it was an orgy of stories, roses, tiaras, and tears emceed by a low-voiced male announcer who, jabbing an arm, pointing a finger, began with this question: "Would *you* like to be queen for a day?" A variant on the sob sister articles that used to guarantee a female byline in newspapers, it presented five women who, wringing their hands and dabbing their eyes at suitable intervals, engaged in a verbal competition as to who had the saddest tale. The audience made the final judgment by applauding, and this applause was quantified by a crude device that measured vibrations, known by its pseudoscientific name, the clapometer. We would pile on top of each other on the sofa, the four girls: me with a book, Jacqueline and Christina applying nail polish, Maureen unobtrusive and silent, along for the ride. Raymond by that time was always off in his own orbit, isolated from the rest of us by age and temperament. If Michael joined us, we got him to be quiet and sit still by telling him to hold his breath and clench a handful of smoke from our mother's cigarettes in his fists as long as possible and maybe it would turn into a friendly elf.

"Maddy, write a letter," I would be urged by my sisters. "See if they want Mom on the show."

As far as I know there is only one complete *Queen for a Day* episode still in existence. It is excruciating to look at, the abasement of the women as they spar for material favor. In it, the first contestant is a "pretty married lady" who really admires her father-in-law and his ability to fix things. She'd like to get him some power tools.

Then, a break to promote a skillet that performs nine different kitchen operations. Despite the middle-aged, domestic nature of the prizes, we oohed and aahed along with the studio audience.

Next, a housewife from Indiana, hoping to get a clothes washer and a dryer for her large brood.

Another break, in which a woman in a corset swivels her torso, advertising a "comfortable, but effective foundation, tightly boned for more control." Ads that hinted at female anatomy always prompted an overblown reaction on our part. "Gross," we would say, clutching our middles. "Help! I can't breathe."

Next, someone who lives in a trailer wants a house and some food: "We sleep on the floor, and we'd give anything to get out of it." Another woman hopes to get a "secret meeting with my real mother because I was three days old when she had me adopted out," and someone else dearly desires "a bicycle for my boy."

Each day's potential queen not only got her specific wish, but also would receive a variety of other booty, including such things as matching luggage, a trip to someplace warm, a dinette set, a sewing machine, and a new dress for after five, "an iced blue sheath with threads of gold." One of the best bonus gifts was five minutes of unimpeded free shopping in a supermarket. Sometimes there was footage of a former queen with a shopping cart on a spree, and that's when we would shout, "Meat! "Meat! Go to the meat aisle, stupid." Michael used to think we lived in the United Steaks of America.

Who would it be this time? The one who wanted the tools or the washer/dryer or a house and food or a secret meeting or a new bike for her boy?

In the midst of each show's deliberation, I would mentally draft yet another inquiry: "Perhaps you'd like as your guest a mother of six from Granby, Massachusetts, to appear on your show. I know she's available because she's *my* mother . . ."

I imagined her on television and hoped that the scent of her fame might perfume the rest of the family. The house would become a wonderland of free new stuff. We would all experience a windfall. I, for instance, would change dramatically overnight, be able to do cartwheels, have no fear of the high board, win at arm wrestling, and give up the earth colors I had favored basically since birth. Even my looks would change: gone would be the girl with limp brown hair and glasses, replaced by someone jazzy and intriguing, born to boas and feathers.

By then we realized we had two versions of our mother.

Which mom should we send?

The first version could go on the show and in her Best Speaking Voice, she could explain that the price of living in a house with two living rooms was high in ways that were hard to predict. The roof, the furnace, the faucets: you never knew what might need fixing next. She could show the studio audience those family scrapbooks, all that haiku she encouraged us to write, the handwritten menus from breakfast in bed, family portraits done in crude crayon.

The first version would be in what we called her Chatty Cathy mode, named after the doll that spouted set pleasantries when you pulled a string. She could talk about how she had been recently chosen to serve on the committee to bring books to Brightside, a nearby orphanage whose very name dictated the kind of beaming, up-with-people outlook expected of its denizens. She would dress smartly in a suit from Best & Company, and she would make a hardheaded request for money for college tuition. She could tell the audience that in junior high school, she was quoted in the newspaper along with other members of a social studies class during National Education Week as saying, "Education is a gold mine for those who wish to make good. Brain is the bank, knowledge is the money, success the interest. Make large deposits!"

In the Shea family all four children, two girls and two boys, went to college during the depression. One son became a lawyer, and the other got his doctorate in food chemistry, once writing a scholarly article for a scientific review, the very title so dry and uninviting as to certify its erudition: "Corn Distillers' Dried Grain with Solubles in Poultry Rations." She herself had attended state teachers' college at Bridgewater, Massachusetts, where she wrote high-minded essays with Topic Sentences, such as, "Tolerance is a delightful virtue and should be considered worth acquiring" and "The proposal that there be some changes in the type and number of courses offered students at Bridgewater has been regarded as heresy by some, but, by many of the thoughtful students, an idea worthy of consideration." She even got an A in economics.

And then, she could add, with a slight downward tilt of the chin, that none of her children could go to college anywhere without a scholarship.

Or, we could send to *Queen for a Day* our other mother, the second version whom we called Miss Orange Brown when she was out of earshot, the one who was edgy and disgruntled, who threatened to send *us* to Brightside when we were, as she put it, itchy and out of control, the one who felt inadequate as a single parent, especially trying to raise her sons, suspecting she had more of a knack for daughters, the way you could be better at crusts than at fillings. This was the mother who acknowledged it would have been easier if she'd just had two of us and then, pausing, would also admit, "The problem is, which two?"

In our family we had no real twins. Yet we were paired by our mother in a variety of dyads: Raymond and Michael as the boys, Raymond and I as the big kids, Jacqueline and I as the older girls, Maureen and Christina as the younger ones, Maureen and Michael as the old baby and the new baby. The four girls were often thought of as one entity: conflated and confused with one another, elided, a blur of bony faces and straight hair. "Four roses and two thorns," we used to say, proud in our solidarity.

It felt, sometimes, as if each child had a signature defect, a trademark blemish. Raymond was too quick to anger. I was aloof and likely to scold. Jacqueline was generous to a dizzying degree. She always worried about everyone else's welfare, making comments like, "Poor little birdies. Poor birdies have to go to the bathroom outside." Diapers for robins: no one person could save the planet on any scale, especially on the one she envisioned. Christina could be social to a fault. She was always seeking definition outside the family. She looked different from the rest of us; her neat pretty features and dark cap of thick hair elicited from strangers tributes to her beauty, leaving the other three girls to languish in gawky silence. She had an efficiency about her that shamed the rest of us. All her life she has made lists, including a schedule for one Christmas in which she designated the time between 10 and 10:15 in the morning to "eat an orange slowly." Our mother used to say that when she grew up, Christina should be secretary to the president of Chase Manhattan. Maureen was too self-effacing. She wore glasses and was easily ignored in the fray. Once we thought she was lost, and we recruited the entire neighborhood for a frantic search until she was discovered, in a sleepy heap, in back of a couch, its skirt a makeshift blanket. We used to call her "Slow Mo" because she had a maddeningly self-sufficient way of doing everything at her own pace. Maureen was so undemanding as to have almost turned herself into a rumor of a child rather than a real one. I used to love to hug her, my private doll. Michael was also undemanding and sometimes appeared to copy her vanishing act. His favorite game when he was a toddler and I was in the third grade was to grab me at the waist from the back. As I turned around and around in circles, asking, "Where's that whippersnapper?" he would laugh at his implied absence. Because of his position as the baby in the family and the misfortune of possessing an easygoing nature, Michael's flaw was that he was too easily framed. A fire from a chemistry set, a broken bicycle, fingerprints in the icing. We always tried to hang any suspicion of misconduct on him first.

When *Life* magazine had a picture of an embryo on the cover, I asked our mother about birth control. "Birth control," she answered, harried, moving about the house to scoop up some mess or another, "that's something your father didn't believe in."

But if you knew our mother, you knew our *Queen for a Day* scheme was ill fated. She would never go on television and unburden herself.

The idea that we would even consider such a possibility for a second was proof of our inferior moral nature, our slipshod ethical standards, marking us as people who cared more about loot than dignity.

She viewed our suggestion as preposterous.

She quoted Shakespeare, "He who steals my purse steals trash, but he who steals my good name steals all."

She quoted Anonymous: "Fools' names and fools' faces oft appear in public places."

Catholics might confess, in formulaic language, to a shadow, in the dark, but not on TV.

"I'm Irish, from New England," our mother often said, to justify the double whammy of reserve that formed the backbone of her character. Her allegiance to certain standards of conduct reminded me of an obscure lady patriot named Barbara Frietchie, the subject of a poem that was taught as great literature in our elementary school: "Shoot if you must this old gray head . . ." but don't you dare tamper with Old Glory. Our mother's Old Glory was not a mere piece of fabric festooned with stars and stripes but rather an invisible tapestry composed of everything she held dear and defensible, including language itself, against whose debasement she held a constant vigil. In her mind, words deserved the same thoughtful placement and balance as Belleek vases and chiseled crystal. We could not shut a door; we had to close it. Clothes were not dirty: they needed to be laundered. We couldn't sleep over someone's house; we could sleep over *at* it. She observed the mass's shift from Latin to the vernacular with a heavy heart. She insisted that strangers address her as Mrs. Blais, explaining that it made her feel neither more comfortable nor more at home to be called Maureen by people who hardly knew her. Self-respect was predicated on fierce silence. One time she told us we could be as modern and godless as we wished. If we wanted to go to psychiatrists, that was our business. She had only one caveat, which, if you thought about and acquiesced to, would surely erode the spirit of, if not totally cripple, the entire enterprise. Her solitary stipulation: "Just don't mention me."

"Did your mother ever remarry?" is another one of those questions often posed by strangers for which the short answer, by its very brevity, maligns the complications of the reality.

Quickly, the answer is no.

For a long time, her brother, our uncle Dermot, served as the emergency infusion of a male influence. He spent most weekends at the house from when our father died until the early sixties, when he took a job in state government running the newly established Consumer's Council.

At the time, his work life consisted of adjudicating insurance claims on the road throughout New England. He was not married, and he had that awkwardness common to people without children who are forced to spend time in their squealing company, like being made to write with the wrong hand. Once he backed up in the driveway and ran over one of our cats. He was so shaken that he went out and bought us all presents: game books with mazes, boxes of 64 crayons, homemade potholder kits.

He was often stricken with a low-grade flu requiring canned soup, plain toast, ginger ale, and a generally quiet atmosphere for a cure. His passions were for politics, history, and his hi-fi, which we were not allowed to touch during his absence or in his presence. It was in the same category as the front door and the front stairs, off limits to greasy fingers and dirty feet. He tried to distract us from our usual high-minded pursuits such as burping competitions with slide shows in the Green Room of the One Hundred Most Beloved Works of Classical Art. He liked to listen to opera and war music, both at a high volume. He often raised his voice above all the squabbling to lecture us about the

Civil War and famous figures he admired from history and sometimes about the nature of childhood itself, on which he was an
expert because he himself had had one. Dermot was the designated disciplinarian, the person our weary mother tried to
threaten us with all week until his arrival on Friday evening.
"Who's been bad?" he would ask soon after arriving. "Who needs
a spanking?" We would all run for cover. Raymond, in particular, was the object of endless orations: "You have to stop creating turmoil, and go with the program. What makes you think
the rules don't apply to you?"

Dermot believed, as if no one had ever before enunciated
the concept, that children underwent important imprinting. If
they were given certain experiences of surpassing happiness,
those memories would sustain them in adulthood. These experiences took the form, almost exclusively, of fresh air. We were
to spend as much time outside the house as possible. Fall weekends were spent raking the leaves on all four lawns, a task complicated by its endlessness, thanks to the leaves that kept blowing
down from the Congregational Church across the street on a hill,
giving Pope John XXIII's so-called spirit of ecumenism a run for
its money. Dermot advocated trips to anyplace there was water
and on a couple of occasions helped subsidize lakeside vacations
in Sunapee, New Hampshire. He especially liked Groton Long
Point, Connecticut, on the Long Island Sound, where the sea
was a tonic, a restorative, the ultimate pick-me-up. At the time
we used to visit, G.L.P. was filled with Catholics from West
Hartford, Connecticut, and Longmeadow and Springfield, Massachusetts, and the talk had a comforting familiarity, with frequent allusions to Boston College and the Cross as well as the
excellent basketball being played by those boys at Providence.
We children could be let loose under somewhat controlled circumstances, choosing the beach where we wanted to swim: East,

Kiddie, South, Main. At any one of them, for years in succession, the portable radios all seemed stuck at the same tune, filled with cornball longing, about seeing someone in September, when the summer was finally through. Main Beach was the most popular, partly because of its boardwalk, a concrete span that echoes the curve of the half mile of sand and is lined with clapboard dowager cottages so close to each other that some of the windows are smoked and so close to the sea that most front yards consist of small stones instead of grass. On the sunniest, hottest days, towels would cover the entire beach. Two ropes stretching a decent distance into the ocean defined the swimming area. A small wooden raft, a few hundred feet out, was the farthest anyone went. Our mother could not see the raft without mentioning a favorite short story she had once read. "I think it was in the *Atlantic Monthly*. It was by that Jewish writer, you know who I mean."

In our house "that Jewish writer, you know who I mean" generally translated into Philip Roth.

"It was about what you would call a lower-middle-class family in which the father was a tailor, and he worked very hard, and every summer the family went for two weeks to Long Island—at least, I think it was Long Island, because it was definitely the ocean—and I imagine they were at a Jewish resort, because back then so many places were restricted, not that I approve, but that's the way things were, and every summer his son and all the other boys, the sons of other hardworking men, would try to swim out to the raft. Like lemmings, they got nearer and nearer each year, but it was always understood that by the time they got out to the raft and could finally dive from the high board, by that point they would have gotten too old to be on vacation and before they knew it they would be spending their summers in the hot city just like all their fathers, and what was so touching is that they kept trying to swim toward a fate they could not really have wanted."

Maureen Shea Blais, artist of melancholy, doyen of brooding. When most people see a raft, they see the dictionary definition, a floating platform often equipped with a diving board and usually secured in such a way as to remain relatively stationary at a reasonable swimming distance from the shore. She saw what Roth saw: the sorrow of what it is to be alive. She should have been a writer. What other profession reveres gloom to such a degree?

She did in fact write one children's story, and for years we were led to believe that if only *Bubblelini* could find a publisher, we would finally have a solution to all our money woes. We would be like people who invent what becomes a common everyday device, like the zipper or the ballpoint pen; we would be rich forever.

The story went something like this:

Once upon a time there was a little girl whose name was Bubblelini. Now, Bubblelini was not like the other little girls. She didn't like to go to school, she didn't like to go to birthday parties, she didn't like to go to the store to buy new dresses, and she didn't even like to watch TV. In fact, her mother had to make her watch TV, every Friday night for half an hour.

There was only one thing Bubblelini liked to do in the whole wide world and that was to . . . blow bubbles!

Mainly, her life was filled to the brim with us.

Sometimes she would appear to break down and a kind of exhaustion would overtake her face, elongating it farther than nature intended. Irish faces tend to be either like hers, all lines and angles, or round and muffiny, circle upon circle. We'd be eating dinner, and in the midst of delivering to her lips a bite of food in a slow sorrowful arc, she would tell us: "The problem with children is that they start to leave home the moment they can crawl; yes, they do. Before you could talk, when you were just toddlers, I could almost hear you plotting: how can we get away?"

She would pause to take a pensive breath.

"Except for Jacqueline, sweet little Locky Lou. You always said you'd live in a cabin with me. But Ray, you've been head-strong and footloose for years. And, Maureen, I never gave you permission to baby-sit for those people on Sound Breeze. Madeleine, don't you ever lift your head out of a book? Even whales have to break the surface for oxygen every now and then. And Christina, dear little Christina, with your perfect blank face: whatever are you thinking? And you, little Michael, scooting into your sisters' arms instead of mine. Oh, I'm not deaf. I'm not without a certain radar. What I don't hear I can see in people's eyes: poor Maureen, the broke widow. Some of those women can be so self-satisfied just because they have husbands who are obstetricians at a Catholic hospital, and we know they'll never want for work, or isn't it great, the Hanrahans are buying a house on the Cape with one of those sickeningly cute names like Uneeda Rest or Happy Daze, and someone else is getting a cabin cruiser. Or there's that Meg Rafferty, sitting on easy street, so thrilled to be one of the package store Raffertys, think-ing I can't see the soupy look of pity in her eyes when she glances at us during mass when her mind should be on loftier matters. You know what I call them? I call them the smuggos, the com-placos. I won't give those people the satisfaction of the truth, and I swear, I'll take the razor strap to you children if you so much as breathe a word of any of this outside the house. I want you to say we're doing just fine, thank you."

She poked at her bun with a pin to secure an errant clump of hair.

"At least now you know what to say if anyone asks."

If anyone asks: the very notion was enough to put us on our guard. Other people's curiosity, even if well intended, was the equivalent of fighting words. It could only mean that our lives were going to be interpreted in the harshest possible light. It was our cue to circle the wagons and hunker down against the enemy.

"You might as well face it. Your mother's never going to remarry. I'm going to stay a widow forever. I'm not the type to find a new husband."

In fact, we faced it early on. What fantasies of a stepfather I entertained took on the irritating dot-to-dot vagueness of some generic physician who sang "Waltzing Matilda" while fixing the tires on our Schwinns, who bore the faint odor of sweat and Chesterfields, and whose stubble during a chaste good night kiss would supply a giddy transport.

Our mother kept up a good front, for instance, watching her figure to the tune of eating the same punitive lunch every day, a banana and a cup of skim milk.

She loved fashion and would flip through the pages of the women's magazines for outfits she liked, sighing with longing when she saw ads for dinner gowns, dresses described as "a column of crepe with a tunic embroidered with matte bugle beads— no glitter, just the subtle gleam of color on ice."

"Oh," she would say, "doesn't this sound dreamy?" quoting from another ad: "'Graceful, flattering, and cool as a sea breeze is this colorful summer dress with white daisies all over the bodice, while an attractive little capelet to be worn casually over the shoulders completes the costume. Gay as a lark!"

It was the notion of the capelet that got to her, you could tell.

There are photos in which she could have been mistaken for a movie star, wearing a scarf and sunglasses, dangling a cigarette, at the beach. Despite her striking looks, my mother was not the type to flirt, to bat her eyelashes and pretend that everything some guy said should be put on a billboard, next to the Coppertone and the "Which twin has the Toni" ads. The women in the fifties who tended to get a second chance in the marriage sweepstakes all knew how to turn their men into heroes of the most down-to-earth situation. *You should have seen the way Al changed that flat* or *I shudder to think what would have happened if Phil and Scott hadn't been there to figure out which way was Vermont!* This became clear to me when the father of a girl I knew dropped dead of a heart attack and her mother did not skip a beat, summoning the kind of raw energy that soon translated into a wardrobe of capri pants and mohair sweaters and dates galore.

We became, in effect, her second husband. We courted her with pictures of flowers and odes in her honor, studying her like a painting, often exploring her bureau drawers; one was filled with lace collars, shawls, and snoods—we thought she had her own private collection of spider webs. She said she had access to another dimension, and we believed her. She liked the idea of seances and Ouija boards. In the bureau with the spider webs she also kept a deck of telepathy cards marketed by Duke University in the fifties. She liked to test us to see whether we had inherited her Braille for the beyond. She held up the cards and kept a record of how many times we could correctly guess the shapes on the other side, hoping we would exceed the law of averages. I wished she had more access to this dimension and was not so easily befuddled by childproof caps on aspirin or following directions for defrosting or finding a channel on a portable radio. She had a pretty low standard for judging whether someone had mastered destiny itself, and it had to do with the ability to self-serve gasoline.

Like all suitors, we eventually came to see her defrocked.

We took note of a certain frailty. Once when we were older and my mother went to visit Jacqueline, who could not greet her in person, there was this note:

> The television is set for the Channel 3 news. I am almost afraid to give you instructions because it is so easy to turn on, and somehow you'll anticipate it should be complicated. Just pull out (gently) the little switch on the bottom. That is all.
>
> Also, the red tea kettle is full of water, ready for tea if you want it. There is wine too.
>
> If you feel like taking a bath, you should be all set.

The letter was signed "Jay" and followed by several postscripts.

> P.S. There are clocks all over the house, on the living room sill, kitchen and bedrooms.
>
> P.S. The thermostat is off. Please feel free to zip it up. It's in the dining room on the wall.
>
> P.S. The wine may be a little sour. Please taste first.

She thought of herself as a pansy forced into hard duty as a perennial. Although she soldiered on, it appeared at times to be an act of pure will, as if her feet were stuck in taffy. Her very sensibility was at odds with the upbeat nature of the postwar mentality. Behind her back we called our mother not only Miss Orange Brown, but also Our Lady of Sorrow. In her life, Maureen Blais had her fair share of loss, presuming fair shares exist. But as if the actual cataclysms weren't enough, she kept an invisible Rolodex of minor disappointments, a democratic hodgepodge in which she welcomed the traumas of people she barely knew, virtual strangers she met while returning a book to the library who told her about someone's distant cousin in Cincinnati who was "a touch catatonic" or someone else's kin down in Washington who got fired from his job with the State Department because he believed in UFOs. She hated to see certain styles change and longed for the triumphant comeback of face powder, dotted swiss, and tomato aspic at summer parties. The Blessed Mother had ten sorrows, but my mother could challenge her to a duel any day: everywhere she looked she found evidence of ineffable sadness, the mateless mitten discovered after the winter thaw, the sight of baby grass stirring in a spring breeze, the sound of a child scratching away at a violin, the hum of the wind in an empty parking lot.

In my memory, my mother had only two dates.

One with an extremely short judge. I think it was a blind date with a confirmed bachelor put together by well-meaning friends. I was predisposed to be a favorable member of his jury. At the time I possessed something of a law-and-order streak, and I liked the notion of what it would be like having a man who dispensed judgments for a living as a new member of our household. At the very least we would become more organized. We would have paper routes, maybe even get a pencil sharpener that worked. At night at dinner we would hear harrowing stories about hardened criminals and learn the fascinating difference between injunctions and torts.

The evening he arrived to take her out we all crouched on the upstairs floor, peering through the railing, like so many miniature, pajama-clad convicts.

"Quiet down," I told the others. "You don't want to make a bad impression."

When they refused to stop whispering, I told them that the next time we had mashed potatoes, I would take their portion and squash it in my hands.

Rampant giggling.

"Stop now, or else if there's an accident when we're driving, I won't let you look at it."

Suddenly, a hush.

She was descending the stairs.

Did she really sashay down them like Loretta Young in one of those dresses in which the bust is delineated and the skirt is all swoosh? Did she and the judge really drink "highballs," the most adult drink in the world, distilled, we thought, from the essences of grown-up activities, such as complaining about taxes and making small talk and registering to vote? Did she serve, as I am certain she did, cheese squeezed onto Ritz crackers topped with—and this was the cosmopolitan touch, the clever home-entertainment trick encouraged by the magazines—pimentos?

Our mother floated out of the house on the petal of an imaginary tulip, and returned, it seemed, far too soon, deflated. It was like a fast forward in a nature film when the plant shoots up, exfoliates, and then droops in mere seconds.

Afterward, all she said was, "You can just imagine the kinds of verdicts he was likely to deliver on days when he was feeling self-conscious."

Not much later, she had a date with a dapper sort of fellow with a trite Irish name, something like Paddy O'Rourke, who hung around for a while and then faded off into the New England sunset, unconvincing even as a memory, like trying to summon the feel of snow in July.

After that brief encounter, she gathered her four daughters and told us sternly, "Girls, I want you to listen, and I want you to listen carefully. I have something important to say, and I'm only going to say it once."

Out of the dregs of a doomed relationship arose gallant and memorable an adage.

"Never, and I mean *never*, trust a single man with a station wagon."

Chapter Six

In the Company of Sisters

DURING THE SUMMER OF 1957, I DREAMED OF GETTING AWAY.

We were housebound. My grandmother was in her sickroom, and there were no plans except to sit and wait for death to arrive, a vigil as tiresome as it was terrifying. Only our grandmother's room had an air conditioner, its rumble another kind of tribulation. The house was filled with the routine of death: the fatigue in the faces of the living, the pharmaceutical odors, the ticking silence, the constant trade in basins and towels and chips of ice.

In age she had faded, this woman born in Ireland, my namesake, the mother of two sons and two daughters, Maureen, Kevin, Dermot, and Eileen, two boys, two girls, a "rich man's" family. My impression was that we children hastened her death, not deliberately, but because the constant noise and commotion unsettled the nerves of someone who liked a quiet game of bridge, whose piano playing was said to be of concert caliber, who was referred to, more than once in her life by people unknown to each other, as a Perfect Lady. To a ten year old she had a distant, ceremonial air, like a pope.

The newspapers that summer were advertising cooked hams, ready for the Independence Day holiday, for 43 cents a pound. Two pounds of peaches for 39 cents. *You'll Never Get Rich* with Phil Silvers, *Gunsmoke*, and *To Tell the Truth* were on television. Movie theaters proclaimed, in snow-capped letters, that they were "air-conditioned year round." *Peyton Place* and *Compulsion* were among the best-selling novels; if you preferred nonfiction, you could read *The FBI in Action.* A man named Khrushchev, short and snarling, dominated the foreign news. A man named Castro was organizing rebel troops in the hinterlands of Cuba. The Catholic Church had a new rule: You had to fast only three hours before receiving Communion. In the magazines there were ads for airlines, with stewardesses wearing white gloves and Bulova watches promising miniature meals in the clouds, with real silver and actual glasses. The ads, with their promise of a larger world, had a special ability to torment.

My mother became distant and distracted in the face of her mother's mortality. Seeing her move about the house, in a drained, hesitant manner, was like watching a Technicolor movie reduced to black-and-white in slow motion.

There are certain laws that govern the universe:

Nature abhors a vacuum.

The happiest apple falls by virtue of its own patience, not to prove a point.

The wise child times her supplications wisely.

Waiting until that moment at the end of the day when my mother sank into her favorite perch in the living room and lit a cigarette, sensing she would be a soft touch for anything that lessened her load, I wangled two weeks of Girl Scout camp. I had seen a leaflet with a smudgy black-and-white photo of its placid pond; it beckoned with the promise of shade and solitude. My mother agreed on the condition that Jacqueline accompany me, a condition that was easy to accept because I was used to feeling responsible for her and the others. When I was first exposed to the notion of a guardian angel, which is to say, a spiritual pilot attached to another human on a twenty-four-hour-a-day basis, I asked if everyone had one.

Yes, I was told by my mother.

"Including Jacqueline?" Again, yes.

A cloud of confusion filled my head, suddenly yielding to the hard bright light of recognition.

"Am I him?"

I started packing for camp weeks ahead of time, cramming my duffel with flashlights and bug spray, emergency Life Savers, and some stationery with a picture of a poodle and a legend I thought of as the height of literary sophistication: "A pen and some ink and here's what I think."

All the while I imagined I was leaving for a much longer and more dramatic interlude.

Boarding school, the Alps.

"You can come," I told Jacqueline, "but you better behave."

I was probably closest to Jacqueline, mainly because we shared a room, a forced umbilical from which we never fully recovered. With her I was guilty of a series of lower-case tyrannies. She remembers how I made her turn off the lights at night when I wanted to go to sleep, forcing her, among other indignities, to study the catechism in bed in the dark, a challenging endeavor because although we sometimes had batteries and we sometimes had flashlights, we never had both at once. Together she and I would take the Street Railway bus the six miles to Holyoke; the fumes from the bus caused us to gag, but they also underscored prosperity as shoppers were deposited and removed in a constant dialysis. We might take in a show at the Victory or the Strand or the Suffolk unless they were featuring one of those stupid mushy movies with grown-ups in pajamas chasing each other. We visited Woolworths for a thrilling lunch consisting of chocolate milk, grilled cheese sandwiches, and our favorite part, manna beyond any conscious expectation, the free, unsolicited pickle. Afterward, we would go to Child's Shoe Store, where our neighbor, Mr. Brooks, was the manager, and play with the x-ray machine, which revealed the bones of our feet in big goopy shadows, a forerunner of strobe lights and Lava lamps. In front of Child's were a series of oversized, permanently mounted brass footsteps, certain in their stride.

My role with Jacqueline, as I interpreted it, not necessarily accurately or fairly, was to get her to shape up. Instead of praising her for her good nature, I took advantage of it. Our exchanges were filled with elaborate sighs, eye rolling, and toe tapping on my part. I responded to her heartfelt remarks with pat phrases.

"Do you think a person would go to hell if she stole candy bars for her little sisters?"

"That's for me to know and you to find out."

"Someone wrote inside my math book and I think it was Michael, and now my teacher wants me to stand in the corner."

"Tough toenails."

"Can I look inside your diary just this once?"

"Mind your own beeswax."

I greeted any endeavor on her part with a scowl. "You think this is a science project?" I said when I discovered she wanted to put a recently extracted tooth in a glass of Coca-Cola with a sign that said, "Decay." "You think that kind of lazy attitude is what we need in the U.S. of A.? No wonder the Russians are winning. You HAVE to make something better than this, something that gets people to sit up and notice."

"Like what?"

"Like something with flashing lights or toads or an explosion." Thus, I inspired her in a doomed enterprise in which she actually tried to devise an electric toad exploder.

She and I were in constant races to see who knew all the words to songs like "Silhouettes" and who heard of the Beatles first. We both adored Annette Funicello, the most popular girl in the world, and when I sent our idol a fan letter with half a piece of Juicy Fruit gum (I couldn't resist chewing the other half myself), I let Jacqueline read the two-page "Greetings from Disneyland" form letter I got back listing all the rides and attractions, but not until she had made her bed and cleaned up her side of the room. Although these Greetings were no more than an advertisement, they had the cachet of coming all the way from California, and we pretended there had been a genuine personal exchange.

I called Jacqueline "Slowpoke" for all to hear as we trudged home from school. At night I wouldn't let her climb into bed unless she had laid out her outfit for the next morning for inspection. We even readied our toothbrushes, with a squiggle of toothpaste dispensed in anticipation of saving time in the morning. We rearranged our furniture constantly, so that sometimes the beds were both against the back wall, sometimes they jutted forth next to each other, and sometimes they were arranged like the letter *T*. A radiator in one corner rumbled and hissed throughout the night: we draped our clothes on it so they would be cozy and warm in the morning. Of course, mine were closer to the grill. Tucked behind the crucifix above the radiator were the dried-out palms we had gotten at church on the last Palm Sunday, and during one especially pious interval we even had a vessel with holy water for blessing ourselves every time we entered or exited the room.

"You've got to be more ladylike," I would tell her. "Watch how you sit."

"What's wrong with the way I'm sitting?"

"Remember how Mrs. Guild told us to cross our legs at the ankles? Jacqueline, you've got to be more careful."

I lowered my voice and turned around to make certain the younger children weren't eavesdropping.

My tone was shocked and stern.

"Jacqueline, you don't want people to see your England and your France, do you?"

In the company of my sisters, there was no mistaking me for anything but the oldest.

There was a kind of sick power inherent in my role as Oldest Sister, and I embraced my despotism. Whenever any of them said or did something that was the least bit foolish or ill advised, I would say, "At least I'm not mental, like some people."

A NO TRESPASSING sign decorated my half of our shared bedroom; violators were charged a fee of one cent. When my sisters got old enough to retaliate verbally, they called me a battle-ax, and then transmogrified my name into Mad, Mad, Maddle-ax. As slurs went, it had a cleverness even I had to admire. But it did not stop me from retorting with a semi-nonsensical phrase I'd seen in some book or another: "Why, you insignificant piece of psychological ingenuity! How dare you insinuate that I should tolerate such a diabolical insult?"

At camp, my first reaction was one of guarded disappointment. Everything looked faded, like a party dress worn once too often—the grass, the main lodge, even the American flag hoisted with all due ceremony in the mornings. The empty cabins with their bare bunks and orange-crate nightstands appeared in desperate need of the giggles of girls. The screen doors had no springs, so of all the sounds that registered during that two-week stay, none was more insistent than bang, bang, bang.

The first evening at dinner we were introduced to the concept of what was called the "No, thank you serving," an elaborately tendered yet invisible portion of whatever food it was we did not want to eat. I tried not to gag as the dishes were collected at the end of the meal and the leftovers scraped at the long table where we sat on benches. I didn't see Jacqueline during those first twenty-four hours or so, busy as we were discovering the lay of the land, the nature of our individual tasks (sweeping the cabin, setting tables in the lodge, removing branches from trails). When we finally reunited, the very sight of me caused first her lower lip to tremble, then her eyes to fill, her body to shake, and finally she gave herself over to a weeping fit beyond all understanding. In me she saw the possibility of succor; in her I feared the weight of responsibility. This was my first major escape and what happened became the prototype of most of my other escapes: flight always included a ball and chain, a sense of responsibility, of a task left unfinished.

When Jacqueline was little, the summer sun tented on her face in the form of freckles. A jangling collection of kneecaps and elbows, she often appeared airborne. Sometimes for a lark she would pretend to be Helen Keller, clenching her eyes shut and poking her ears closed with her fingers. She's always been gentle, given to whimsy. One time during elocution when we had to recite the phrase "the horns of elfland, faintly blowing" as if we ourselves were faintly blowing horns, she concluded by saying, "toot, toot," and so she earned Mrs. Guild's most imperious look of complete, nearly fatal, dismissal.

When someone once asked Jacqueline, "If I had no head and no arms and no legs, could I still go to second grade?" she said sure, and I remember berating her for not being more realistic.

It may have been the overwhelming realism of camp life, the absence of any pretense of elegance, that violated her sensibilities: the plop of the basic food groups on the plates at meals, the communal cheer, the ghastly stink of the outhouse.

Some of what repelled Jacqueline about Camp Sandy Brook also repelled me: the fluid boundaries between people and their bodies in a camp setting, the damp, fetid shower room. What I liked, which was simply lost on her, was the militaristic overlay, the predictability, the rigid schedule from reveille to taps, the precise and equitable division of labor, the songs and traditions and s'mores. I enjoyed visiting the Trading Post during strictly allotted times to buy stamps and postcards. I ended all my letters, "Happy Hunting Grounds." During craft time I easily convinced myself that baskets made from Popsicle sticks were something special. The false and exaggerated rivalries between cabins seemed to me real and true and urgent. I wanted ours to win the talent show and the scavenger hunts and all those endless cabin inspections. Tone-deaf, I nonetheless sang with gusto at campfires the plaintive, "Peace, I ask of thee, oh river," and the old standby:

> *Make new friends,*
> *But keep the old.*
> *One is silver,*
> *And the other gold.*

At camp, I became, well, famous. So great was my enthusiasm, so fulsome and nonstop my tributes to the fresh air and the scouting spirit, that when a lady from the local newspaper came to camp to do a feature story, she interviewed me as well as four other equally vocal campers. To this poor reporter, who, as a woman, was probably not allowed to cover real news (I still vainly search for her byline to this day: Enid Schwartzwald, where are you?), I chatted about the thrill of bag lunches on hikes and the opportunity to make new friends from other cultures, meaning two towns over. I praised the food, which on the day of her visit, according to her own account, consisted of "light scrambled eggs mixed with bacon, bread and butter, peanut butter, lettuce salad, tapioca pudding and milk."

The more confidence and celebrity I gained, the more home-sick Jacqueline got, unable to eat eggs and pudding, or to sleep, moping continually. She was delivered, tearful, to me several times a day by her counselors. My spirits sagged when I saw her approach, a thin, pitiful, almost eight-year-old girl with teeth even bigger than mine, racked by sobs.

The worst outburst occurred after we had gone to church on Sunday. For some reason, our home-base Catholic church was chosen by the camp as the one to attend. I floated in, wearing my Scout uniform, happy in my green and yellow anonymity. Jacqueline made what was for her the fatal error of scanning the congregation for familiar faces. Our mother! Her best friend Eileen! Christina and Maureen! (And what of our grandmother? Was she still sick, was she still alive?) You couldn't talk in church, and when we filed out, there was no lingering. Later, Jacqueline would describe the feeling as nightmarish, liked being trapped on a screen inside a silent movie. Back at camp, the counselors encouraged her to give in to her tears, not necessarily the wisest strategy, in that she soon became hysterical. The more she carried on, the more she guaranteed that she would be brought to me, a quivering cargo.

I pretended to drip with sympathy.

"Poor little thing," I cooed, but as soon as the counselors left, certain that my nurturing manner was just the tonic for her sinking morale, I seized her by the shoulders and read her the riot act:

"Shape up, pip-squeak."

Rage filled my lungs, knotted my throat, clenched my hands. She was not human but flotsam, out to cramp my Camp Sandy Brook style. Couldn't she see how busy I was, I demanded, arms akimbo, eyes glaring, as I gestured toward my orange crate with its stack of projects demanding my attention: a half-decorated beanie, an unfinished spatter painting, a wool octopus still in need of several limbs.

A practitioner of tough love before it had been invented, I gave her the stern dose of home she needed.

"You're entering that talent show tonight whether you like it or not."

She heaved her frail shoulders up and down, but at least she stopped crying.

"But," she whimpered, "I have nothing to wear."

"Yes you do," I said. "You brought a bathing suit, didn't you?"

She nodded.

"You can be . . . a beauty queen. Just wear your bathing suit and the shoes you brought for church and walk on stage and turn to the judges and say," and here I did my best imitation of Mae West, gleaned from old movies on TV, "'Come up and see me sometime.'"

She gave me a baleful look.

"Let me hear you try."

Jacqueline was nearly skeletal as a child and acted frightened of taking more than her share of anything, including oxygen. Out of her skinny self came the unlikely words, "Come up and see me sometime."

And then, just to show me she was really trying, she added this extra touch: "Sonny boy."

"Hey, that's great, that's really great. I'm jealous."

"Really?" she said, brightening considerably.

"Really. If you keep this up, I'll let you borrow my skort." The skort was a combination skirt and shorts, a peculiar hybrid garment that enjoyed fifteen minutes of popularity that summer. "Now, come on. Chin up. You'll be one cute cookie tonight."

The minute I could see that she had calmed, I kicked her out of my cabin and sent her back to the Bluebird Division. "I'm sorry," I said, affecting an air of busy distraction, "but now I have to double-sheet my friend Louise Vlash's bunk"—how I loved that name, Louise Vlash!—"and then I want to finish making my homemade braided belt."

When at last she shuffled her way across the stage that night, raising her head to utter her big lines, the audience clapped and stamped its pleasure, an overreaction that thrilled her.

On the last day of camp, my cabin mates and I exchanged addresses and written expressions of good luck. I possessed at the time an Autograph Hound, a stuffed animal covered with a light canvas fabric suitable for writing on. Mine was in the shape of a dachshund. My cabin mates signed it, claiming that we were the best campers and this was the best summer ever. We urged each other to write letters, and someone wrote on my hound what I considered the unspeakably clever exhortation "D-liver, D-letter, D-sooner, D-better."

Back home the aimlessness of summer kicked back in. Sometimes I sabotaged my sisters' diaries by writing fake entries, but in time even that lost its luster. We practiced setting our hair in pin curls and with orange juice cans, and we tried to start a fan club for Tab Hunter. I was big on memorizing commercials: "One out of every ten Americans is mentally ill" and "Save now for the college of your choice" and "Crest has been proven to be an effective decay prevention dentifrice when used in a conscientiously applied program of oral hygiene and regular professional care."

In late August our grandmother died, and I tried not to contemplate her absence any more than I did the absence of my father. This was out of what I now think of as a protective mechanism: loss, dwelled upon, can expand and strangle. But her image returned to me at unexpected times, as when I smelled her favorite food, lamb chops, cooking, or when I heard certain strains of music by Chopin, with its discreet merriment.

Fifth grade began with the creation of relief maps of the United States with a concoction of salt and baking soda and water, and camp soon faded from conscious memory. If you ask Christina or Maureen what they remember about our going away, they both say, "You were always going away and getting to do everything first. It just blended together." Jacqueline maintains to this day that if camp was not the most traumatizing episode of her life, it was one of them.

Fifth grade was the last year that I remember *playing*, in that fierce way in which children's play is its own work, almost a full-time calling.

In some ways, we raised ourselves, policing and admonishing each other as we dashed about in our unarchitected Keds, chomping on Bazooka, wielding what power we could due to superior strength or age. In a manner that is hard to imagine today, when our lives have too much asphalt to envision that much prairie, we roamed the outdoors, building forts, finding treasures like an old-tire swing deep in the woods, returning home at exactly six when the Congregational Church pealed its bells. We moved about in packs, tow-headed, cowlicked, sticky-fingered proof of American prosperity.

We foraged in neighbors' gardens for tomatoes and radishes and cukes in season, picking them from patches without permission, wiping the dirt on our shirts, entering their strange, sweet, tart, juicy kingdoms. In the fall we gathered hickory nuts and cracked their shells with the heels of our shoes. In the spring we dipped our fingers into the buckets collecting sap from maples. In June we sucked the juice from rhubarb.

In an occasional flurry of civic duty, we put on plays in the Town Hall, the plot of which never varied, thanks to Shauna and Sharlene Brooks, who were born the exact same day as Prince Charles: "The Trouble with Twins." The proceeds went to the Red Cross, which was either our favorite charity or the only one we'd ever heard of. We played King of the Mountain on the huge piles of dirt that accompanied the constant construction projects of the fifties.

Not all our fun was pristine. When houses on the common became empty, we would break into them, moving as silently and weightlessly as we could through the shadowed rooms, enjoying the felon's deepest thrill of floating above and beyond the rules. We smoked pilfered cigarettes, whose real allure was not the corruption of our lungs so much as the joy of playing with matches. We made crank calls: "Is your refrigerator running? You better catch it." We tried to get little boys to pee in front of us. We played in the cow pond several fields beyond the one in the back of our house, harvesting frogs for potential dissection. For sport, we chased cows with apples, hoping to ruin their milk, and we spat in the sap buckets of a mean neighbor.

We tormented Jimmy Parker, a one-eyed man who lived in someone's shed, who dressed with odd formality each day in a suit, often festooned with a weed in the lapel, his best effort at a carnation. He roamed the town with a burlap sack in which he placed the grass he liked to pick while singing, "Here she comes, Miss America." Jimmy Parker would be in a field by himself, picking through the blades, deep in conversation with an invisible companion. "Jiiimmmmmmmyyyy," we would shout and then hide, so that when he stood up from his labors we would be outside the range of his one good eye. He would turn around in a befuddled lunge. Just as he cocked his grizzled chin toward the source of the sound and moved toward it, another child, equally hidden, would shout his name, so that we forced him into a dizzying circle until finally we would get bored and run off. Why did we taunt Jimmy? Were we, as the nuns told us, driven to wrongdoing because we bore the mantle of original sin? Were we repaying the adults in our lives who abandoned us to our own resources, trusting too much in the blinkered somnolence of a small town? Or was our aggression merely fear in a different guise?

When people died in the fifties, their deaths were not usually discussed, but they did die, even the children. There was slim, blond Catherine, who had a wasting disease and who could be seen on Saturday afternoons making her confession, surely a negligible enterprise given what must have been her overall purity, accepting penance like the rest of us; and Terry, the boy from up the street who dressed up like a pilgrim and held Christina's hand on stage all during one Thanksgiving pageant, stricken with leukemia, gone by the time of the pageant the following year. There was the Polish boy, run over on his bike by a truck while the family was on vacation: it was a matter of him or his sister, everyone said. She was on one side of the road, he was on the other, and the truck had to turn. One or the other. Something about this story held a particular terror for me. Children folded into the surf at crowded beaches, they got polio, and they climbed inside abandoned iceboxes and shut the door.

We were not daredevils, and so we were spared the worse fates. One late March day when the sun was struggling to be strong and we welcomed its silent caress, a gang went skating on the cow pond. The ice had a glassy blueness with an extra layer of liquid on top. Underneath it was bumpy and disappointing. It was especially unpleasant if you fell down because you soon felt the water soaking through your cloth parka and your wool leggings. We were sick of winter and wished for the disrobing of spring.

> *April love can slip right through your fingers*
> *So if she's the one*
> *Don't let her run away.*

We sang the words of Pat Boone a.k.a. Mr. Dreamboat, after which Jacqueline broke into "I'm just a sweet old-fashioned girl." We joined hands and spun around, building enough momentum so that the last person on line could be released into a glorious solo spin. We cracked the whip. When it was Jacqueline's turn to be on the end, the usual cry of joy was canceled by a splash and a yelp. Her seamless glide had ended with a plunge. My sister's head, swathed in a cap that tied beneath her chin, bobbed up out of the water. Every piece of ice she grabbed broke off.

"Stand!" someone shouted. "Stand! It's not that deep."

"No, don't stand!" someone else shouted. "It might be quicksand." That was always the rumor we entertained about the cow pond, partly to heighten its drama on summer days when surrounded by buttercups and violets. It had a puniness we found almost prissy.

Her head went under again. We lay down on the wet ice, imitating the rescue scenes we'd seen on films in Health, forming a line. One of the Brooks twins was closest to Jacqueline, and she grabbed her by the arm, helping her to slither onto the surface, with all of us yanking her to the nearby bank. Tearing off our skates as quickly as our fear would permit, we helped Jacqueline with hers and shoved her boots onto her feet. We half carried her back to the barn at the edge of our backyard while someone raced into the house to get her some dry clothes.

We make a pact among ourselves, a vow of silence.

We were used to independence, used to the idea that what we did from three to six on school days and on the weekends and during the summer was our business.

Drowning was the worst thing, but being caught not drowning could very well be next in line.

Chapter
Seven

If Anyone Asks

"RAYMOND IS SO LUCKY, IT JUST SLAYS ME," I SAID TO JACQUELINE JUST before the fall of 1958, when he had what I came to think of as his Camp Leo luck all over again. I was wearing pedal pushers and pretending to faint from the injustice of it. Raymond was gearing up for yet another adventure. This time he was off to Mount St. Charles Academy in Woonsocket, Rhode Island. Once again, I watched in envy as he packed his trunk.

Raymond was going to the same school our father had attended. He had a formula to follow: football, Holy Cross, medical school. The grown-ups kept saying, "Best thing for him . . . discipline . . . structure . . . male atmosphere . . . buckle down . . ."

Throughout his time in elementary school, Raymond's behavior in the classroom resulted in our mother's being called to the school for conferences. Raymond fidgeted in his seat too much. He bothered his neighbors. He did not stay on task. Back then she was still trying to fight back. We knew that, because whenever she went to those conferences, she wore a hat.

Raymond's two years at Mount St. Charles were probably
his last sustained good times.

"Dear Mother," he wrote in a letter filled with cheer and
goodwill, "I am glad to hear Uncle Dermot is on his way
to Washington. I hope he has a good trip.

I'll be waiting for the stamps to arrive. They will be
welcome.

Why in the world did you get a blackboard? I know
my chores well enough by now to tell you what they are:
rake the leaves, mow the lawn, shovel the walk, empty
the trash, bring up the wood, put the girls' bikes away
et cetera et cetera et cetera and so forth.

I bet Derm brings back a lot of news from Washington.
Give my love to Liz and the girls and Mike.

Another letter dispensed with preliminary chitchat and began
with a triumphant roll call:

> Religion: 81%
> English: 88%
> Algebra: 94%
> Science: 96%
> Civics: 88%

Well, I made the honor roll and not one subject
under 80%. Wait till Derm hears! He'll flip! I did!

I saw my name with a little star next to it like this!
*BLAIS, RAYMOND M.

At first I thought that, like the last time we got
marks, it meant I failed two or more subjects. I was sick
until I saw the marks. Then I thought how surprised you
would be when you saw the marks.

We wrote to him, about how we lost our teeth and scraped our knees, which had to have iodine, a crucial detail, proof of the seriousness of the injury—IODINE—which we never spelled the same way twice. We told him that Christina could do the hula hoop. "Mike has one too," we reported, "but he can't do it too good yet." Maureen wrote a poem: "Wind, Wind, Please blow my Kite." We told him how we went to Forest Park. Mike was afraid of the lions and tigers. We saw pretty birds. We saw Santa's reindeer. Every letter ended with the same basic reminder: "Do good work in school."

It was never clear why Raymond wouldn't stay at Mount St. Charles, but after his sophomore year he refused to return, first begging and finally demanding that he be allowed to stay home. The argument that he should remain at Mount St. Charles because he was doing so well was the same one he used to come home. Once back at 5 Center Street, he entered his junior year at the public high school. That spring, just when he turned sixteen and it was legal to leave school, he did.

America is geared toward nothing if not toward creating high school graduates. Dropping out became fashionable later, when doing your own thing was an acceptable mantra, but at the time of Raymond's action, it was a fringe gesture of despair reserved for certified juvenile delinquents, for boys in black leather jackets with Camel cigarettes tucked into the rolled-up sleeves of their T-shirts, their hair arranged in greasy dunes thanks to Brylcreem, and for the girls they knocked up.

"P.C.," Dermot would call him, short for "privileged character." And the rest of us chimed in. It was plain irritating, Raymond's inability to toe the line.

"But what," said my mother, "will people think if you leave school?"

Up until the time of my brother's decision to leave school, our mother was still proceeding with her head high, sustained by the fantasy that my father's death had not changed the course of our future. But now the worst had happened, external proof that her stewardship as head of the family contained a grievous flaw. It was a manifestation that defied hiding, that could not be spruced up in a Christmas photo.

At the public high school, where I would be enrolling in the fall as a freshman, the word was out. My brother had left school. Was there a contagion in the family? How could I be trusted not to do the same?

I was told I could take four, but not five, classes. If my brother couldn't finish high school, perhaps I should think twice about college. That callous triage hit home. Maureen Shea Blais would show them. Their snub became her fuel. For years, since the school had opened in 1956, our mother had thought of sending my sisters and me to the Ursuline Academy in Springfield, run by the smart nuns. The Ursulines were not the worn-out, scary nuns of popular lore, dried up, with vague, saltine cracker features, exploited women put in charge of overpopulated classrooms regardless of whether they liked children or had a gift for teaching, the kinds of nuns who were sour and literal and who believed in the supremacy of the Church and the implicit virtue of Good Penmanship as the universe's two leading principles. The Ursulines took pride in their own intellects and in the intellects of their charges.

Ursuline was the school with which parents all over the Pioneer Valley, and in the hill towns, and even across the border into northern Connecticut, threatened their daughters if they didn't behave. At least some of the enrollment consisted of girls who possessed what was known then as a "faulty temperament" or a "wild streak," though it's difficult to imagine just what *wild* meant in that constrained world. But our mother, acting on the decidedly modern concept that packaging counts, told us that this was a place for *la crème de la crème*. Only the finest young ladies worthy of the most rigorous spiritual and intellectual training were allowed to go to "the academy," as she always called it, as if it were a female West Point.

The summer before school began I was sent a pamphlet on which I wrote my name in big, careful, loopy letters, proud and proprietary, and the words "Important. Must be taken care of." It was titled:

Reading List
for
Students of
Ursuline Academy
of Springfield

I pounced on this list the same way I seized upon the convent-school uniform, as part of my grand scheme to cut loose. It was summer and, despite being stuck in one of those mythical muggy interludes, I wore the gray flannel jacket all one morning, practicing the right way to get the white collars of our camp shirts to rest over the collar like two sleeping doves. Finally, exasperated, probably close to suffocation at the sight of me, our mother pointed out, in a voice hot-wired with false patience, that the only other person she'd heard of who swaddled herself in wool on a similarly unendurable boiling day was, of course, Lizzie Borden. She was always fascinated by Lizzie Borden's patricide and matricide, which, considering that she was, as she so often pointed out to us, both our mother and our father, struck us as distinctly against her self-interest: "It's the choice of weapon that is so compelling," she always said. "A gun or a knife is one thing, but an ax shows a very distorted personality."

I was a typical teenager. To me my family consisted of a group of demented individuals united in their passion for invading my privacy, hampering my style, and pointing out my faults with the hideously accurate radar bred of intimacy.

My plan was to read my way out, to tunnel through hundreds of books to a better fate.

This reading list was no mere mimeographed sheet with a few tried and true titles from the era, like *Hiroshima* and *The Bridge of San Luis Rey*. It was fourteen pages long, consisting of about thirty titles per page of suggested readings.

We were not actually expected to read each and every book. I observed on the back page, once again in careful fat script, a notation as to the "minimum requirement" for fourteen year olds entering their freshman year:

3 classics
2 biographies
2 novels
1 communism
1 spiritual life
_____
9 books

We were also, according to my notes on the back cover, called upon to prepare index cards containing the title of the books we read and the name of the author. We were to "state briefly one fact about him," and then, in accordance with the proposition that "a good novel should be an inspiration to its reader," we were to name two ways in which the book had been an inspiration to us.

Communism?

Spiritual life?

The former included titles like Whittaker Chambers's *The Witness* and Herbert Philbrick's *I Led Three Lives*.

These many years later, the category of books on the list that causes me the most amusement is called "Personality and Conduct of Women," with titles such as *The Rosary and the Soul of Women, Planning Your Happy Marriage*, and *Girls, You're Important*, all written, I cringe to report, by men. (Where are these works now? Once bright and urgent and modern, they are surely as moldy and forgotten as attic detritus, as old lace, as dead dolls, as crippled lamps.) For some reason, aviation was a big subject back then: *Last Flight* by Amelia Earhart; *Listen! The Wind* by Anne Lindbergh and *The Spirit of St. Louis* by her husband, Charles; *Night Flight* by Antoine de Saint-Exupéry; and the one I probably preferred to all the others, *Skygirl: A Career Handbook for Airline Stewardesses*, written in 1951 by someone named Mary F. Murray. What a comforting name, warm as scones, solid and sincere. Under "Science and Nature," we could learn about the sea around us, about the flowering earth, and about Louis Pasteur and the microbe hunters. "Art and Music," a mere ten entries, was heavy on biographies: Mozart, da Vinci, Michelangelo, Bach, Brahms, Schubert, Beethoven. Under "Personal Narratives" there were sixteen choices, all taking World War II as their theme, including works such as Mark Tennien's *Chungking Listening Post* and Heinrich Harrer's *Seven Years in Tibet*. "Biography" occupied nearly four pages, and was divided by first, second, third, and fourth years but also subdivided into "men of heroic stature" and "women of heroic stature." Inspiring men for first-year students included Thomas Edison, Father Flanagan of Boys Town, Nathan Hale, Cardinal Newman, *Walter Reed: Doctor in Uniform*, and Father Junípero Serra. Inspiring women included Saint Angela of the Ursulines, St. Bernadette, Francesca Cabrini,

Clara Barton, and Harriet Tubman. By the time you reached the third year of biography, the categories had expanded to "converts," with books such as Gladys Baker's *I Had to Know* and Bella Dodd's *School of Darkness*.

Converts: that special quarry, human proof that we were right all along.

Fiction was saved for last, perhaps because it was the most unruly, the most potentially revolutionary. (Wasn't it Orwell who called the novel a "Protestant art form requiring a free play of mind"?) Even before we were allowed to select our two novels with their two points of inspiration, there was a daunting hurdle entitled "Preliminary background," a list of twenty-six books we were already supposed to have read, including the childhood classics of *Peter Pan, The Secret Garden, Little Women, Alice's Adventures in Wonderland, Robinson Crusoe, Heidi, Bambi, Treasure Island, Lassie Come Home, The Adventures of Huckleberry Finn, The Adventures of Tom Sawyer, The Prince and the Pauper, Gulliver's Travels, Penrod, The Swiss Family Robinson,* and *Rebecca of Sunnybrook Farm.*

Fiction for first-year students was once again divided and organized: classics, standards, supplementary titles, and modern books, featuring *Uncle Tom's Cabin* and *Seventeen* (classic) and the works of James Fenimore Cooper, that old fascinator, especially for girls (standard).

The modern books were for the most part disappointing in the way of trinkets in a cereal box, having stirred inflated hopes, but there were a few breezy titles that my younger self would surely have found enticing, such as *Come Be My Love* by Lavinia Davis, *Going Steady* by Anne Emery, and *Marcia, Private Secretary* by Zillah MacDonald.

That summer of 1961, just before Ursuline, when I wasn't baby-sitting for the magnificent sum of thirty-five cents an hour

(I still think I deserved fifty cents), much of which was squirreled away in the hope of purchasing a new Villager outfit, or going to see *Psycho* with my girlfriends, I could be found more often than not with my nose in a book.

The list was as self-satisfied as it was innocent. Although we did not know it at the time, the world in which reading was required to yield two examples of inspiration and one point of high interest was a vanishing one indeed. The nuns loved predictability, admired neatness, lived for alphabetic order. But my goal as a reader was neither grandiose nor noble nor alphabetical. I read because I liked language more than I liked music or sport and because I had a simple desire to learn the facts of life, physical and emotional. I read in order to understand how it is that men really treat women and vice versa, to get definitions for cowardice and passion and revenge. I read about whiskey (Hemingway), whores (Salinger), rape (Harper Lee). The heroines I liked stole and schemed, they eavesdropped and they told tales in the name of higher truths. The heroes were no better.

In short, I read because the world seemed various and dangerous and complicated, not alphabetical. People weren't always nice and high-minded and predictable in person, and I didn't expect them to be that way in print. I enjoyed a little dirt with my uplift.

"If anyone asks how long you're going to stay at Ursuline, just say it depends on how you find the commute," our mother said.

The commute was indeed a complicated formula. It involved several buses as well as cadged rides, during which time I memorized declensions and wrote essays about how "three things especially conduce to a habit of prayer: physical withdrawal from mind and memory, willingness to learn from the advice and examples of others, renunciation of restlessness and frivolity." I was also supposed to tell people that I liked wearing a uniform because it cut down on my clothing allowance, which might have been handy if I had had one.

At around the same time I started at Ursuline, our house-keeper Elizabeth Cavanaugh left for a nursing home. She was always a puzzle to explain to people outside the family, the close-ness of her connection. Though rough in her speech and without much education, her common sense sustained us. One time when I was six years old or so and the feisty Brooks twins, both excellent athletes, ganged up on me and started punching from both sides, it was Lizzie who said, "For goodness' sake, punch back." When I did, the twins' father came down to the house to thank Lizzie. Whenever we wrote compositions for school entitled "My Family," she always occupied her own stellar category. She was far more than just the extra mother or grandmother. She was the source of total uncensored approval, a wizard with flour and butter and optimism. She never uttered a harsh or impatient word. She led a shadowed immigrant life in service to others. Paid a modicum of a wage, she saved nearly all of it to the penny, often redirecting the cash back to us.

She would die in January of 1965 from complications of Parkinson's disease. Lizzie, who seemed without age, was suddenly aged. The person who had given us around-the-clock care required it herself. Because the home was within biking distance, we visited her often. She had the front room on the first floor, which made it easier to receive us, huffing from the exertion, hoping for a piece of candy or a quarter. Gone from the house was the paraphernalia we associated with her: beer (she had a glass each night before her dinner, which she ate alone, at her insistence, before we had ours), corn pads, basins for soaking sore feet, jars for storing hairs removed from combs, Irish sweepstakes tickets, support hose, flesh-colored girdles of a breathtaking intricacy and magnitude, mass cards, and an army of ointments meant to soothe stiff, swollen limbs. Sometimes she gathered the strength to send us letters in shaky handwriting. "Dear Madeleine," read one such letter, "I am glad that you are happy. I hope you always will be. Be a good girl you are pretty in fact you all are. No reason why you wouldn't get along together. Show the people that you was brought up nicely."

There it was, in plain frail English, the directive that would be the backbone of the family crusade: show the people.

After a year or two of doing nothing other than hanging out, dreaming of sports cars and rock bands, Raymond decided on a course of action that, it was universally agreed, would straighten him right out. He would join the air force. Where Raymond's own blood uncle and the Christian Brothers of Woonsocket, Rhode Island, had failed, the armed services would step in. In that time-honored tradition in which young men of uncertain prospects are administered a massive inoculation of who's who and what's what, Raymond would join the military, and the military, keeping up its end of the bargain, would make a man out of him.

No more sleeping in until midday.

No more odd hours.

No more making some kind of mixture in the kitchen just before dawn, usually, for some reason, lasagna, seeming to conscript every pot and pan and spoon in the effort. Instead of being Lizzie's sunlit haven, Cloroxed and caffeinated, the morning kitchen was a bloodbath, with red sauce smeared all over the sink, the stove, the table.

When Raymond was feeling crossed, his speedometer worked at an adrenalized speed. It was as if the chaos he must have been feeling inside had to detonate. He would seem to rocket from zero to sixty in an instant, becoming a human rocket, a reckless Sputnik flying through the house, fists flailing, verbiage spewing, no brakes on the horizon.

He flew into fits at provocations big and small.

No, my mother would say, you can't have money.

No, you can't have the keys to the car.

No, you can't slam the doors like that.

No, you can't drop out of school.

No, no, no, no.

He was in the thrall of some force within, an unleashed misshapen squalling infant.

He would threaten us with physical force. By the time he was seventeen, he was six feet one, taller and bigger and stronger than everyone else. He didn't have to use even a fraction of his strength to frighten us with it. Even though he was always threatening collisions, we developed that bird radar for mysteriously avoiding them, absenting ourselves from his line of fire as much as we could.

We would ask him to stop.

We would yell at him to stop.

We would beg him to stop.

Still his wrath grew, and still the words disgorged.

I would be sitting at the dining room table, with the French doors on one side closed, and the swinging door to the pantry also swung shut. Tab was the drink of the hour for young girls, a new low-calorie invention whose name was said to be an acronym for "totally artificial beverage." I would have my Tab in a bottle by my side, purchased with my own money, as well as *Seventeen* magazine, which I devoured, wishing I looked like the perky girl on her bike or swimming in a white (white!) bathing suit in the Tampax ads, wishing I had the courage to use Tampax, and consoled by a world in which the biggest problems concerned acne and boyfriends. This was where I studied after school for two hours before dinner and for three after dinner. The mahogany table had large clawed legs. It provided a commanding surface, plenty of room to spread out all the textbooks as well as whatever novel I read from every night after I did my homework.

The exact words he would shout are lost to me now. They exist in my memory as shapes, ugly chunks of sound hurled against the thin curtain of our lives. These thudding missiles were the code words for all the people who were after him, who were responsible for giving his enemies plastic surgery so that they would all look like his friends.

Fleur de lis, I would memorize for French class. That means lily.

Agricola is Latin for farmer.

An isosceles triangle is one in which there are two equal sides.

For theology, I would write a composition: "The efficacy of the Sacraments do not depend upon the worthiness of their ministers."

For English, for a teacher with the stately, extravagant name of Mother Mary of the Incarnation, a term paper: "The Structure of the Scarlet Letter: Scaffolds Real and Implied."

Then a list of prepositions, *in, cum, sine, ab, ex, de, pro*, memorized in order to recite like a cheer in Latin. "What do they have in common?" our teacher always wanted to know. "They all take the ablative," we would answer as a group.

Back to French: a *trompe l'oeil* is a trick of the eye.

My gaze soaked up the symbols in my books, the squiggles and slashes and dots and circles.

Still the words continued, the sick stew of sound.

I tried to ignore the commotion, above all, not to lock eyes with my mother because whenever I did, her expression appeared hollowed out, disemboweled, stricken, as if she were recalling the innocence with which this all began, a woman delivering her first baby, ordering birth cards with a tiny blue bow. How did it get from here to there, from his first sentence to this ricochet of venom?

In May 1962, after only twenty days at Lackland Air Force Base, Raymond was asked to leave. The reason was confusing. Either he didn't obey orders, or he did obey orders that no one else had heard.

"If anyone asks," our mother said, "tell the truth. Tell them that the air force discovered there was something wrong with his ears."

Uncle Dermot would say, "Maureen, you're paying too much attention to him, making him too much the center. If you're not careful, he'll take the rest of the children down with him. You can't shelter him forever."

His argument was matched in unassailability by her own.

"He's my son. I'm his mother. I'll do what I can to help him. He needs me."

Dermot would try again and meet with the same steely resolve.

And, maybe, one more time. Same gambit, same results.

After which Dermot would sigh and shrug and return to whatever Bruce Catton book had just won his gaze.

"You can't," he often said, "fight city hall."

Chapter
Eight

"Serviam"

WE WERE, IN A WAY, SAVED BY THE NUNS.

My mother had driven me to Ursuline for Mission Day, a chaste little carnival that had in my opinion only two advantages: classes were canceled, and we could wear normal civilian clothes. Throughout the day a girl in a white dress, wearing a crown, circulated the gym, dispensing robotic hellos. She was our Mission Day Queen, elected solely on the basis of her goodness, which meant she had, during private consultations about her spiritual future, let it be known that a religious vocation was not entirely out of the question and, also, that her favorite color was blue, the same as the Blessed Mother's. A car was raffled. Elaborate exhibits showed foreign children in uniforms studying at Catholic schools supported by events like our fair. There would be scads of offspring, barefoot and brown, standing in front of smiling parents with downcast eyes. The parents were forever being quoted as saying that as long as you had faith, food didn't matter. You could purchase pictures of saints and pricey rosaries and little pins with the school motto, which was the same as that of the Jesuit school attended by Stephen Dedalus in *A Portrait of the Artist as a Young Man,* "*Serviam,*" Latin for "I shall serve."

Mother Francis and our mother discussed literature that day. Not much later, a phone call came.

Ursuline was expanding; lay teachers were needed to complete the staff, especially at the coed elementary school level. My mother's salary of $270 a month would be sweetened with free tuition for all four girls. At the time, the starting salary for stewardesses at United Air Lines was $325 per month with the potential of a $90 monthly bonus. This would solve my commuting problem: she would be our chauffeur. And now all the Blais girls were guaranteed that Ursuline gloss.

On the surface the biggest differences between Ursuline and public school were the absence of boys and the uniforms: those ugly gray blazers, box-pleated green gabardine skirts, loafers, and nylons. But more than that, the nuns had a way of micromanaging our social interactions, ensuring that even the sorriest girls had some kind of circle. Someone who in a different school would have been ripe for hazing, given her assorted social handicaps—such as never shaving her legs, never closing her mouth, or possessing a retarded aunt—even she had friends. The nuns made a point of informing us that the more humble and penitential our behavior in this life, the more days we could lop off purgatory in the next through a complicated system of plenary and supplementary indulgences. Their main disciplinary strategy was to treat misdemeanors as if they were felonies. You earned demerits if your nylons sagged or had runs: a messy outer life announced an equally sloppy inner one. In between classes we walked in silence in single file. Lunch consisted of a bleak sandwich composed of a lonely piece of see-through meat. Most of us were so hungry we kept secret bags of chips and candy in our blazer pockets, which we learned to extract piece by piece during class and consume noiselessly without ever being caught.

One time, some girls got suspended for playing Spin the Bible with some elementary school boys on the bus. Their faces were stricken and frightened when they were summoned one by one from their classrooms to explain themselves to the principal.

Encouraging kissing games was bad.

Using the Bible for twisted purposes was worse.

The combination of the two?

Unspeakable.

At each report card, the students who were well behaved got a blue ribbon to wear on the sleeve of their blazers. Girls who were good, and bright to boot, got blue and gold ribbons, and once in a while a brilliant sinner merely got the gold, a cold secular trophy revealing a weak nature and an underdeveloped conscience. Our grades were arrived at with pinpoint precision: Math 86.7%. When I flunked a major chemistry final during my senior year, the grade was written on my report card in red ink: "67%." I asked Jacqueline, "Do you think Mom will be mad?"

"Try her," said Jacqueline.

She wasn't mad at all. "Don't worry about it. You won't need science. I never did."

At Ursuline, we were, most of us, the children and grandchildren of immigrants. The Cuban girls were the only genuine newcomers. They showed up overnight, mysteriously, shortly after the Bay of Pigs, their only baggage their colorful pasts, musical accents, and pierced ears. The principal, the daughter of a Bronx cop, used to brag, "This is a dictatorship, not a democracy," which must have been especially disappointing to them. When we prayed, we listed our intentions, and after Conchita and Mercedes arrived, we added our hope that someday they would get good enough in English to dream in it.

Our last names were Marinello and Giamalvo, Cosgriff and Glynn, and Conway and McCarthy. Although in 1960 a Catholic was elected president, we still imagined we were living on America's margins, fearful of quotas and closed doors.

It was also a tricky business, back then, the education of girls. No one worried about our sabotaging ourselves with bouts of low self-esteem; society had ensured that that would be redundant. We knew our education had a hot-house ornamental quality. After disappearing into our grown-up fates, all that Latin and all that business with Bunsen burners would be useless. We were to marry: Jesus, a man, or Service to Others in the form of spinsterish devotion to jobs at, say, the soul-eroding Registry of Motor Vehicles or in mournful classrooms filled with interchangeable unruly pupils year after year. If we didn't watch out, our intellects would be like all those Christmas trees on curbsides in January, denuded, discarded, and the impulse to duty and good deeds would be all we had left. We prayed in Latin, English, and French. Amen with a toga, amen with a baseball cap, amen with a beret.

Very few of our mothers worked outside the house. The fathers had Chevrolet dealerships or they practiced medicine or they did legal work for the diocese. Tiny, freckled, with a high, happy voice, a girl named Connie Breck, about whom everyone said *She has good hair, thank God*, was our only celebrity. Her father was a shampoo and hair conditioner magnate. This was the golden era of the famed Breck ads, with their idealized girls with gleaming hair and glowing complexions, fixtures in every reputable magazine with a female clientele. "Who is the girl in the Breck portrait?" the ad would ask itself. "She's a teenager in Tucson, a homemaker in Fargo, a career girl in New York. She's like you in many ways. Loves the things you love . . . home, family, children. Most of all she loves to be loved."

It really said that: *Most of all she loves to be loved.*

We asked Connie how it was that each Breck girl possessed the exact same degree of prettiness as the next. At first she wouldn't tell us, holding us at bay until finally, clearly against her better instincts, she relented and whispered, in strictest confidence, of course, what we took to be a well-guarded company secret: "It's all in the lighting."

The nuns gave us lessons in graciousness. Now that a Catholic president was in the White House, our horizons as young women had suddenly expanded. They saw us all as future Jacqueline Kennedys, an amazing leap when you consider that we all had Frito breath. But still they persisted in seeing us in the most hopeful light, the way the Irish describe vicious downpours as nothing more than an overactive mist. Maybe we too would marry a world leader, in which case we had to know where to stand in a reception line, how to curtsey before a monarch, and what to say during conversations with men of substance at a state dinner. "What would you do," we were asked, "if by chance you were seated next to a nuclear physicist? What would you say to him?"

Our blank faces must have been frustrating.

The nuns provided the answer. "Talk to him about himself and his work, of course. Find out where he's from. Ask: What's nuclear? What's physics?"

"Girls, here's something to ponder," said the priest who was leading our weekend retreat. "What age would you be if you could be any age at all?"

We were all fifteen. Our answers did not vary much. Sixteen, seventeen, maybe twenty-one.

"Does anyone want to be younger?"

No one did.

"An infant, perhaps?"

Again, no takers.

His face lit up: bull's-eye. "No one would ever choose to go back to being a baby, yet that is exactly what Jesus Christ our Lord and Saviour was willing to do when He came down to earth in order to die for our sins. That's just one more example of the kind of sacrifice He made so willingly, and look at you, not one of you willing to be even one day younger. How many of you have heard the song that goes, 'To know, know, know him is to love, love, love him'?"

We all knew and liked the song, by a group called the Teddy Bears.

We all guessed, correctly, that he was about to ruin it.

"What does it mean? Does it mean that the more you get to know a boy, the more you like him?"

We exchanged glances: this guy was a real genius.

He moved in for the kill. "The same is true for our Lord, you know.

"Some of you, I know, are wondering about the ways in which you can honor the Lord. Every day, He gives us the opportunity to honor Him in large ways and in small ones. Let's look at one of the small ones: lipstick. Many of your parents have asked that you wait until you are older before you start wearing lipstick. Why? Because you are vessels of the Lord, you are His handmaidens, and the wearing of excess color can be an invitation to lust. A modest amount can be an enhancement in a much older woman, but you girls are still very young and surely nature at this stage requires no enhancement. It will ergo be considered a violation of your uniform if you paint your face in an excessive manner. We must constantly remind ourselves that we have been conceived in original sin, and we are born into a state of darkness, from which the Lord in His infinite mercy has seen fit to rescue us through the Blessed Sacraments of Baptism and

Holy Communion. For these blessings we must offer constant thanks and daily witness, through prayer and in our actions. Our lives must be conducted in a meritorious fashion so that eventually we can enter the Heavenly Kingdom ruled by the almighty risen Lord and we can achieve the highest goal of mankind: we can bask in the Beatific Vision, the dazzling light of His goodness.

"The eating of meat on Friday.

"The missing of church on Sunday or on Holy Days of obligation.

"The failure to perform one's Easter duty.

"The tragedy of marrying outside the faith.

"These are the large transgressions with which we are all familiar. But sometimes I fear that in our enthusiasm to avoid these sins we relax our vigilance against Satan's less dramatic beckonings, the small moments that are also sinful but perhaps not as public in their depravity. I am talking about some of the thoughts that might occur to you as you bathe. I am referring to the sin of self-pollution. I am referring to the all too popular custom of close dancing, to driving around in cars sitting on the laps of boys, to the lure of liquor in all its cheap perdition. Convertible automobiles, racing toward pleasure: a prime example of the insidious nature of Temptation, arriving as it does in the finest of outward apparel, masking its rotten core. The serpent did not appear in a swamp; he came to Adam and Eve in a garden. Let us now pray to our Blessed Mother for divine guidance to recognize Satan in all his guises, great and small. Mother, most holy, tower of strength."

Every first Friday of the month as well as on Holy Days of obligation, we celebrated the mass. Because the altar boys were at their own schools celebrating their own masses, we females were allowed as an assembly to give the response to the priest, and to this day when some middle-aged man is discovered to be an altar boy of that vintage, I will challenge him to see who can remember the most liturgical responses, a contest I sometimes win, my one shiny nickel, the verbal equivalent of a three-point shot.

Once and only once, as I recall, a priest was brought in to hear everyone's confession: I've wondered since then if he didn't have a secret task of ferreting out a rumored pregnancy.

We filed into the makeshift confessional, reciting the boilerplate offenses for girls our age:

Bless us, Father, oh how we have sinned: We listened to the radio after lights out, we snuck a cigarette from our mother's purse, we sipped some beer at Polly's New Year's Eve party, we stopped at Friendly's when we said we were coming straight home. And then pausing, our voices becoming softer and more serious: we touched ourselves, we allowed ourselves to be touched. More details: the edge of someone's underpants had been stroked by a boy on the dock outside Doreen's beachhouse in Old Lyme one summer night, a bra had been loosened from its mooring after dark in some boy's car. The vision of all of us in our turn confiding to a dark, shapeless creature, dressed in robes, seated inside a box, has a lingering air of the absurd and frightening and the kinky: Samuel Beckett meets the Inquisition meets *Penthouse* magazine.

For people who had taken a vow of chastity, the nuns certainly enjoyed talking about sex a lot, only they called it fancy names like "concupiscence" and "the marital debt." Out-of-wedlock babies were a major obsession, and the nuns all had well-thumbed pamphlets, supposedly actually authored by a fetus before it died in an abortion. They would reach inside the billowing black folds of their habits, extract the pamphlet, and read details about each of the fetus's developmental triumphs, such as its first little kick or faint heartbeat, leading up to Month Three and the startling revelation "Today my mother killed me."

The nuns believed in something called moral hygiene, a loophole that meant that even if you were inclined toward wrongdoing, you could cleanse your soul with really good deeds. Every now and then we got to go on class trips, but it wasn't like at the public school, where the kids took big yellow buses to Mountain Park or Riverside and got to ride on the Cyclone all day and gorge on cotton candy. We drove around in kids' mothers' station wagons, and our excursions were designed to result in a corporal or spiritual work of mercy. And we didn't sing fun songs like "99 Bottles of Beer on the Wall," either. We sang songs like:

> *An army of youth*
> *Flying the banner of truth*
> *We're fighting for Christ the Lord*
> *Heads lifted high*
> *Catholic action our cry*
> *And the cross our only sword*

One time we brought brownies and root beer to an orphanage, where a little boy who kept scratching his head tried to sell me a slingshot. Another time we gave homemade sock puppets to some people at a hospital who drooled and made noises you couldn't understand, but which the nuns said meant thank you. Then it was off to a home for veterans. During "Jingle Bells," an old man reached into his pants and started singing along, the same words but totally off key. Later, he asked one of the prettiest girls if she liked sarsaparilla, which he said would put hair on your chest, and then collapsed into a smoker's hacking laughter at the word "chest." On the way back it was decided that we made a mistake when we sang secular songs about reindeer and white Christmases and we should have stuck with the holy ones with their calming emphasis on sleeping infants. The orphans and the sock puppet recipients and the old soldiers were united by one redeeming characteristic: they were all Catholic.

One nun stood out as possessing a gypsy streak, our mother's benefactor, the French teacher, Mother Francis Regis, or Franny, as we called her behind her back. Franny was by far the most temperamental and, as a result, the most invigorating of our teachers. Her favorite dictum was, *"Pensez-y and profitez-en."* Think about it and profit from it. She was Miss Universe for *le mot juste.* She had those frequent displays of impatience that often characterize teachers of foreign languages, and her way of showing it was to recruit some sorry specimen to stand in front of the room and be the object lesson for the words that embodied our failings:

Mademoiselle is messy.

Mademoiselle has holes in her clothes.

Mademoiselle has scuffs on her shoes.

Franny reserved the worse circle of hell for mumblers. "How can it be," she would rail at some girl whose natural-born shyness caused her chin to be devoured by her neck, "that despite all my best efforts I have failed so totally to turn you into an exhibitionist!"

Franny was also the drama coach, a title she welcomed because it gave her the chance to travel from Stockbridge to Boston, to cut loose and indulge certain flesh-driven cravings. It was well known that she never refused an offer to stop along the pike at Howard Johnson's for the all-you-can-eat fried clam special.

When she wasn't goading us to do better, she would invite us into her special club involving male-female intrigue. She was the driving force behind our tea dances, awkward daylight events in which the partners were often students' brothers and cousins, with the exception of the occasional paper boy innocently delivering the *Union*, only to be collared by a large nun and ordered onto the dance floor. While inside the school we were shuffling our feet to the music, Franny would be standing at the door, scanning the horizon for more male recruits. These dances were always held in the winter, and she would pretend to be drawn to a snowfall. "Ah," she would say, quoting, I believe, James Joyce, "the filigree petals, falling so purely, so fragilely surely," clasping her rosary against her bosom, secretly praying, "Dear St. Ann, send a man."

Although not in the world in the least, she was clearly drawn to it. She told a story that was both confused and sorrowful about how as part of her religious training she was cloistered for a year in the early 1940s, cut off from all communication. During the war, while transferring from one convent to another by train, she entered a car filled with soldiers close to her in age.

"Pray for us, sister," they said.

"Of course I'll pray for you. Is there any special reason?"

"You know the reason, sister. We're going to war."

She gazed at them and did not dare ask, "What war? With whom?"

She hid *Life* magazines under her mattress because in the convent they amounted to contraband, filled with shocking information about parties and the Pill and movie stars of dubious virtue. She would sneak them into class, drawing them forth from the folds of her habit, and whisper, "Look here, girls."

"Brigitte Bardot," she would tell us, "is a famous French actress. Let's hear you say it right."

Bridge Eat Bar Dough, we would reply.

"What's the terrible thing that happened to Clark Gable shortly after he filmed *The Misfits* with Marilyn Monroe?"

"He died of a heart attack."

"*En français, s'il vous plait.*"

"*Monsieur Gable est mort d'une attaque du coeur.*"

"What kind of woman is Marilyn Monroe? *En français, s'il vous plait.*"

"*Une femme fatale.*"

We followed Franny, those of us who also wanted to break loose, to various contests in which we intoned passages from *The Hunchback of Notre Dame* ("Sanctuary, sanctuary") and invoked the oratory that preceded the death by hanging of Irish Freedom Fighters, as well as reciting the more maudlin poetry of William Butler Yeats, including "The Ballad of Moll Magee." This doomed soul, Moll Magee, had the horrible misfortune of lying on top of her infant baby and suffocating him after a long day of work at the salting shed.

> *So now, ye little children,*
> *Ye won't fling stones at me;*
> *But gather with your shinin' looks*
> *and pity Moll Magee.*

Franny was the coach when I entered the Voice of Democracy speech contest and helped me write a tribute to Herbert Hoover, that often overlooked statesman, who as a child helped support his widowed mother with a paper route, working his way slowly but surely to the top, becoming president of the United States, then through his actions helping to create a depression, thus affording millions of other youngsters the chance to follow his lead and raise themselves up by their bootstraps.

The dramatic selections for the girls of Ursuline were always safe, laudable, and above all clean. Other students from other schools performed the more daring works of Edward Albee and Tennessee Williams, who would have been considered too modern and transitory and crass for us to study formally. Albee's Everyman on the bench in *The Zoo Story*, who felt that sometimes you had to go a long way out of your way to come back a short way correctly, and Williams's flighty character in *A Streetcar Named Desire*, Blanche Dubois, the one who depended on the kindness of strangers. Who needs their shabby posturing? There was something suspect about them. If you saw them walking toward you, you'd think: Iffy, iffy.

To the Blais family, the Kennedy White House was proof that we had arrived. If, as it so often seemed in our world, the highest status accrued to families with a priest in their ranks, because then you had your own special pipeline to the divine, having an Irish Catholic in the White House had the same feeling of privilege and intimacy. The whole nation had been shrunk to something smaller and more manageable, to parish. One of ours was at the helm.

We followed the entire presidency, of course, but we were most enamored of Jacqueline Kennedy's televised tour of the White House. She had grace and class; what's more, she wasn't afraid to express her opinions, telling the audience: "When General Grant became President Grant, he put false, elaborate timbers across the ceiling and furnished the room in a style crossing ancient Greece with what someone called 'Mississippi River Boat.'" In that famously breathy voice she praised Gilbert Stuart's portrait of Washington but also complained, "So many pictures of later presidents are by really inferior artists. . . . I just think everything in the White House should be the best." Of course, we concurred.

At home, we played a game based on the Kennedy women. Our mother wanted to know which one she most closely resembled.

We were honest.

"Not Joan," we said. Too young and too fluffy.

She seemed to agree.

"Not Ethel, either." Ethel was too toothy and too tennis, anyone?

Again, no argument.

We paused when we came to President Kennedy's wife.

Maureen Shea Blais looked up, hope flashing.

We knew we would hurt our mother's feelings, but we all need to face facts. "Not Jackie, either." No, not Jackie with her perfect hair, perfect pearls, and perfect life.

There was one right answer: "Rose," we said with a flourish, yes, yes, yes, Rose, with her hats and her head held high, her daily mass and her constant campaign teas for her baby, Ted.

The static-swaddled crackle of the voice of the principal came over the intercom: Mother Mary Austin, announcing the news that the president had been shot.

"There has been terrible news about President Kennedy. The president has been shot."

Stunned, silent, without being told, we knew we should fall to our knees onto the hard linoleum, a torture we gladly endured because after all Christ had allowed Himself to be crucified for our sins and you had to ask yourself, which was worse, and we began to pray for his recovery. The prayers of course did no good: Kennedy died soon after we heard he had been shot, but still we remained kneeling, shifting gears, praying now for the repose of his soul, as if there could be any doubt that someone as handsome as he was, from our own home state no less, a devoted father and family man, a believer in the one true holy apostolic faith, would have any trouble whatsoever getting into heaven. "Think about it," said one of my classmates, like all of us a sudden expert on the subject of eternal salvation. "If anyone deserves to bask in the Beatific Vision, surely it is President Kennedy. We are talking State of Grace to the nth degree."

At home, we spent the weekend watching scenes of the first lady climbing on top of the car, ruining her suit with blood, wearing, if truth be told, that unflattering little hat. Later, we witnessed the commotion at the jail when Oswald suddenly slumped over and Jack Ruby was arrested for his murder. We watched the funeral cortege—a new big word—with the riderless horse clomping down some big wide street in Washington. The horror and the spectacle were a leavening force, humbling evidence that everyone could have it tough, even the high and mighty.

Clichés are the most self-respecting of phrases; you don't get to become one unless you embody an extreme and unassailable truth. The more I thought about the randomness at the heart of human existence and the more I contemplated the bullet that killed Kennedy, shot from the textbook depository, the more anxious I became. I said three Hail Marys to myself at the drop of a hat, and I made the sign of the cross all the time, unremarked, in the palm of my hand. I knew a girl at Ursuline who liked to invent forms of penance. She put rice on the stairs and walked up them on her knees; at school she would offer to sharpen everyone's pencils. I thought if I wanted to enter a similar black hole of pain and frustration, I could always try to match all the socks in our house.

In Franny's class, for weeks on end, the formal study of French was suspended.

Instead, she read the accounts of the funeral out loud:

The terrible ordeal of Mrs. Jacqueline Kennedy reached its
final phase today.
    The widow of the dead President, still bearing up proudly
three days after her husband's murder, chose to walk instead
of ride behind the caisson bearing her husband's body to the
funeral mass.
    Before that, the 34-year-old Mrs. Kennedy, who marked
her 10th wedding anniversary in September, made her third
sorrowful trip to the Capitol in less than 20 hours this morning. This time it was to accompany the body to St. Matthew's
Cathedral for a low Pontifical Mass.
    Mrs. Kennedy left the White House shortly before
10:30 a.m. EST, to go to the Capitol. There she stood on the
steps as the flag-draped casket was slowly brought from the
Rotunda and placed on the horse-drawn caisson. A dirge
sounded in the background.
    She visited the casket in the Rotunda three times and
kissed it twice.

"Girls," said Franny, smuggling forth yet one more piece of
paper from her capacious sleeve, "I have here a quote
from the *London Evening Standard* that says it all: 'Jacqueline
Kennedy has given the American people from this day on the
one thing they have always lacked—majesty.' Repeat after
me."
    And we did, our voices lingering on the word "majesty" as if
it were a crown in and of itself.
    My sisters and I did what insecure people so often do in
the face of overwhelming external events that have no clear

link to their lives: we found a connection. As fatherless children, John-John and Caroline were now, on some level, like us, a blood brother and a blood sister. Our feelings were mixed. While it was heady to be considered in their category, it also made us less singular. They would know, as we did, death's great contradiction: the profound presence of those who are forever absent.

Chapter Nine

Din Din

THERE WAS A NEW MUSICIAN NAMED BOB DYLAN WHO HAD A SONG MY more renegade friends liked, called "Blowin' in the Wind." My sisters and I practiced the Watusi, the Frug, and the Hully Gully in case we got invited to a discotheque. We joked about the changes in our bodies and spoke of them in code: a bra was a cotton harness, shaving our legs was mowing the lawn, and we didn't get our period, we got our punctuation mark. In my purse I kept a pack of Newports, entirely for show. I got my driver's license, but I was so worried about working the clutch that I failed to learn how to use the rear view and side mirrors, so I could not drive unless I had a minimum of three passengers interpreting traffic patterns to the right and to the left and someone else looking permanently backward. My favorite character in literature was Flannery O'Connor's Misfit in the story "A Good Man Is Hard to Find," who said about an irksome grandmother, "She would of been a good woman if it had been somebody there to shoot her every minute of her life." I took to quoting foreign phrases, including Sartre's famously smarmy existential maxim

"*L'enfer, c'est les autres*," meaning "Hell is other people," after which I would glance at my family, trying to imitate our mother's trademark glare, which combined flames with daggers and which she used to try to reel us back in whenever we trespassed beyond her notions of acceptable boundaries.

I loved the movie *What Ever Happened to Baby Jane?* with its splendid theme of sister torture. Bette Davis plays the blond, ringletted child star who at the start of the film demands ice cream in exchange for performing a cloying version of an excruciating song, "I'm writing a letter to Daddy, to Daddy in heaven above." I made Jacqueline see it with me, and she earned my admiration when, as the film nudged toward its denouement, she predicted, correctly, that the final scene would include ice cream at the beach. Jacqueline was changing, for the better. She was getting smart, and funny. "Din din," we would say to each other for years afterward when it was time to eat dinner, quoting what Bette Davis says to her valiant crippled sibling, Joan Crawford (in a rare turn as a victim), as Davis diabolically delivers to her room a tray with a covered dish in which there rests a nicely garnished, exquisitely presented . . . rat.

But when it came time to write an application essay for college, I reverted to someone who ached to be dutiful, remarking how I had been a Girl Scout through the ninth grade, and how as a member of the Mission Club I got to take a bus the previous summer all the way to Notre Dame University in South Bend, Indiana, for a "truly fascinating" national convention of Mission Club members, although I thought it would be indelicate to mention that the source of all that true fascination was in the dorm rooms, which were equipped with curious sinklike devices called urinals. Then, to cap, clinch, and clear all, these sweet lies: "Two of my favorite activities are to read the dictionary for the fun of it and to do as much volunteer work as possible." The entire morass of self-deception and self-promotion was headed by the title "*C'est Moi.*"

When I told the principal, Mother Mary Austin, that I wanted to go to one of the Seven Sister colleges and to major in English and to minor in psychology, her face paled and she began to tremble. "You want to study what? Psychology?"

She made it sound naked and undulating, not in the least something you would study.

"Surely, you are not inclined to expose yourself to the works of that man," she said.

"You mean Sigmund Freud?"

"*That man,*" she said weakly, unable to befoul her lips with the pronunciation of his name. I could sense from the alarm in her eyes that such an exploration was unlikely to occur except over her dead, her martyred, her mutilated body.

"Tell your mother I must speak to her immediately."

In solemn, urgent whispers, they stood and conversed above my head while I sat politely at a desk. Together, they decided my fate like two Mafia *donnas,* their hands and lips moving in a cadenced code in which mumbled words and sentence fragments were easily translated, the one by the other.

"Full tuition scholarship . . . our motherlode institution, the College of New Rochelle . . . appropriate areas of inquiry . . . proper influences."

Everyone has a moment or two of pathos she would give anything to be able to undo.

I insisted on applying at Smith anyway, and when I went for my interview in one of those classic New England college buildings, gloomy, high-ceilinged, smelling of decaying paper and rectitude, I could tell within the first minute or two that I had no business being there.

The questioner was an older woman, thin, flinty, more interested in a stack of papers on her desk than in anything I had to say.

What did I say that day that made me so deeply unappealing? Could it have been my suffocating earnestness? Did I sprinkle French and inflated diction and even Latin into my spiel as much as possible, saying something like, "I grew up across from the *bibliothèque*, in a small *Edenic* community, where although we did not personally own a *cheval*, we did know many *agricoli*." Did I overemphasize the Catholic aspects of my education, which is to say, did I mention them at all? Morning meditation. Marching in the St. Patrick's Day Parade in Holyoke. Praying for heathens. Maybe it had been wrong to check the financial aid box, to tip the institution off to the depth of my financial need. All I know is that I have never felt so deeply invisible in my life.

When April arrived and I received one of those thin little no-dice envelopes, it was hardly a surprise. What rankles now more than anything is that for several years afterward I told people I had been put on the waiting list, unmindful of one of life's most important lessons: If you're going to lie, at least lie big about something important.

"You've been trying to sell yourself to us all your life, you might as well sell something else," said our uncle to Raymond after he announced that he had found a job. It was hard to tell whether Dermot was being encouraging or just the opposite.

Raymond's job would take him door-to-door, peddling encyclopedias.

He was drawn to the unpredictable rhythms of that line of work, its seesaw nature, the mountains and valleys inherent in trying to make a sale.

"Let's just say a novena and hope this works out," said our mother.

Once again she saved the documentary proof of his success, including a mimeographed piece of paper proclaiming that "a star has been born."

In person, salesmen often have a certain amount of bluster and a slightly forced, almost preening, formality. These salesmen had in it their prose as well:

"Ray Blais started working for us 3 days ago, and so far has written 3 orders (one order each day he worked). Ride 'em, cowboy!"

In May of 1964, from the northeast division of Encyclopedia Americana:

> This letter will serve as a confirmation of your appointment as Field Manager of our canvass operation.
>
> May I take this opportunity, Ray, to not only congratulate you but to outline to you my thinking in regards to your promotion. Ray, you are embarking on a wonderful career which you so deserve, but it is imperative that you take stock not only of yourself but your prior working habits. I can assure you of one thing—that working with men is a rewarding as well as frustrating job. Unless you are the model of dependability, you cannot, regardless of your sales ability, gain their respect which is so important for any manager. I have told you on many occasions that without exception you are the best salesman in my division, but if that ability is not utilized properly it is wasted. I strongly recommend that you set up a plan and then you follow this plan.
>
> You will be paid, Ray, a weekly overwrite of $10.00 per order on all orders from your crew. You will also be paid a monthly production bonus of $5.00 per order for

25 net orders per month; an additional $8.00 bonus for
35 net orders per month and a $10.00 bonus for 40 net
orders per month. You will be responsible for all charge-
backs of your men, to be charged at the going rate. As far
as expenses are concerned, they will all be paid for by my
office with the exception of your automobile.

Ray, you are in a position, starting today, whereby
you can easily earn $15,000 in the next 12 months. All
that you need do is put to work your abilities. Welcome
aboard. Let's show them what can be done.

Another mimeographed pep talk:

Meet Ray Blais, a resident of Granby, Mass., who started in
the selling field immediately after graduating from Granby
High School. [At some point Raymond did get a G.E.D.]
His sales career started with Colliers. He soon realized after his association with other book men that Americana
offered the most. Colliers' loss was our gain. Ray has been
a consistent producer in the Springfield area right from the
beginning. His willingness to cooperate with his manager
and his eagerness to work with new men perhaps is best
exemplified by the training job he performed with Fred
Joslin. Ray's big goal at this point is a Corvette and I'm certain we'll all have the pleasure of riding in this Corvette very
soon. One of Ray's greatest assets is that he is willing to set
a goal and then willing, at all costs, to work towards it. Earlier this year, he was instrumental in having a set of Americana donated to the Governor of Massachusetts' favorite
charity. The publicity from this gesture was immeasurable.
I'm confident, as Ray progresses in our business, that he will
be a man to contend with in the future.

Raymond was out of the house more than he was in it, eventually spending time in Boston and New York City and Puerto Rico, selling. We had less and less in common. I knew little of the details of his life, and he knew little of mine.

For Raymond, and our family, the superiority of encyclopedias to some other product sold door-to-door was their inherent respectability. When displayed on a shelf in a living room, especially in an otherwise modest or even impoverished setting, it didn't matter whether the books were ever opened or not. They stood for ambition, enterprise, ardor. A better future. Somehow, in our collective desire to lunge after the rosy version, we did not dwell on what it must have been like for Raymond to go from door to door: the bad hours, the food on the run, the twinge of discomfort upon entering strange neighborhoods, hoping to lasso a star. We believed in those letters to the letter, failing to detect their overblown tone, the gassy oaths of big money and armies of underlings.

When I left in the fall of 1965 for the College of New Rochelle in New York, known at the time as the you-can-drink-when-you're-eighteen state, my sisters gave me a gift of personalized stationery with my name misspelled, and our mother, cashing in scads of books of S&H green stamps, presented me with a fleet of hard-cased red luggage that I lined up in order of diminishing size. In what strikes me today as an epic blunder of nomenclature, this brand of suitcases was named after Amelia Earhart. One of my first friends at college looked at me, looked at the luggage, and said, with a slow, knowing nod, "If I were leaving home for the first time in my life and my mother gave me luggage named after the most famous missing woman in history, I'd think twice."

In addition to the usual classes, we had special presentations. We could hear an address entitled "The Catholic College Graduate: Opportunities and Challenges of the Business World" by

Miss Patricia Carbine, then assistant managing editor of *Look* magazine, or we could attend a panel discussion with married women called "Christian Marriage: Is the Ideal Possible in the Real World?" or we could hear a talk about the "Physiological Aspects of Marriage" with a Catholic woman doctor.

All it took was a few months at college for me to transform into a beatnik stereotype, favoring a wardrobe that consisted of a black leotard, a Danskin wraparound skirt, and Capezio flats. I wanted to be a sad-eyed lady of the lowlands, with a pilgrim soul, who lamented the death of the universal soldier, but who might someday cheer up and send in the clowns. I yearned to develop a style that I hoped would be seen as original and worldly. My novel strategy was to declare everything to be either pathetic or bourgeois. For that first Christmas, I made a list of what I didn't want: not a beaded Orlon cardigan, not a Cos Cob dress made out of Dacron ("The fabric that never sleeps"), not anything from Peck & Peck. I left reminder notes to myself: *Be one upon whom nothing is lost*, and *Live by language* so that Time itself, which W. H. Auden said is "indifferent in a week / to a beautiful physique," would be on my side. We still had religious retreats, and the priests still warned us about the devil quoting scripture for his own purpose, neglecting to give us what would have been a useful update about boys from Fordham and Fairfield quoting Ferlinghetti. The Fordham boys in particular had a foolproof argument for their advances: "JFK used to do it all the time."

Of course, I came home for all the major holidays, a college girl in a camel's hair coat deigning to drop by.

"You don't have to," our mother would say. "I only want you here if you think you'll enjoy yourself. The last thing I would like is for any of you girls to dance attendance on me."

"She doesn't mean it," Jacqueline whispered. "What she means is: 'Dance, girls, dance.'"

At night there'd be the usual rustling of the newspaper.

"Now, listen to this, girls," our mother might say. "A mother in California dumped her three kids on the median strip and just kept driving toward Mexico. The oldest of the children, who is seven, informed police that the mother got fed up when they wouldn't stop horsing around in the back seat." A short pause to string on a side remark like a bead. "I wonder why she didn't think of leaving them at a gas station. It would have been a lot safer.

"Oh, look here. One of the churches in Holyoke is discontinuing bingo for the duration of the winter, worried that a senior citizen might take a fall. How I hate that expression, 'senior citizen.' I don't care how old I live to: I forbid anyone using that expression around me. Here it says the oldest resident of South Hadley is getting the Gold-headed Cane. If they tried to give that damn thing to me, I'd refuse it. They try to make it sound like such an honor. What kind of honor is it to be next in line?

"Dottie Wilson is moving to Florida. She was quite the dame, quite the gal. First woman I knew to wear overalls. I haven't thought of her for years. For her wedding, someone gave her a big pot for making homemade baked beans. She got famous for them, hauling vats to all the Girl Scout functions and the annual Congregational Church fair. It always seemed like such an odd gift."

Pause. She knew how to get a laugh.

"For a bride, I mean."

Meanwhile, time continued its inevitable process of self-erosion. As quickly as the house had once filled with babies, it was spitting out gawky teenagers. One by one, we launched into our parallel existence.

"The hard part," said our mother, "is that there is always one last time for all kinds of tasks that involved you children, but

you never actually know when it is: the last time you're begged
for a coin for the gum machine, or asked to tow someone's sled,
to retrieve a tooth from under a pillow, to buy a pail and shovel,
to tie a shoe. It comes and it goes in total anonymity, like the
final flake of snow at the end of a storm. One last time."

Still, she labored over the scrapbooks, now including those
moody college photos popular at the time of barefoot girls hug-
ging trees, taken by our Art Major friends who tried for a cunning shadow-ridden effect or something oddly angled. There is
one of me, from a profile, featuring a prize possession, long dangling earrings that someone had sewn out of watermelon seeds.
The world of fur hats and matching muffs had faded from empire. Sometimes a letter we wrote to those still at home merited
inclusion. One letter that I sent to Jacqueline would surely have
broken the clapometer for insufferability:

"I had to write a letter because Giles Fletcher (seventeenth
century poet) loses all appeal on cold dark Friday nights," it
began.

"The best thing about staying in on a week-end is that you
generally delude yourself that you owe yourself some pleasure
and relaxation since you so effectively denied it to the outside
world," it continued. Did I really believe that? The letter nattered
on in its breezy, bratty way, ending with a vocabulary list, the
better for my sister to get high SATs:

Learn, J.!!!
    (1) Pindaric: characteristic of a Greek lyricist
    (2) rhetorical: studied, labored, overdone
    (3) amanuensis: one employed to write from
        dictation
    (4) Laputan: devoted to visionary projects
    (5) putsch: secret plot to overthrow the government

I asked her, "Do you have any opinion on the not so peaceful peace march in Washington?" I further wondered, "Isn't this a great letter? Is it, as Eliot says, 'lovely and justified'?"

I want to say I don't believe I ever wrote that, but if we are characters in our own life, it makes sense. The same deluded individual with buck teeth and eyeglasses who wrote to Grace Kelly about looking like her might also mislead herself into believing that haranguing someone with a vocabulary list is "lovely and justified."

In 1967, Jacqueline left for Marymount in Virginia, then a two-year college.

During one of my visits home the following spring, my assignment was to help Christina with her college essay.

"My goal," I said to her, "is to make you sound like an unusually articulate person as opposed to a merely normally communicative one."

Christina was the sister who had all the fun, who really did almost go to Woodstock except she didn't want to share her toothbrush with strangers. She interrupted our session to take at least three calls from friends, to buff her nails, and to lay out the next day's outfit.

"When you talk," she said, "you sound just like a book."

This was not a compliment.

"What a miscreant remark," I shot back.

I decided it would be easier to simply write the essay for her.

"While I find myself enamored of the moderns (i.e. Updike, Bellow, Greene), more often than not my most undivided attention is devoted to the writers who fulfill the classical exigencies and honor all the old Aristotelian values of plot and setting and at the same time have crafted their sentences with lapidary precision. . . ."

"I can't send this. I don't even know what you're talking about."

The next fall, Christina went to the College of Our Lady of the Elms in nearby Chicopee. During her stay she renamed it Our Lady of the Tree Stumps because of a campus-wide case of Dutch elm disease. Like the rest of us, Christina helped finance her education with work study. Her job was janitorial, and she often joked about graduating *magna cum broom*. Yet even from headquarters as geographically marooned as the Elms, she managed to spend weekends skiing at Stowe or attending regattas on the Charles River.

With only Michael and Maureen still at home full-time and with Raymond dropping in and out according to his job prospects or the lack of them, by the next fall our mother's days had taken on their own deflated routine. One letter read:

> Over the week-end I have planned dry cleaners, the
> Ware factories outlets for a sweater for me, the South
> Hadley Common for the Columbus Day fair, correction
> of school papers, out to dinner with Peg and another
> friend, big catch-up on important correspondence, yes,
> you're right, I'll probably get to one third of the whole
> thing. Oh, yes, I forgot, GREEN STAMP trip. Funny the
> patterns one's life assumes. The list I just made is a pretty
> accurate description of the way I spend my leisure non-
> school hours.

Maureen wrote to Jacqueline about financing her education at Marymount in Virginia. "I have a $1000 work study thing, and a grant of $700 more. But I have to get at least $900 or a thousand more. Does it cost $3200 or $2800? I thought you said $2800. Did you?"

In 1969, Maureen worked out the finances and left for Marymount in Virginia, while Jacqueline transferred to the four-year
Marymount in Tarrytown, New York.

I enrolled at Columbia Graduate School of Journalism. That
summer, in New York, was a time of nightmare and dream unleashed with equal force. My first apartment was unit 3J, Lau-
reate Hall, on the north side of 119th Street, between Amsterdam
and Morningside Drive, shared with a friend from college who
wanted to be an actress. We both sought to redefine ourselves
as women of stature. We hoped to learn about wine and to meet
some interesting atheists. Our mothers were worried about having their daughters footloose in such a heathen place, warning
us especially about The Village, which they knew for a fact was
filled with what they called "drug addicts and other charming
types." To save money, we tried to learn how to cook, sometimes
calling down to the doorman to see if he knew whether salad
dressing took three parts oil and one part vinegar or it was the
other way around. Inside our small, dark apartment, where the
cockroaches were fruitful and multiplied with a vengeance night
after night, we led the frugal lives of most young women new to
the city, packing snacks in our purses and walking long distances
to avoid subway fares.

But outside apartment 3J, the world was filled with screaming headlines, events in boldface, underlined and capitalized.

The dream came first: Man on the moon. Who could forget
the watery image of men in swollen suits as they progressed like
fat stick figures across the TV screen? We hooted, of course, at
everything that Nixon did to attach himself to the event, especially when he called it "the greatest week since Creation."

"Overblown," we said, "self-congratulatory. Maybe even
blasphemous." We couldn't believe that our government was

taking all the credit, with not so much as a passing nod at Euclid, Newton, Galileo, Copernicus.

We also saw that objects didn't have to travel a great distance to change history. One day before the moon landing, nightmare: Ted Kennedy drives off the bridge at Chappaquiddick.

And then another dream, Woodstock. Of all the songs at the festival, the "Feel-Like-I'm-Fixin'-to-Die Rag" by Country Joe & the Fish caught the mood—nervous, mocking, iconoclastic— of the half-million young people who slept outside on farmland in upstate New York under Nixon's moon.

And then, one August day, some hippies killed some movie stars. Charles Manson took his place in that strange American galaxy, the Richard Speck Hall of Fame.

The turmoil was so vast that any family turmoil took a distinct second place: jet engines drowning out the chirps of sparrows.

Two years later, Michael left for Cape Cod Community College and later for Rutgers University in Camden, New Jersey, and Maureen transferred to the University of Maryland.

Each one of our educations was financed by a jury-rigged combination of scholarships, government grants, work study, and student loans (our negative dowry, we called them). The rule of the day was you got a diploma if you didn't burn down the school and graduated with honors if you actually went to class. Our reduced circumstances had a nifty camouflage in the era itself: the detachable poverty that most students affected in the late sixties and early seventies. "You are wealthy," said some famous philosopher of living simply, "in proportion to what you can do without." Materialism was the crass province of boozy grown-ups who had traded their dreams for lookalike lawns in the suburbs, the very people who had gotten us into racial discord and into Vietnam. It was considered noble to pretend to be poor and to be able to get by with one perfectly weathered pair of jeans, but faking destitution usually stopped short in the face of a faulty carburetor or a throbbing tooth or cheap shampoo.

Our mother fielded the dunning calls from the banks and sent out notes to us like this one: "It was disconcerting to have a telephone call from the bank this morning about your loan. Mr. B. said your payment is over three months overdue and he really should turn the loan over to a lawyer. If you can't make a payment, let me know. I will have to lend you the money, as it's too much to get these calls, especially the first Monday of the New Year. I understand your financial pressures and I am willing to help."

Even with my degree from Columbia, the first years out of school were a painful apprenticeship in which many long steps were taken backward in order to grovel forward however infinitesimally. Most of my early jobs were more effective at showing me what I didn't want to do than what I did. In Boston in the early seventies I had a five-week tryout at a Hearst newspaper so cheap that there was no air conditioning, just a cooler with lukewarm water and a supply of salt pills. One day, I was sent out to a hospital to cover the vigil of some children still in their plaid school uniforms waiting to see their father, who had been shot during a robbery. I called into the city desk to say there was one boy and two girls.

"Did you get their names?"

"Of course not."

"Why not?"

"They looked scared. The boy was crying. I didn't want to go up to them."

"What do you think you're being paid for?"

"I'm sorry. I don't even know what to say."

"It doesn't matter what you say. Just bullshit with them."

I hung up.

I returned to the waiting room.

I stared at them and I circled them, but I could not think of a single way to break through the bulwark of grief that was building up in the room as each bulletin about their father's prognosis presaged the worst. I returned to the paper with an empty notebook and with the hard-earned realization that although I probably didn't mind interviewing people after a tragedy, I did not want to talk to them as one unfolded, a distinction that might seem trifling but which led the way for me to confine my efforts to feature stories rather than breaking news.

It was a matter of marking time before I would be let go.

One afternoon, I was asked to write a poem to accompany a car rental ad during leaf-peeping season. I was given the assignment at 4:30, and when it was time to punch the clock at five, I asked if I could take it home and work on it overnight.

The editor snapped at me.

"Who do you think you are? Shakespeare? All we want is a little foliage ditty."

Another editor, one of the seemingly interchangeable gray-faced men with sagging jowls who sat at a desk in the center of the newsroom, surrounded by smoke, added his opinion: "Newspaper poets only need half an hour."

These men radiated despondency. Their organizing principle appeared to be disappointment. The parade had passed them by, and now they had nothing but contempt for those who were riding the floats of public attention. They could not bear the eruptions they were witnessing all around them: blacks asserting their rights, young people refusing to go to war, women demanding a life beyond making Patriot's Pudding Jell-O in the kitchen. They reacted with disgust at Angela Davis's raw racial call to arms. "Look at that hairdo," they said, ridiculing her Afro. "Bats could live inside that." A story came over the wire services about a school principal who called girls into his office and made them jump to see whether or not they were wearing a bra. An editor brought it to me to read, and when I was finished, he said, "Let's see you jump." Whatever passion for self-expression had brought me to this job was certainly not being satisfied by it, although I did get one bit of excellent advice. In a puff piece about the opening of Mama Leone's Restaurant in Boston, I used the words "colloidal chemistry" and even worse, "culinary." Another reporter cringed when he saw it in my copy, later slipping me a note: "The word culinary is best used only in the S.S. Pierce Christmas catalogues and even there, with grave misgivings."

Chapter
Ten

Cheap Symbolism

"BE NICE TO RAY. HE NEEDS TO KNOW YOU GIRLS SUPPORT HIM, MADDY. Take him out to Friendly's for a big beef cheeseburger, that's what he likes. Ask him how the new course is going," my mother would say whenever Raymond had taken on a new endeavor that was finally supposed to open the door to a stable future.

Sometimes he dreamed of running a vegetable stand, and he would study pictures of produce. "Your good fruit man," he would say, "knows the name of every apple in the world." If he had managed to make it as a fruit and vegetable and plant man, he would have aligned himself with a proud local tradition. It is a bedrock belief among the residents of the Connecticut Valley that its land is the richest in the world—something to do with the quality of silt from the river—and no soil anywhere, not even in Italy, creates produce that equals the perfection of tomatoes, peaches, and sweet corn. If consumed at the same meal, at the height of the season, they constitute their own holy trinity.

At one point Raymond studied graphology in the hope of becoming a handwriting analyst. When I asked him about it, my voice was overly cheerful, like a sunflower or a red-breasted bird.

"It's a definite science, you know, not just some flake thing. Catch someone when he's writing down his John Hancock. Watch the way he crosses his *t*'s, and if he uses funny marks instead of dots for his *i*'s, you better steer clear. Worst of all is someone who leaves the bottoms of *a*'s or *o*'s open. That's when you should head straight out of town. Matter of fact, I'd run like hell. Take a bus to Omaha if you have to. Those kinds of people," he would say, "are mass murderers."

Unfortunately, there wasn't as much call for handwriting analysts as the teacher had led him to believe, especially one who saw apocalyptic rampages in each and every squiggle.

With Raymond I had learned it was a good idea to censor the subjects we discussed, knowing how easy it was to set him off. One treated him the way you sometimes see parents of an only child treat their offspring, as a prized orchid or as an experiment that failed. He would often pose some supposedly rhetorical question such as, "If you were a landlord, would you rent to me?" to which the only possible answer was a resounding, unequivocal "yes." It had become increasingly clear that certain topics had to be avoided because they might rile him, including religion, politics, and almost anything in the news. One of the few safe subjects was the valley itself where he had lived all his life. Did he think the braided rugs at Thorndike Mills were a bargain, was he still a fan of the strawberries at Sapowski's, when was it exactly that the restaurant at the Notch went out of business?

I also learned to wait for the right time for a conversation, the precise moment of equipoise when he would neither snarl at nor dismiss somebody, when his thoughts were not ganging up on themselves, when they were beige rather than magenta, flan rather than curry. Listening to him meant listening to what he had to say, not what you wanted to hear. It required a radical act of self-abnegation that no doubt proved of service in my work as a newspaper journalist, though it would have been hard to figure out how to include it on a résumé. Specialized skills: "Can deal with her brother = can deal with anyone."

"I keep reading articles about runaway housewives," our mother said one Thanksgiving. "Women who think if they have to wash one more dish or pick up one more dirty sock they will lose their composure altogether. One lady I read about skimmed off ten dollars a week from the household expenses for a year and hightailed it to New York City. She got a room at the YWCA, where she said the down-to-earth conditions were a relief from the racket and the bickering she had to put up with at home— kids fighting over TV shows nonstop, refusing to pick up after themselves—and spunky gal that she is, she got a job as a cook at one of those $1.19 steak restaurants. Sure, she's working hard, but now, she says, at least the customers appreciate her efforts and she gets a regular paycheck. She said that if you add up everything a woman does to keep a house afloat without the slightest compensation, she should be given a salary of fifty, one hundred thousand dollars a year, minimum."

We had just seated ourselves, and her cigarette was still lit. The talk clearly interested her more than the turkey. It wasn't that she was looking for a fight. She was simply baffled. A book called *Beautiful Lofty People*, filled with word snapshots of people who faced life with intensity and integrity, had recently come to her attention. Is that what it meant to be beautiful and lofty nowadays, to embezzle from the family kitty and run away? She had dolled up for the evening. She favored in those years a modified Bohemian look, so she had on dangly earrings, and her dress was a cotton print, some kind of batik. Across her shoulders she had tossed a shawl with just the right amount of insouciance. The table had not merely been set; it was in costume. Out of her arsenal of fine possessions, she marshaled only the top artillery for the occasion: the Haviland Limoges dinner plates, white with gold rims, the wedding band pattern, heirloom from her mother. We were supposed to take special pride in the paintings on the wall of people we had never met, with creepy eyes that appeared to shift on the canvas.

"At least *I* never did what those housewives are doing. At least *I* never ran away. At least *I* never joined a commune."

We four girls looked at each other. Is my memory right? Were we all really dressed alike in bright orange granny dresses, or is that just some horrible hindsight slander?

As if, we told her, *a commune would have you.*

"And what do you mean by that, dearie dots?"

Our answers came out in the usual choral rush, with each of us trying to top the other. I cannot say who said what when, but I remember the rapid-fire gist of it perfectly:

"Mom, honestly. You'd hate it. Everyone wears unisex clothes."

"And no more Salem cigarettes. You'd have to smoke Acapulco gold."

"Which, in case you don't know it, is a very intense form of marijuana."

"You'd have to eat an exclusively macrobiotic diet of brown rice."

"Ditch the American eagles and the gold draperies. Paint all the rooms black."

"Hang up a poster of Castro."

"And Che."

"Listen to rock."

"Copulate as a gesture of friendship."

"Stay up all night talking to boys about ways to get out of Vietnam."

"Suggest that they might want to get braces."

"Or shoot off a toe or two."

"Or, artificially induce tachycardia by not sleeping and eating horseradish and chili."

"Commiserate with them about their lottery numbers."

"Explain that girls don't always say yes to boys who say no."

"And, if you go back to college, you'll have to insist on canceling your regular final so you can take an interdisciplinary, ungraded test, the purpose of which is to determine how well a person reacts to being alive."

By now we were giddy with our own humor.

Michael, unamused, said, "Pass the potatoes."

"They're fattening."

"But they have iron."

"So do nails."

"Eat a nail then."

Our humor was willful, mocking the stoned quality of so much of what passed for conversation in our age group. "Far out," someone would say, only to be gently corrected. "No, not far out. Far fuckin' out."

"How much," asked Jacqueline, driving the riff to a pleasant end, "would this Waterford glass pitcher be worth if it weren't cracked?"

"A thousand dollars," we all answered.

And then, suddenly, Raymond looked up from his plate, his face almost shiny with sweat from shoveling down the turkey and the dressing and the cranberry, a voraciousness not to be lightly crossed. The rest of us had barely begun.

He had perked up at the mention of potatoes. Not only had he exhausted his options at the encyclopedia companies, but he was also bouncing from one get-rich-quick scheme to the next. Recently, he had heard about a sewing factory that was going out of business, and he talked our mother into subsidizing the purchase of hundreds of wooden spools. He had an idea that he could get us, the girls, and our friends, especially the ones who were art majors, to paint them some old-fashioned hue and re-sell them as candlestick holders. Huge heavy shipments, which we pretended to ignore, arrived at 5 Center Street daily.

"Potatoes," he said. "A most versatile vegetable. You can fry them, boil them, bake them. Eat 'em sliced, diced, or mashed. Use them in soup, stew, or shepherd's pie. I'm not just pulling your juggler's vein." His face was now like a furnace, glowing with the gravity of his commentary, the words building on them-selves, tense and interlocking, roiling and urgent. "If George Washington Carver had worked with potatoes instead of pea-nuts, he wouldn't be the famous Negro he is today." And then he said it again, and again, and again, laughing louder with each recitation, a wheezy private laugh that took over the table, enter-ing into the stuffing and into the gravy, so that before long one fork and knife after another was placed silently on the right side of the plate, blade in, as we had been taught, while quietly we removed ourselves and our dishes from the room.

Later, while we were cleaning up, we sang "We Gotta Get Out of This Place" by the Animals.

"Save the cranberry sauce," I said.

"Save the cranberry sauce? Rest assured, cranberry sauce, redemption is on the way," said Jacqueline, who bowed her head and placed her hands, palms down, over the bowl, murmuring, "Repent, repent."

Our mother poked her head in.

"Girls, I want you to come to the living room as soon as you're done. Maureen is going to recite Robert Frost's 'The Death of the Hired Man,' aren't you, Maureen?" This was Maureen's signature piece for the speech contests at Ursuline, which, we had just learned, was going out of business in the era of Free Love. Apparently, the market for young girls willing to wear white gloves and attend afternoon tea dances and contribute to the Mission Bank on a daily basis had dried up in the same sweep of social change that was causing housewives to hit the road and young men to flee to Canada. More grace gone, more vanished standards to lament.

Maureen nodded and giggled. She had just won a regional contest.

"Maureen," we said, "first you were the belle of Bondsville, and now you're the toast of Munson."

Maureen's deep alto could have belonged to any of the sisters.

> *Mary sat musing on the lamp-flame at the table,*
> *Waiting for Warren. When she heard his step,*
> *She ran on tiptoe down the darkened passage*
> *To meet him in the doorway with the news*
> *And put him on his guard. "Silas is back."*

Later that night, our mother went into the Green Room, as she so often did on the holidays, and sat at the piano that always needed a good tune-up and played songs that ranged from the old-fashioned "I Don't Want to Play in Your Yard" to the predictable "Danny Boy" to the lighthearted "The Entertainer" from Scott Joplin's *Ragtime*, a selection that would later be known as the music from *The Sting*. Lost in old chords and the happy thunder of major keys, she shed a certain severity. For a moment, the footloose tinkle of Joplin's music transformed the cold, heavy house with its groaning pipes and drafty windows, heating it up with sound itself.

"Sadie, Sadie, married lady."

At last, we had the opportunity for a true last hurrah, a last hurrah of such extraordinary pedigree and vintage that no more would ever be required.

A Blais daughter was getting hitched, and the wedding would be performed at the Immaculate Heart of Mary Church, followed by a reception at the house in Granby.

June 23, 1973. Christina's vows would be the excuse to grant the house one last facelift and one final blast of consecrating ritual before it went, as it was slated to, on the market. Raymond designated himself the official fixer-upper of the house. With the help of a friend, he would strip off and replace the wallpaper, repair the crack in the ceiling, even install a new sink. Often these home remedies threw into relief all the other work that needed to be done. "Gresham's Law," our mother would say, invoking the one practical financial concept that lived on after that good grade in college economics. "Bad money drives out good money. We should just sell the house now and stop trying to fix every square inch." But as often as she said it, she refused to act on it, persisting in giving him money to make repairs that led to the need for even more repairs.

We spiffed up the house as best we could, with some necessary skimping. The barn, for instance, was repainted but only on the side that showed. Christina was supporting herself and her fiancé, who was still in school, on the salary of a part-time nursery school teacher. She turned to me to get money for a root canal and flowers.

Her husband-to-be was a man of boats, sailing them, refinishing them, insuring them, selling them. "His mistress," Uncle Dermot kept saying, to everyone's dismay, "is the sea." Together, the young couple had the vigorous clean-cut looks of people in an L.L. Bean catalog. They dressed alike in Izod shirts, khakis, and Weejuns.

Whether as a gesture of respect or one of penny pinching, or both, Christina consented to wear our mother's dress. When she went to get her wedding dress out of the hall closet less than a half hour before the ceremony, she accidentally imprisoned the heirloom avalanche of satin our mother had worn with such hope on her wedding day. The doorknob slid off in Christina's hand, like a tooth so ready to go it extracts itself.

"Ignore the cheap symbolism," we told her. "You know they can't start without you."

Someone got a neighbor who was known to be handy, meaning he could remove lids from ordinary jars without expecting a government commendation. "This little Phillips-head should do the trick," he said, and when it did, many future prayers were pledged to the causes of his choice.

After several last-minute showers, we were all late arriving at the church. Uncle Dermot's hair was damp as he led his niece down the aisle, and our mother had also dressed in haste, so that her bun appeared to have only the most precarious allegiance to her skull. It was the era of loud polyester prints, and throughout the Immaculate Heart of Mary Church were women wearing floor-length dresses with designs that varied from the geometric to the botanical.

After the ceremony, the couple left on a trip to Nova Scotia. They were both only twenty-two. They moved to Glen Olden, Pennsylvania, where they lived in an otherwise unoccupied house owned by Christina's father-in-law. It makes no sense that houses that are dark on the outside are necessarily dark on the inside as well, but it was true about this one, the feeling of discomfort fed by the hulking furniture. We all have free-floating memories of the poverty that afflicted us in those first few years on our own. I was once diplomatically passed by as a bridesmaid at a dear friend's wedding because it was understood that I could not possibly bankroll the pink silk dress with dyed-to-match pumps. Jacqueline remembers owning a single pair of operational shoes. Maureen, in her first year as a teacher, would buy a family pack of chicken every Sunday, freeze each piece individually, and then eat one piece per evening until the next Sunday. Christina and her husband were joined in Pennsylvania by Michael. The house had heat but no hot water. While Michael and Christina's husband headed off to school at Rutgers, Christina would sometimes arrive at work early in order to wash her hair, hoping it would dry quickly in case the director dropped by. Jacqueline recalls visiting Christina in Glen Olden and marveling because Christina had became "an expert, an utter expert, at making Bisquick coffee cake, and while it was cheap to make and it wasn't nutritious, if you were to buy it, it would cost a fortune. I remember thinking: Here's someone who isn't taking poverty lying down."

The first time Raymond went to Northampton State Hospital, in the winter of 1974 after he had a psychotic break in the middle of a plant store where he was hoping to find work, wasn't necessarily the worst, or the longest, of his stays. But when he was let out, we could tell that omething had changed in his life for all time. At Northampton he experienced the traitorous nature of his illness to the fullest: the alleged cure only made it worse.

It was Raymond's bad luck to go to the hospital at the very moment in its history when it had the fewest resources due to the policy of deinstitutionalization begun under Kennedy with the best of intentions and often the worst of results.

All day long in the open wards, filled with smoke, there was an impromptu theater, a floorshow of the disenfranchised. On display were the ten percenters (remember that old ad? One in every ten Americans is mentally ill), the unlucky elect who'd spent their lives being just the type of person kinfolk, and many others, can't abide. The attendants were few and far between, and they had the defeated air of workers who were putting in time for money—and not much at that. The day staff complained, "You know nights. Nights don't care about nothing." And the night staff had the same high regard for the day workers. The odor was foul and stale, like that of an overcrowded, overheated kennel.

An old man lay on the floor, kicking his legs, writhing, saying the baby was coming any minute.

A woman kept asking if anyone had found her ticket. She carried a soiled tote bag with the names of world capitals written all over it: London, Tokyo, Rome. She walked in a continuous circle, addressing imaginary porters: "No, no, I'll carry my own bags, thank you."

A tall, pale, thin man of indeterminate age also circulated throughout the room, pausing in front of one patient, then another, holding still, making his eyes bulge, and finally moving on.

He was a camera.

Someone else kept trying to eat cigarette butts. No one tried to stop him, though everyone must have wondered, in a mild uninvolved way, what would happen if one of the butts turned out to be lit. An ancient woman, whose wrinkles had wrinkles, said her mother would be here "to spring her loose" any minute. The man with the butts said, "Your mother's still alive, I'm calling Ripley's."

"I'm on fire," said the human camera, moving his hands quickly, as if to douse the flames, but of course the blaze was all in his head.

The staff, such as it was, muttered over charts. We learned to decipher their private vocabulary.

"Elopement precautions" meant someone might try to escape.

"Watch out for sharps" referred to the fear that a patient might possess a pencil or scissors or even a plastic fork and use it as a weapon.

"Vitamin H" was the nickname for Haldol, the psychotropic drug administered in big-time doses with big-time results. The patient is calmed but often afflicted with side effects such as impotence, dry mouth, drowsiness, and tardive dyskinesia, a shaking condition similar to Parkinson's.

"Everyone here is nuts," Raymond said to us in a whisper. "Shrinks too. The one this morning thinks he's so smart, he didn't even know today's date, the month, the year. Had to ask me. Idiot didn't even know the name of today's president. You know what else he didn't know? He didn't know what it means, 'Don't cry over spilled milk.' Has to ask me to explain it. Has to ask me 'How are a cat and a dog alike?' Wants to know if I'm walking down the street and I find an envelope addressed to someone else, all sealed up and stamped, what would I do? Another thing this joker wants to know: do I ever hear things or see things that other people can't hear or see."

"So what did you say?"

"I told him time doesn't matter. By the way, Einstein agrees with me, and he was no slouch in the genius department. President's probably Eisenhower and he's probably out playing golf. Thing about milk is, so what if it spills. Just pick it up, for Christ's sake. That's how I got to be king."

"King of what?"

"Oh, you can't trap me. Listen"—his voice slowed down, became almost confidential—"I want to make a phone call, but they wouldn't let me, especially after they found out where to."

"Well, where to?"

"Where else? The moon."

He began the frantic pacing that often preceded a shower of fists on whomever or whatever happened to be in his orbit. The eyes lit up with a fierce red glow. The speech was pressured and quick and interlocking, the words spewing out in chunks, stuck together like pieces of a cheap jigsaw puzzle.

"I haven't slept in three days. I can't sleep at night. Here are the facts. Everyone here has a pillow. I'm in a loony bin. Anyone could suffocate me, and whenever I bring it up, they call me paranoid."

When Jacqueline visited, he said to her, "These people think I'm crackers. Fine. Bring me some crackers."

She made the ill-advised error of doing his bidding and, worse, doing it incorrectly, bringing him the wrong kind, Triscuits, not Wheat Thins.

He was livid, opening the box, dumping its contents on the floor and on her.

She brushed the crumbs off and backed away.

Raymond started screaming about how he was going to have her name removed from the visiting list. The notion that at that point in its history Northampton State Hospital, overwhelmed as it was, was capable of maintaining and monitoring visiting lists was further proof of his disorientation.

The doctors tended to be foreigners who didn't speak much English, only compounding the problem. There is no blood test for what was wrong with Raymond. Diagnosis was made through observation and through listening. But how could doctors with a limited command of the language being spoken by their patients distinguish a word salad from a legitimate complaint from a bizarre delusion? In any event, they rarely agreed on what was wrong with Raymond, acting as people do at the concession stand at the movies, immobilized over whether they should choose M&M's or Twizzlers. They went from one opinion to another. They had a flavor of the month. He was schizophrenic. He was borderline. He was manic depressive. He was schizoaffective. With all the labels, it would have been a lot more convenient if he had had multiple personalities as well.

We were changed, too, by Raymond's hospitalization, changed utterly. No longer could we pretend to ourselves that his behavior was the result of some gargantuan streak of obstinacy. He was sick, and if we weren't careful, he'd make us sick too. The world took on a different cast, even the news, which now seemed filled with the spectacle of mental illness in action. People whose judgment is flawed and whose sense of reality is fractured are often thrust into split-second fame. Sometimes the spotlight is due to a display of goofiness or bad luck on a world-class scale. They stand naked in the middle of the road giving away money. They stalk the wrong celebrity. Their bright idea is often everyone else's worst nightmare.

A woman is arrested in a botched scheme to trade her tot for a car.

One day a mild-mannered loner with a shotgun decides to thin out the cat population in his barn; next thing you know, it's police officers in our nation's capital.

A social worker is stabbed by a distraught client on a city street as she heads to work at eight in the morning.

A man pushes a woman he has never met into the path of an oncoming subway.

A passenger tries to break down the door of a cockpit on a crowded plane so he can prove that he, too, can fly.

If you have a brother like my brother, you develop cop sonar. You bristle at and quickly decode even the slightest skirmish on a street corner. You register tone and nuance in the voices of strangers. You become an automatic compendium of dreadful occurrences.

The prejudice against people like my brother is both extreme and widely countenanced. At one point a few years back, some homeless people took to sleeping on heating grates outside a dorm at Harvard. The students often brought them food from their dining halls, free falafel wadded up in napkins, distributed in a spirit of charity. An administrator thought of a clever way to evict the interlopers, and he enacted his plan in the middle of a cold snap in January. He ordered the installation of high, curved bars over the grates, ensuring that no human being could ever again panhandle that warmth. What few objections were raised died down quickly.

For our mother, the most painful part, beyond the facts of Raymond's illness and his hospitalization, was the lack of money for a better placement. She thought that if she had the cash to send him to a posh private facility, his prospects would improve. She heard about one in New York where each patient had his own room and every day there was a structured event: "Monday's bingo, Tuesday's card games, Wednesday's crafts, Thursday's self-esteem, Friday's movies, Saturday is in-town privileges, and Sunday's chicken." It was nothing like Northampton, where every day was a unique excursion into the abyss.

It was not always that way.

When the Northampton Lunatic Hospital for the Insane opened in 1858, it occupied 172 acres of the best real estate in town, with views of the Holyoke Mountain Range. It was conceived with the highest of intentions and out of the noblest of motives. Everything was top of the line: fireproof masonry, steam heating, running water, and gas lighting.

An address that was delivered at the laying of the cornerstone by Dr. Edward Jarvis could not have been more humane or more high-minded. Occasionally, portions are reprinted in local newspapers and magazines, and I have no quarrel with his words:

> Many are in the highest state of bodily health and vigor, most are strong enough to care to provide their own sustenance, while some are sick and need the care of others.
>
> There is a general and acknowledged obligation resting on mankind for the strong to protect and aid the weak,— the rich to provide for the poor, the wise to guide the foolish,—the healthy to nurse the sick,—and the sound in mind to cure and care for the insane.
>
> The higher the state of civilization, the more these obligations are recognized . . .

The hospital would be a haven, he said.

> If the fallen house, the broken fence, the rusty implements, the weedy field are monuments to the improvidence of the proprietor or occupant, how much more should neglected and permanent insanity be deemed a monument to the faithlessness or inhumanity of those who should have provided the means of healing.

You of this town and these counties can and will do much for the prosperity and comfort of this new Institution. You can cheer, support and strengthen it, you can pour the oil of joy on its machinery and give the power of confidence to its operations, and we doubt not, you will do so, and then this Hospital will ever have reason to rejoice, that it is placed in the midst of an enlightened and a generous community.

During its early days, the hospital offered bowling, billiards, religious worship, classes in rug and basket making, and boating on the Connecticut River. There was a reading and smoking room, and assemblies were held on a daily basis. The hospital had its own football and baseball team.

It would have been wonderful if Dr. Jarvis's high-flying sentiments had reigned indefinitely, but the history of the treatment of the mentally ill in this country is one of slow, downward-spiraling neglect and abuse, culminating in the state hospital that gave my brother such a terrifying experience.

In Raymond's Northampton, patients in disjointed, sad outfits roamed the room. Velour caftans were teamed with hiking boots, sneakers with evening gowns, pajamas with formal wool vests. At Northampton, patients were not allowed to keep their own clothes. Every few days or so a huge pile of laundry would be hauled into the ward, so that each person could pick through the mound anew for something to wear. This policy only aggravated the loss of identity that patients were experiencing by the very nature of their sickness.

Raymond used to write about what happened, over and over in letters, as if to crack the puzzle of the depth of the betrayal he felt:

When you arrive at Northampton, you are told when you ask to make a call, you have no rights. You are stripped of your clothes which are gone forever and given state clothes which are worse than the Salvation Army rejects. They are rags.

They give the same drugs they use to put a race horse to sleep. You go around in a daze and can hardly talk. If you do speak out, you are put in a seclusion unit, a small cement room with a small window, no toilet, you excrete on the floor and then you eat your food from a tray on the same floor. The board of health should investigate these people.

Chapter
Eleven

"Quiet, the Mustard Is Boiling!"

JUST WHEN YOU THINK YOU'VE HAD YOUR *LAST* LAST HURRAH, THINK again.

It was the final Christmas eve in the house across from the library, and all of us were on hand for what Jacqueline called "the body count."

Our next-door neighbor, a retired schoolteacher named Miss Gertrude Taylor, dropped by, as she did every year. And this year, as in all the others, she was offered a cordial, and she accepted it with madcap glee, a spinster on a prim binge. In retirement, her two passions were African violets, which she grew in boxes on tables throughout the house, and making her own fudge and homemade candy using unlikely ingredients like mashed potatoes to great effect. She was one of those reticent Yankees whose idea of an expansive conversation, one in which all parties are engaged in what she considered to be a heated exchange, was to say, "Least said, soonest mended."

Dermot stood by the fire, his white hair adding an air of distinction and his square black glasses giving him a disconcerting resemblance to Barry Goldwater. Like a politician, Dermot loved to expound, and this evening, with its high quotient of built-in emotion, was a perfect opportunity to launch into one of his "what this country needs" speeches.

"Remember that Christmas about eight years ago when it was sixty degrees out? Nobody appreciated it because oil was still cheap. People aren't waiting in line anymore for gasoline, and they are taking it for granted. What this country needs is a good strong energy policy, and I don't think Ford is the one to give it to us. He has to spend too much of his own energy living down Watergate." Then, turning to our neighbor, "Wasn't Watergate something?"

"Least said, soonest mended."

He looked back at the rest of us. "I blame it all on these kids and their peace candidate, McGovern. What we really needed in 1972 was someone like Humphrey. You can trust Humphrey."

"The reason Mom and Uncle like him," said Jacqueline, under her breath, to me, "is because he's always giving speeches about how his family had to sell their house during the depression."

"I heard that," she said. Our mother's eavesdropping skills were finely tuned. "You joke about it, but I've been wondering what Rose Kennedy would do if she had to sell her house," our mother said. "The hitch, of course, is that Rose Kennedy wouldn't be able to understand. She has had too much practice with national tragedies, and not enough with normal problems, like money."

That January, she called our neighbor Mr. Brooks, who had left the shoe business for real estate, and asked him to put the house on the market. She let him pick a fair price, and he could show the house anytime as long as he gave reasonable notice. She threw up only one barricade. She could not bear the thought of any scoundrel in a vehicle who just happened to be chugging by on Route 202 being able to observe that the house where comfort and happiness abounded was now on the chopping block. She refused, in a gesture as maddening and impractical as it was admirable and steel willed, to permit a sign in front of the house that said FOR SALE.

The house sold for about three times as much as we paid for it in 1950. The new owners had young children, and they put a pool in the big backyard. We were told that the man was going to use the barn as the showcase for his electric train.

After we paid taxes and a large heating bill, the sum from the sale was not such a windfall. And there was no financial redemption on the horizon, no publishers panting for *Bubblelini*. Our mother and Raymond moved to the woodsy outskirts of town to a raised ranch with a sump pump to keep the lower level from getting too damp. Raymond's room had belonged to a child, and the wallpaper still had a drummer boy theme. "If anything went wrong in this house, that's just the kind of detail," said Christina, "that would be snatched up by a certain kind of reporter."

Raymond continued to have "episodes," as we came to call them, and the family that took notes on itself continued to document them. I had relocated to Florida, and a letter dated April 25, 1979, from Jacqueline shows how hard she and our brother Michael were trying to get him help.

> Dear Madeleine,
> It all began Easter weekend. Michael spotted a breakdown while Mother and I could have easily seen it as just a *new lease on life*. Ray went on a diet, gave up drinking etc. Then he stopped eating and sleeping. Mike wisely banished Mother from the household and next we heard Ray was up in Rutland, Vermont. Mike called Tim

Murray and Mike arranged for Medicaid. We got up to
Rutland, and everyone agreed at that point that it was
the best breakdown Ray ever had. Ray said this himself
upon getting into the car. Ray and Michael did not talk at
Ray's insistence.

Unfortunately, the Mercy hospital was inadequate to
the care Ray needed at that point. His psychiatrist
recommended shock therapy, and Ray became totally
angry at the suggestion.

Anyway, Ray got transported to Northampton, which
has changed. For one thing the recreation room is co-ed.
We saw Ray's social worker, who looks like Rhonda
Meister [a petite friend from Ursuline who joined the
convent for a spell] and is just as conscientious. They've
diagnosed Ray as manic-depressive of the manic kind.
Mother is relieved to think it's genetic. She was glad to get
some concrete information on Ray, a whole lot better than
a Freudian approach ("Your husband died, Mrs. Blais.
Hmmmmm."). Secondly, Mother was saying last night, "I
think things are going to work out and don't think I'm
acting *manic* about everything, because I'm not." She must
have excused herself from a manic frame of mind at least
five times. Also, Ray looks great, honestly, handsome. He
grew a mustache sometime between Rutland and The
Mercy and got his hair cut. His mustache is a nice full
semi-circle and very trim. He did say one or two genuinely
funny things when I saw him yesterday, e.g., when he got
married he'd rent the biggest (manic) cathedral and
Mother and I could sit alone in the back.

Mother is getting used to the idea of retiring to the
beach and I fully expect you to find an eligible husband

from the elderly Miami dating scene. Michael requests a
retired history professor (like uncle but with more of a
sense of humor), but I'd settle for an ex-jewelry seller.
Also, Ray tells Mother he can't come home and Mom
tells Ray he can't come home, so at least they are in
complete agreement for a change.

A letter dated May 14, 1979, shows how hard my mother
was taking the news of yet one more setback:

I have just received notification from the hospital that
Ray is going to be committed by the state for a six
month period. This was necessary because he can't be
depended on to stay voluntarily and he needs to be
there that long in order to get him on the right program. Michael went up to see him yesterday. Guess he
was quite unreceptive. The social worker told Michael
that he will probably improve, but we can't expect
miracles. I don't, but I am bitter about the fact that this
should have been done years ago and maybe with the
right treatment, he could have done better. That's
where money counts. Ray is now at the bare minimum
of his lithium intake (sort of like getting a D– in a
college course). He talked to his psychologist and the
psychologist said the lithium is having a dramatic effect.
Not a cure-all but very efficacious. Also, and this
kills me, Ray could have had it all along. It's just that
Northampton State did not utilize it, because they didn't
want the trouble of monitoring it. I don't want Ray to
know this. Isn't it sad? I just hope he gets calm enough
for Maple House and leaves me alone.

In June, from Springfield Hospital, Raymond began a letter to me with the salutation—unusual for him in that he had the kind of healthy respect for religion that permits a person to leave it out of as many situations as possible—"Jesus and God Bless You!" He wrote that he had heard that the new owner of the house in Granby might need a repairman:

> Maybe I'll get the job. He's a really good guy. The last time I saw him I said I'd go to work for his company and he said I'd have to marry his sister. I said that's too high a price. It's our house but I think it has a jinx on it since Daddy died. You and I were the only ones to know that perfect life. Dermot thinks he knows everything and all mother did was make birthday cakes. Some way to make a man out of me. Things will be better once I leave here and get a business started. I hate being in the nut house.
>
> Whatever you girls can do I love you. Jay you can forget because she's too self-centered.

The letter concluded with an offer to pray for my happiness. Raymond was released from the hospital and hung around the valley. He did not want to go to a halfway house because he did not want the structure and the rules, or the stigmatizing and labeling. When he was functional, he was just functional enough, as one social worker put it, to "pass." He stayed in Massachusetts, while our mother headed down to Connecticut. It was one of those difficult lost summers.

Jacqueline wrote that she would be moving into a small rented cottage with our mother:

> I think I will survive the summer very well, if only Mother doesn't cook chicken and leave the carcass

hanging around in the fridge in anticipation of a couple of dinners, and mmm mmm, homemade soup. The other stuff, the bouquets of Kleenexes, overflowing ashtrays, and dishes put back on the shelf before they have fully dried, is such a familiar routine I am well rehearsed. The chicken, however, becomes a new affront every time.

The timing of Raymond's breakdowns was textbook. They always took place in the late fall, heading into the holidays, or in the spring.

But it wasn't every fall and it wasn't every spring.

Whether he was on medication or not, he would send us letters with his Christmas list starting in October. In this letter he is calm, and he begins it by lampooning his more runaway desires:

> Corvette.
> Cottage (three bedroom on Maine coast).
> Use of American Express card for 30 days.
> Trip to France.
> Should I add more?
> Anyway, back to reality:
> X-large knit shirts, long and short sleeves
> X-large crew neck sweater
> Pants 44 inch waist, 30 inch legs or longer, can be
>   hemmed
> Coat 46 long
> Could also use socks, maybe a gift certificate for
>   shoes
> Last year you surprised me and I like surprises.

However, the clothes list should give you something to work with.

With the money you have sent so far I got a good
pair of winter boots and some Levi's. I'll call you this
week-end and see what's going on. I should get a lot of
use out of both. (The boots and Levi's.)

I got a beautiful plant yesterday for the apartment. It's
a Bolivian Jew about four feet long. I only paid $3.50 for it
wholesale. It would have been fifteen at a florist. It's really
big and you need a big window for a plant that size.

I'm off to the mall to see my friend and for lunch (a
hot dog). Only trouble is I'm there twice a week and I
think I'd like it better if it were once a month. It gets old
fast in the malls, especially if you go twice a week
window shopping.

One more thing.

A three-piece suit.

Love,
Ray

A three-piece suit always implies a fourth piece: a reason to wear
it. How Raymond longed to be part of the bright world of com-
merce and connection. That never happened on a day-in, day-
out basis, but occasionally a reason to dress up did materialize,
such as for my wedding in May of 1980.

The wedding was held in a small Catholic church in Connecticut where most of the family had migrated. My husband-
to-be was Episcopalian, and we joked about how the bride's side
of the church should have a banner "Guns for Belfast" and his
should say "No Irish Need Apply." Each of our mothers supplied
us with her own guest list. On my side: Shea, O'Sullivan, Walsh,
Murray, Mahoney, Donahue, Collins, Welch, McCormick,
Teahan, Cosgriff, Glynn. On his: Christian, Phelps, Stokes,
Hawkins, Chamberlin, Chapman, Duncan, Gardner, Ketcham,

Harriman, Harrison. We found an organist who could play "Jesu, Joy of Man's Desiring" and a caterer who called hors d'oeuvres "pick- ups" and asked if we wanted paper plates and paper napkins or did we want real. We said real.

I'd met my future husband at the *Trenton Times* in New Jersey, where I was a society reporter. Not only did the title have a false sense of glory, it was also a true contradiction in terms. The events that I covered included such high-level glitz as a Polish debutante ball and an Easter egg hunt at the Trenton Y. When I arrived in Trenton, I told myself it was time to grow up and buy a car. The executive editor asked whether I preferred a domestic car or a foreign car. He had two people on the staff who could help me either way. At the time, this decision was highly politicized. Vietnam had not yet ended.

A domestic car meant support for the domestic economy, which on the one hand helped pay for a racist war in Southeast Asia, but on the other hand provided a living wage for all the hardworking guys in Detroit.

A foreign car was a vote against "Amerika," spelled with a *k*, and all her fascist ways.

The first expert was a middle-aged ex-Marine with a crew cut and with four children in the suburbs. He was an authority insofar as he covered the Trenton Speedway.

The second expert was single, tall, athletic, funny, liked to read, and was an expert on foreign cars insofar as he possessed a Porsche that was always breaking down on the way to assignments. Also, he had heard of Martha's Vineyard and Bruce Springsteen.

The next day I signed the papers for an orange VW Dasher that said "Dasher" in huge black letters on the side.

Eventually, my future husband was offered a newspaper job in Florida and one in Alaska. "The perfect existential choice," he called it. "You could either burn or freeze to death." We both emigrated to Miami. Although it has always had a renegade streak, with its welcome mat constantly out for gangsters who could afford their own private islands, Miami then was mostly known as a sleepy pastel backwater brimming with timid retirees who lived for their early-bird specials. The Cubans were still considered a quaint subculture, here on loan, with *piñata* shops, thick, high-octane coffee, and elaborate coming-out parties called *quinces* for their fifteen-year-old daughters. South Beach was filled with Jewish refugees who sat on deck chairs on porches in front of the decaying art deco hotels, patting their canes like pets, living on fixed incomes, hoping that the diminishing supply of pennies and minutes would have the good grace to run out simultaneously. The police who walked the area called it "raisin patrol," and the most common reason for stopping someone was for driving too slow.

We got to Miami just as it was doffing its old skin. The narcotics trade was just heating up. It got so bad that drug dealers dumped each other's bodies by the side of the road on such a routine basis that this practice became known as "felony littering." A gunshot at the temple was called a "serious headache." The autopsies revealed that the victims usually lacked the U-gland, standing for "upright." Miami was on the verge, by the late seventies, of transforming into the city it is today: loud, brash, bold, shocking, and a total original. America's teenager, as it is sometimes called: spiked, branded, pierced, and out of control.

My first vision of Florida, coming in on the auto-train, won my chilblained New England heart for all of time: the near impossible flatness of the thin-lipped landscape, the dancer's stance of the loose-limbed trees dotted with oranges and lemons and mangoes, the sun that day after day has the same bright greet-

ing, a solar cuckoo, *hello, hello, hello.* Miami was the dream opposite of New England. It was not a place where you could ever
under any circumstances imagine anyone saying, "Least said,
soonest mended."

People court in whatever way works for them. I once interviewed a famous editor from the *New York Times* who said that
in the twenties he and his wife had no money, so they used to
find a pretty spot outdoors and read out loud to each other: "That
was our way of making love."

We sealed our engagement by covering the Ted Bundy trial
together.

The *Washington Post* contacted us separately during a merci-
fully brief period in which we were both freelancing, which can
be interpreted as a time when we were both footloose and light-
headed with self-invention, which is to say, broke and unin-
sured. The national desk was looking for a story that pointed
out all the issues. The Bundy trial was supposed to make great
strides in the field of forensic dentistry and would John mind
taking all that recondite expert testimony and boiling it down
into cogent prose that could be readily accessed by the masses?

I was called by the Style section and asked to do a color piece.
What was the defendant wearing, did he make eye contact with
his girlfriend, what was the mood outside the Metro Justice
Building?

In one of my color paragraphs, I described Miami that June
as being short on rain and short on mercy. A man at a movie
theater had actually stabbed another patron to death because
he tripped over his feet trying to find a seat. It was a time when
the nerves of all citizens were frayed. The "mean season," I called
it. We ended up melding the two pieces into one, we thought,
seamless account, our first and only joint byline until the children came along.

To our wedding we invited friends we'd met in the newspaper business who now lived up and down the East Coast. Many said yes, which impressed Dermot, who kept saying throughout the festivities, "I've not seen a wedding like this since the war—so many people from out of town. No, nothing like it since the war."

At the rehearsal dinner, we had seated people next to each other because they ate fast, or they had lived in Providence at one time or another, or they might fall in love. Although it was never in question whether Raymond would be invited to the wedding, I was worried that he would do something to undermine the event. At the time I had many friends who had postponed marriage because they couldn't stand the thought of inviting any number of people to an actual public ceremony, including their perpetually tanked aunt, the neighbor who compulsively played air guitar, the born-again anybody. Afterward, I came up with a universal theorem about weddings: Someone's going to act badly, but it's never the person you predict.

At my wedding, it was not the distant cousins on either side, not the newspaper friends who were known to be rowdy on occasion, not the people who eat too fast, not my brother.

It was me.

Raymond was fine, even after I made him drive two hours round-trip back to Massachusetts to get the fake front tooth that he forgot to bring.

Brides usually have one of two styles. Either they happily assign every detail of the entire shebang to minions, or they engage in a kind of grotesque overinvolvement best left to others.

"You have to wear your tooth," I told him, as if the day itself rode on that fragment of porcelain. "It's my *wedding*."

Knowing that some people were more comfortable talking to Raymond than others and were even able to take an uncondescending pleasure in Raymond's offbeat creativity and desire to be included, I saw to it that he was seated at the rehearsal dinner next to a man who had served as a Marine in Vietnam, and who knew life isn't fair, and his wife, a nurse, always a bemused compassionate listener. She had a long conversation with Raymond, after which she told me he seemed to be doing very well.

"You think so?" I said eagerly, figuring that if anyone could make a prognosis, it was a trained professional.

"Oh, my goodness, yes," she said. "He told me all about his new business, and it sounds just dynamite."

"His new business?"

"The International Book Search. He told me that he's taken out ads in the *Times* and other places and that the company motto is 'We'll find any book, anywhere, anytime.'"

"He said that? Any book, anywhere, anytime?"

The International Book Search existed in the form of a letterhead on a piece of stationery and in the clutter of the trunk of whatever ailing vehicle Raymond had recently inherited from one of us. He had written to me that he had taken some ads in newspapers, but the prices were generally prohibitive: "By the way, I checked out the *Globe's* advertising rates out of curiosity. Don't Ever Feel Guilty (not that you do) about salary. $150 per column inch. One inch. Unbelievable." He did manage to pay for an ad or two in the *Times*, however.

Letters from foreign professors written in the stiffest, most roundabout dictionary-driven English devoid of nuance arrived at the house constantly: "I respectably seek perchance the collection work of John Galsworthy for study further. With all personals and all regards . . ."

The letters, which went unanswered, were shuffled aside into some dusty corner. They had one advantage over the wooden spools scheme. They took up a lot less space.

"Oh, Beth," I said, "he's right. It is a thriving business. In his head."

She looked crestfallen and pressed on.

"Well, he also told me you might write a book about him."

I nodded my head dolefully.

Raymond made that suggestion frequently.

Whenever he asked me to, I would answer, "Maybe, someday," waffling because I knew the book he wanted written would be a falsification, a libel in reverse. Conceived in the summer, delivered in the spring, my brother led a life that fanned out into one long contradiction of all that early promise. In any official version that would win his complete approval, he would be pictured as healthy, flourishing, a success. I would have been obligated to concentrate on the few years after he dropped out of high school when he sold encyclopedias in Puerto Rico and lived the high life. Perhaps I would have listed his various passions and prejudices, how he liked horse races, spareribs, Miller Lite, smokes, girls, early Woody Allen, Arlo Guthrie, Corvettes, Mustangs, tag sales and antiques and didn't like *The New York Times Cookbook* (which earned his most dreaded dismissal, "flaky"), the movie *Clockwork Orange*, arcane ingredients. One of his favorite expressions was "KISS: Keep it simple, stupid," said with no enthusiasm. He believed that the worst drivers are old men wearing hats. End of story.

The eighties for all of the Blais children except Raymond were a time of acquisition, rather than of shedding, a time of getting.

Better jobs, new houses, our own babies.

Our generation would produce six children in all, born between the years 1980 and 1988, five boys and one girl.

Michael worked at first for the Town of Stonington in Connecticut, in the office of town planner, and then spent about five years as a corrections officer at a women's prison in Niantic. I used to tease him that, after being raised in a household filled with so many women, this job must have felt like divine retribution. Later, he went into computer work, partly because he didn't want to be someone who oversaw other people's confinement and also because he was attracted to the endless tinkering of electronic communication. Maureen got married and bought a house, to whose bare bones she added several rooms, and had two sons. She took a year off from teaching for each baby.

Christina and her husband moved to his mother's former house in the same seafaring village in Connecticut where Maureen lives. For a time the birth of their two boys and the weekend parties with their flow of boats and bonhomie seemed like enough to sustain a marriage that had begun too young. Like Maureen, Christina took time off when the boys were born, but other than that, she continued to cultivate a teaching career.

Jacqueline was the surprise. From that frightened girl who could not bear the extroversion of Girl Scout camp, she turned into a wry spirit. Back in the days when live telephone operators processed collect calls, she answered their question, "And who shall I say is calling?" with one word, "Ishmael." Jacqueline remains the peacemaker and to some degree, the mascot. She is the one who, when our mother said, "You have my forehead," pretended to peel hers off and said, "Here, take it back." She has odd, precise, formal enthusiasms, for croquet, sherry, and grammar. Her first job after college was as a social worker at Belchertown State Hospital in the blind unit, working with children who were both blind and delayed. Later, she got a job putting out a newspaper for a community organization, and that led to the chance to work as a reporter on a small paper. It was the kind of paper where all the reporters got rotated into each other's beats, and the only time we feared for her employment security was when she was assigned to "food and fine dining." She has never been much of an eater and lacked the antenna that would make a person pause mid-bite to question whether tarragon really was such a good idea in this particular sauce or to think twice about cilantro in the salsa yet again. One time she wrote a recipe for which she meant to recommend two bay leaves. Instead, she wrote, "two cups bay leaves," and for days on end phone calls came from concerned readers who said that the amount of bay leaves recommended by Jacqueline would surely poison your average eater, to say nothing of being inedible for all the crunching it would require. When the Gannett chain bought the paper, they snatched her away (as we saw it) and sent her to Washington, D.C., so that now one of the wittiest, most literate people I know lives in the stuffiest, least language-respecting city in the nation.

"You know more than you think you do," is the first line of Dr. Spock's baby book and one reason it is an enduring bestseller. There is nothing a new parent needs to hear more.

As a parent, I did not trust my instincts, or perhaps I trusted them too much, fearful that I would treat my children the way I had my siblings, as intrusions on my valuable time and space. I read every book I could on the subject of parenting, a trendy new verb in the eighties, no less irritating for having hung in and entered the language on a permanent basis.

At night my husband and I actually had conversations that went like this:

Him: "You know, this crying at the end of the day is quite normal."

Me: "Absolutely. They just get a little fussy. As Anna Freud says, that's when their little egos disintegrate."

Him: "Yes, into a fretful noisy collection . . ."

Me: ". . . of needs and reflexes."

Him: "It's that sense of cosmic attenuation . . ."

Me: ". . . that often presages . . ."

Him: ". . . a new developmental milestone . . ."

Me: ". . . and comes from that frustrating imbalance . . ."

Him: ". . . between his sophisticated sensory apparatus . . ."

Me: ". . . and his primitive motor impulses."

Him: "Do you think he'll ever stop crying?"

Me: "God, I hope so."

When I reported this exchange to Christina, she said it was amazing: I married someone who also sounded like a book.

For me the fire of motherhood was, at the beginning, elusive; it flickered on and off. The birth and the caretaking of my firstborn activated the old buried frustrations of growing up in a house with too many babies and not enough adults to take care of them. When the baby was cranky and I was tired, I invariably slipped and called him Michael rather than Nicholas. My friends with babies seemed much more stout-hearted and pioneering as they navigated what I considered the dull shoals of nap time and regular feedings. They were explorers stumbling over new territory. I had a feeling of having been there and done that, not so successfully the first time around. It was slow going, discovering what felt new, to me, about babies, and mostly I found it in long walks, folding my son's infant limbs into a denim Snugli, and as he curled up in the pouch, together we sought adventure and saw the world as a new coinage. He would hear an unfamiliar noise, observe a falling leaf, or notice the pattern in the sun's shadows.

Once, he felt the rain.

Once, he saw the night.

It was our finest time.

A neighbor with three children helped put *my* fretfulness in perspective. She came by one evening with a meal of brisket, applesauce, and salad. (When I think of all the meals I have consumed over the course of a lifetime, why does this one menu remain so clear and concise?) The applesauce was red, and the salad had a newfangled ingredient, roasted pine nuts.

As she stood in the doorway, getting ready to leave, I said: "Susan, I can't sing."

"So?"

"So? So, no lullabies."

I looked at the wide-eyed baby in my arms. He had not taken a nap all day. Nap, I used to tell him: Not Awake Permanently.

"Oh," she said, "this is serious."

She stood still, backlit, lost in thought, as if carefully arranging the stems and stalks of memory in a vase.

"Ah," she said, "I remember now."

And then she proceeded to recite, word for word, a poem by Yeats that she had used with her children from time to time. "Put him down in his crib and say this," she said, "over and over, and soon enough you'll touch his back and feel the even breathing of a sound sleep."

> *The angels are stopping*
> *Above your bed*
> *They weary of trooping*
> *With the whimpering dead.*
> *God's laughing in heaven*
> *To see you so good,*
> *The Sailing Seven*
> *Are gay with his mood.*
> *I sigh that kiss you*
> *For I must own*
> *That I shall miss you*
> *When you are grown.*

During the children's early years, my sisters and I had a shared investment in each other's children and their well-being and in their growth, as peas and milk and sunshine had their merry way with them. The children were a loud phalanx of missing teeth, infected bug bites, scraped knees, and untied sneakers.

Jacqueline, known as Aunt Jay or Play Jay, got them kits that had a scientific overlay: "Why wait a billion years? Make home-made coal now!" When they tripped and fell, rather than chas-tise the children, she would make an elaborate show of rebuking the linoleum, culminating in the stern order, "Floor, go to your room!" She exclaimed over each and every ragtag gift of dead dandelions.

We went to their nativity pageants, expressing sympathy about how hard it was to be Joseph because then you had to put your arm around Mary.

We helped them make volcanoes for their science fairs:

> *one cup water*
> *a quarter cup vinegar*
> *a half cup dishwashing liquid*
> *Pour into bowl with baking soda.*
> *Watch it explode.*

They made the usual childish malapropisms, though in the new era of frank talk and open discussions, their mix-ups had modern twists, as when I heard one of the boys talking about someone who liked to pull down girls' vaginas.

They thought that the job of policemen was to wave, and they thought toll collectors got to keep the money. They called music la la. They said *elemenopee* as one word when they recited the alphabet. They struggled with deep mysteries, such as, were bagels ever alive? We acted encouraging when one of them said he wanted to grow up to be someone who hunts for gold. We would agree not to talk when they presided over play stoves with Tupperware pots and issued orders: "Quiet, everyone. The mustard is boiling."

At one brief point, they each thought my sisters and I were all goddesses and every house in America should have our statue in it.

If you wore a dress with flowers, they would try to pick them.

Chapter
Twelve

A Grudge X-Ray

WE BEQUEATHED RAYMOND THE VALLEY. HE STAYED IN WESTERN Massachusetts, while the rest of us headed south. Because I lived the farthest away, I was his designated correspondent.

There would be long stretches when the communication from Raymond would be resigned, logical, slightly despairing, a not unreasonable response to his circumstances. His letters were sometimes an odd mix of formal diction and inane detail, the bright but blighted mind caught in a limited deadening existence. "I'm so tired of being stuck in Chicopee. For example, Springfield is having a tasting sample from good restaurants and I saw a dish of ziti, broccoli, cheese (three kinds) with sausage and marinara sauce, as an example, all at very reasonable prices, but alas I can't go."

Then, not much later, after Jacqueline passed down her old car so his access to other towns increased:

I hope this turns out to be a long letter. Halloween is over. I didn't buy candy and I was worried about 200 kids showing up. No one came. The front door has a security lock and they probably couldn't get in. Maybe Halloween is passé. You could write a story: razors and poison may be a turnoff.

I met a girl (Jean) at a coffee shop and we see a little of each other. We had Spaghetti at Mel's in Holyoke last night but she is married. It's rocky (the marriage) but I guess our friendship is okay.

Can't wait till x-mas.

Here's my list: shirt large or extra large, underpants forty inch waist, shoes size 12, socks either 11–13 or stretch one size, pants 44 inch waist, 30 inch length.

I'm going to take your suggestion and play it cool with the flowers.

Every time I see anyone in the family, there is some mention of the old house. Wouldn't it be nice if we could rent it for some kind of reunion?

Jay's old car runs good. It gets great mileage and it takes me wherever I need to go. What a pleasure compared to rotten buses and bus drivers.

It's starting to get cooler here. It's been way warm this fall. Tonight is supposed to be the first cold night.

I'm very bored. That's why you are getting such a long letter. I do, however, expect you to respond in kind.

Another time he reported that he and a friend (unnamed) went to the Paramount Theatre in Springfield to see a movie: "The place was magnificent, very large, holds perhaps (ball park guess) six thousand people. It has two balconies and several, if I'm using the correct term, opera or box seats. It's been completely refurbished by the city, with federal aid, I think, but kept authentic with its old architectural charm fully intact."

He continued with his lists, even when it wasn't Christmas. We supplied groceries and the usual stuff people need to maintain their personal infrastructure:

> sweet and lo
> canned stew
> boneless sirloin (freezes well and doesn't take up much space)
> sugar free strawberry jelly
> canned ham (small size)
> A-I sauce
> canned mushrooms lots
> canned corn beef hash
> new broom
> Good News razor blades
> Resolve carpet cleaner
> horseradish
> paper plates
> olive oil.

He also needed objects for his home:

> Mattress (I have foundation)
> pots and pans
> two nice medium height lamps, not a matched pair.

Sometimes, he would shoot for the extras:

> A Pentax camera
> stereo and tape equipment.

And, sometimes, he would shoot for the stars:

> A trust fund.

When our mother attended her fiftieth reunion, in the early eighties, at Chicopee High School, she filed this account:

> One man said he and his wife had just taken their eleven grandchildren on a cruise. I would have been out the nearest porthole. The food was awful: canned fruit salad, green salad with gunky dressing (the waitress spilled some on the sleeve of my green dress), frozen beans, mashed potatoes and capon smeared with pallid gravy, accompanied by a thin slab of ice cream. I sat with three classmates who went to the Alvord School with me. One of them said she'd never forget when our club (six little girls in the fourth grade) put on a show in Kay Mannix's backyard and I did a "Powder Puff Dance." Apparently, I swooped around with exaggerated gestures, powdering my nose. Original, anyhow. She also remembered the boy who sat across from me and was always giving me boxes of jewelry, which he had acquired by selling things. I was always so embarrassed by the gifts, poor kid.

It took awhile, but eventually she sold the second little house in Granby and moved to Mystic:

> Finally, I am going to be all in one place. I have a b-e-a-u-t-i-f-u-l place in Mystic, a unit in a landmark building. It has four large rooms with corner windows (charming). I have the use of a large attic for storage. Floors are hardwood. The house is old (1869) so my furniture will look great. I am on the second floor, hence the attic. I am just down from the library and can walk to church and stores (A&P) as well as have the occasional cup of chowder at BeeBee's. And, it has a fireplace!

Holidays came and went:

I find Memorial Day depressing and Ray's plight does not
make it any better. In spite of the dogwood, pink and
white, the air is heavy for me and lonely. Maybe what I
want is to be a Girl Scout again, back in 1925, and
marching in the parade where we ended up at the
American Legion where we were served the forbidden
fruit of coffee with doughnuts. I really hated coffee, and
we had Lizzie's own doughnuts, much better.

Just read a new life of Oliver Goldsmith. Terrific.
What gaps I have in my education.

"Ray's plight," as she called it, had been compounded by an
incident in 1983 when he tried to get off Social Security and get
a job. He was spurred to do so by a wholesale governmental
review of the cases of people like him, who were suspected of
playing the system in order to avoid taking responsibility for
themselves. The frenzy that this review set off in Raymond was
enormous. He did try to get work, as a grave digger, but the
stamina required for that kind of work went far beyond his store
of energy. The second day on the job he went to a bar in the
evening and fell off a bar stool not because he was drunk—he
hadn't had time for that—but because he was so exhausted. With
his leg in a cast and his financial safety net in jeopardy, he became so despairing that he attempted to commit suicide by
jumping off a bridge in Springfield. We have been told that this
incident was documented on local TV, a kind of bad news/good
news/bad news joke. Bad news: someone tried to kill himself.
Good news: he was saved thanks to the buoyancy provided by
the cast on his broken leg, coming to rest on a small island in the
river. Bad news: he was taken by ambulance to Northampton

State Hospital, a place that by now filled him with fear and loathing in equal doses.

By then, we knew that there would be no miracles for Raymond. He had deteriorated beyond repair, and healing him would be like trying to restore a wilted flower to its original form or paste dead leaves back on a tree. A line had been crossed. Instead, we would have to temper our hopes for him, whittling away our dreams for his improvement to something much more realistic. We would try to keep him from hurting himself or someone else. We hoped he wouldn't thrust us into an unwelcome limelight like those stunned families you see on television.

Sometimes the tone of resignation in his communications shifted to something more dire.

The writing would be scrawled and legible only to trained eyes, eyes used to an onslaught of words, the letters crushed together: "Often I feel with Reagan wanting to save money to finance 'Star Wars' that my suicide was unfortunate only in that I missed. He (Reagan) would prefer me begging on the streets. Please help. Ray." He never forgave the Reagan administration for putting him through hoops, making him get the job that almost killed him. "That man has an absolutely borderline moron vocabulary."

The tone of his letters went back and forth, reflecting his moods.

Threatening: "Some people are harassing me and ruining my life. Some family members are getting involved. If any family member chooses to help these sleazes over Xmas I will depart for home and no longer consider them part of my family."

Angry: "Have you slept on the streets, have you begged for food, have you depended on soup kitchens, your fool loser brother has. Even cheese has an address. It comes from Vermont or Wisconsin. Where were you, bragging your help? I have a life of F-U-C-K-I-N-G poverty. You are no or little help. Reagan loves to hurt poor people. He wants me begging on the streets." And, then, even bigger letters with more underlining and more capitalizations:

"THE THING IS HE NEVER EVEN MADE A GOOD MOVIE."

Even more angry: "Don't ever brag about what you do. Don't feed your nervous ego over me. You do very little. Fuck you. You landed me at Northampton. I don't trust you and I don't need you."

One More Winter: my husband and I found ourselves going back and forth about whether to stay in Miami or move back up north. The years had piled up, eleven in all. We were boggled and shocked at the amount of time, gamblers amazed at their debts. Yet it was unsettling living in a community strewn with bodies of people who lacked their upright glands. Everything that made Miami exciting for a reporter made it dubious for a parent. I remember asking my husband over some roast pork and pounded-out steak at the Versailles Restaurant in Little Havana, "Do you realize, except for the alligators, everyone here is a refugee?"

"So what?"

"They're all running away from something. Bad affairs, of business, of the heart. Dictatorships." I didn't want to get involved in politics, especially at a Cuban restaurant, but I did whisper, "Some of them *were* the dictators."

I cut a plantain in half. "What about us? Why are we here? Are we exiles too?"

At its worst, Miami was a series of huge shopping centers connected by streets ghoulishly empty of people. Our son's first words: dada, mama, dog, bus, bye-bye. Not much later, he said

Burdines, the name of a popular department store. He said Dade-land, air conditioning, South Dixie Highway. Who was he? Who were we?

All over town, you heard racist fears voiced of home inva-sions by hordes of Haitians. The new Cubans from Mariel were called *escoria* and *gusanos*, scum and worms. The elderly Jews on Miami Beach were being kicked out of their condos, forced to move inland, by developers who didn't see the charm in shtetls next to prime oceanfront property.

Guns were common as mangoes. Our closest neighbors, all-American family men with the all-American names of Skip and Bud, both had weapons in their homes. Our son played with Skip's kids.

My job at the *Miami Herald* often meant taking phone calls from the subjects of stories in the evening. I'd be bathing the baby, and there would be someone on the phone who needed to talk, right now, having been led to believe, by me naturally, that the coverage of their story was the most important event in the cosmos.

Mothering and reporting required the same basic ingredient: hanging out, being there. I was having trouble trying to do both jobs at once. The world and the womb, the beckoning of both.

We had another child, a daughter this time. I thought of naming her after Lizzie, but I was afraid that the name rang too deep an emotional chord for all of us. She would be asked to live up to too great an ideal. In the end, I called her Justine, partly because it is the name of a novel by Lawrence Durrell, about a smoky, mysterious woman given over to breaking hearts, and also because it means "justice," and she was born on the first day Martin Luther King's birthday was celebrated as an official holi-day—a fact made clear to me because even though it was a week-day, there was a shortage of nurses on the labor room floor. Also, the name Justine was the closest I could come to combining the names of my three sisters, who, though shaping up into women of stature, were not so ideal as to be intimidating.

I missed them.

I missed seasons, real seasons, the hefty kind, not the tropical version, in which bold scents get bolder.

I missed cider.

The decision to leave had to do with the roots that cling.

It had to do with where to raise the children, and I gravitated back to a setting I knew, having been offered a job teaching at the University of Massachusetts.

But even then there were choices to make. There were two roads diverging in a yellow wood, with imaginary signs.

One said, REPEAT.

The other, REPAIR.

Traditional Irish culture operates under a system of primogeniture, meaning that the oldest son inherits the land. What is also true, but involves less of a legal framework, is that the oldest daughter inherits the people. It was now my turn, and, of course, I discovered the obvious: it was going to be just as frustrating for me to try to control Raymond's illness as it had been for the others. Raymond might go for as long as a year or two without any flagrant breakdowns, only to find that the pressure cooker inside his head had to give off more steam.

One Christmas—after the holiday itself, before the New Year—I got a call. He needed a half gallon of orange juice, a case of beer, a carton of cigarettes, and a bag of chocolate chip cookies. And he needed all of this pronto. I brought them to him. When I got to his place, he was sleeping. I knew where to find his spare key, so I opened the door and left them right inside. The next day, same call, same requests, same scenario, although this time I went inside, picked up the cans strewn everywhere, emptied the ashtrays, swept, and left. He was out. The next day, ditto; call me a slow learner. I kept hoping he'd get through this without another hospitalization, and since he refused to go on his own, what I hoped didn't really have much weight to begin with.

Each time after the first day I checked his meds. I laid them out in piles of the appropriate dosage. On the fourth day, when I called him early in the morning, shortly after six, he sounded more than ordinarily groggy. After I got the children off to their play dates, my husband and I went to Raymond's. "You have to come with me. I can't do this alone, I said."

Unexpected intimacies, not so unusual in a marriage, are often their secret spine.

This unexpected intimacy went the extra lap.

We found him on the floor, passed out, twitching.

Raymond had overdosed on lithium.

Baystate Medical Center in Springfield kept him for five months, first for the detox, then for the bilateral pneumonia that followed, then in chronic care, waiting for an open sore to heal and he was strong enough to leave.

Once he was back at home, another year or two might go by without an eruption. My sisters and Michael and I would be in constant contact. Raymond's illness drove us closer and fostered an interdependency in ways that were not always healthy or desirable. Instead of being little kids fighting over whether or not to watch *Dobie Gillis*, we kept exhausted tabs on who had visited Raymond during his last hospitalization and whose turn it was to visit now, who called him, who sent him money, who let him inside their house and under what circumstances. Christina would cook for him, but only if he ate at Maureen's house. Michael felt, correctly, that he had been left alone on the Raymond Watch for long stretches in the sixties and the seventies, and he would do what he could, but he was busy launching his career and others had to pitch in. Maureen invited Raymond to every major holiday; Michael once described her house as being like the inside of a warm muffin, with its hanging shelf of dishes that always catches the light. Jacqueline had him visit her in Washington at least once, often twice, a year, during which time her friend Hank would take him to the horse races, once remarking that you hadn't seen anything until you saw the look on Raymond's face when he thought his horse was going to win. But even with all of us doing what we comfortably could, there were times when it felt as if we were floundering in a leaky dinghy in a rabid sea. One time Raymond called the Department of Mental Health and delivered a message, which was recorded automatically, complaining about how he had been treated during those early visits to Northampton and how his uncle, who happened to run the Commonwealth of Massachusetts, and I, a major investigative reporter for the *Boston Globe*, the most major investigative reporter ever, were on the verge of personally shutting it down and exposing its fraudulent ways. The friend who gave me a copy of the tape said it showed how profound Raymond's betrayal had been at the hands of the system early on. The very people who could give him help were the people he feared most.

Every parent has a special stockpile of panics, and usually in that stack one distinct source of fear rises taller and sturdier than all the others. People worry that their child will choke on a piece of popcorn, fly over the handlebars, put a tongue on a live socket. When my children were old enough to venture forth from the house on their bicycles, I would beg them to assure me that they would not travel to the nearby railroad tracks. "It's very dangerous," I would say. "It's got to do with the physics of sound. If you are walking or riding on the tracks, you can't hear a train coming from behind until it's too late." I would say this each time with such fresh urgency that it was years before my daughter turned to me and said, "You don't have to tell us that every day."

No matter how hard we tried to prepare ourselves for the cycles in Raymond's illness, it was always a new shock when the disease erupted, as if we didn't hear the train coming.

We would get lulled into thinking there would be no more breakdowns. He had exhausted his particular coupon book for that kind of travail.

Then, a call from the police one Saturday evening when we had company.

"We have your brother in protective custody. We can release him now, and we'd like you to come to the station and bring him home."

Raymond was being detained at the Palmer Police Station because he had called Barnes Airport in Westfield, requesting an ambulance, saying it was a matter of life and death.

It was nine-thirty at night. The image of me trying to pick up my brother in an agitated state and get him up the dark wooden steps to his apartment unnerved me. I said I would be there in the morning.

"In the morning? He's ready to leave now. Is there any other family member in the area who could come get him now?"

"There used to be. But they all moved away."

"You're it? How are you feeling about that?"

Now the cops are shrinks too. I could not tell if I was being baited, or if this was a neutral, maybe even sympathetic, interrogation. I knew how the cops and prosecutors in Dade County used to view some of their less appealing suspects. "N.H.I.," they would say, a term that I thought stood for some little-known legal maneuver until I was apprised otherwise.

N.H.I.: No humans involved.

"It's not always easy. I can't leave now to get him. I have company. I have young children. They need me here at night. I'll call in the morning to see if you still want me to come."

The next day I brought Raymond home.

The police gave me copies of the documents detailing the charges against him. How often in Miami I had looked at documents just like this, with their strange, stilted, staccato language, always astounded anew at how people got themselves into such pickles.

"Mrs. M. called from Video Paradise. Older male subject (Raymond Blais), just in store threatening them."

Raymond wanted one of the women to come to his home immediately: "in 10 minutes or he'll be back to kill them."

Later that day, he called a series of distant family acquaintances with whom he had not been in touch for years to ask them to a nonexistent surprise party. I received phone calls from some of them at home. Although the callers were polite enough to act as if maybe the invitation was genuine, they were in fact trying to alert me to something I already knew: Raymond was going downhill fast. He went back later to Video Paradise to apologize, "saying he is manic-depressive and on medication," and when he was asked to leave, he left the store angry, stopping traffic as he crossed the street.

He frightened some women who worked at Friendly's across the street.

He was taken into custody again and on Monday at the advice of the police, I went to district court in Palmer to get him committed to a mental hospital.

The moment in court went quickly.

The judge took one look at my brother (in shackles, eyes downcast) and one look at me (Joan Vass dress, eyes steady), and the papers were signed without much fuss.

But it still took all day, because I had to wait for a psychiatrist to interview me, in part for information about Raymond, but also to evaluate my motives. When the doctor finally showed up after many hours, I explained that I was there at the suggestion of the police, who believed my brother needed to be hospitalized in that he presented a danger to self and others. This was not the first time I had gone through this spiel, though it would be the last. I knew the doctor was gauging my sincerity, taking a grudge x-ray. Was I on the level, or was I so demented with some revenge scheme against my brother that I had cooked up baseless accusations and phantom complaints simply because it gave me some kind of sick pleasure to see him packed off?

It was a song and dance, even at the best of times.

Song, dance, dance, song.

I reminded myself: follow the formula.

Sit up straight.

Modulate your speech, so that sometimes it's fast and sometimes it's slow, but it's *never* out of control.

Convey that you know something about the problem, but not so much that you are in any way questioning the superior resources of the system and its ability to solve it.

Avoid their words: *enmeshment, designated patient, dual diagnosis, noncompliance*, and stick to your own.

Describe your sense of Raymond's decompensation, the technical word for loss of sound psychological function, with facts, not feelings.

Don't say, "I'm scared of my brother."

Do say, "On Sunday night he threatened violence against a clerk at a video store, who is now afraid to return to work."

Don't exaggerate, but do describe the gradation of dangerousness to the highest grade possible.

All accidental overdoses are suicide attempts.

All suicides are homicides.

Anything is a weapon.

Raymond was at Franklin Medical in Greenfield for ten days. It was his last time in a mental hospital:

"Patient was not threatening during this hospital stay as he maintained a routine of expectations with reminders from staff. Patient is relatively stable medically and psychiatrically."

A chest x-ray raised the suspicion of chronic lung disease.

When I went to pick him up, he seemed in a good mood, or at least he seemed subdued, which is what I often interpreted as a good mood. I called it his pharmaceutical harness. We took the longest way back to Palmer I could think of, going through the smallest of the small hill towns, places like Wendell, mere geographical twinges, but, somehow, the passing landscape was a kind of ballet for his eyes, a visual balm pure and simple.

After that, the physical energy it must have taken to explode mentally was no longer there. I am reminded of a feature story I wrote in the late seventies with the title "When Mommy Goes to Jail," in which the warden told me that usually by the age of thirty the recidivism rate dropped steeply. The women stopped breaking the law.

I was taken aback.

Had they all become model citizens with pension plans who served on the school board and complained about crabgrass?

"Not really. After thirty, they are too old, too tired, or," she said, "they're dead."

As mistakes go, it was sincere and honest, the most annoying kind.

A few years ago, my sisters and I decided that as a project for the holidays to occupy our mother, she should go through the dozen or so scrapbooks and photo albums that had survived as the official documentary narrative of our childhood. She should divide them into six separate story lines for each of her six children. The final entries were made in the late seventies and early eighties when our own babies came. There is a note home from me after the birth of my son, alluding to a booster shot and its screaming aftermath and how someone was dropping by with a prepared dinner but the person was "a frightful cook and I mean frightful. To reheat rice she boils it again." Christina asked my mother to baby-sit, with these instructions on an index card: "Robby eats his lunch which Bob will leave in fridge at 11:00. At 12 or 12:30 he has his bottle (in fridge). At around 1:00 or 1:30, if he has not napped yet just interest him in a crib toy and put him in his crib. I'll be home by 3:50."

And then they stop.

The reason was less mournful than practical.

We began to keep our own records of our lives and those of our children. It is our turn to save the school play program from when the children were in *The Gondoliers* and their drawing of Sojourner Truth and the invitations to bat mitzvahs on homemade paper.

The photos we take are in color but not much less haunting. Just the other day, I paused, pierced deep inside for an instant, with the inescapable truth: the cars in these photos will look old someday too.

In the years since, at our bidding, our mother took all the old albums and parsed them so that everyone got his or her own class photos, in which the boys wore plaid or stripes and the girls all had on dresses with tiny round collars or the big bib kind or jumpers with suspender straps. We have all regretted the impulse that made us think this was a good idea.

When I look at my skinny wedge of the pie or at the abbreviated, hacked-up versions belonging to someone else, it startles me how much I had imagined that their work belonged as much to me as to them. Each separate book ends abruptly, like a hem that's way too short; dismantled, they seem skimpy, even a little pathetic, a mouth with missing teeth.

My sisters and I will be seated at one or another one's dining table, sipping coffee. We will sigh a Blais sigh, shooting air up our face to cool a forehead, and when the silence is broken, it will be in mid-thought, but everyone will know the subject at hand. We all agree: it was a bad idea. The albums are so misleading now. Anyone looking at them would have that maddening sense of having missed the first five minutes of the movie. The crucial context. But she meant well. We were the ones who urged her to do it. Maybe, somehow, we could restore them.

But, then, we have to consider the unrealistic nature of such a task: who really remembers how it went? The actual sequence. It was (how could we have been so foolish not to see this before it was too late!) the aggregate that counted. Before, if you saw those books, you could sense a fearsome force. A huge wind blowing across the invisible landscape of life itself.

The six of us as one.

Now.

Nothing . . . but a bunch of little gusts.

Chapter
Thirteen

The Heaven of Lost Futures

IN THE END RAYMOND LIVED OUT HIS FINAL YEARS ABOVE AN AUTO repair store in the town of Palmer, Exit 8 on the Massachusetts Turnpike. Next door was the defunct Casa de Diablo bar, whose name always makes our mother wince. His subsidized housing was subjected to periodic inspections by government representatives who counted the vents and the doors and the smoke alarms. In one of those typical petty bureaucratic displays of one-upsmanship, their notices always specified the day of the inspection but never the hour, or even whether to expect the evaluator in the morning or the afternoon. He would, of course, wait for them all day, a kind of house arrest.

His place was on the second floor, carved out of the roofline. It had a combination living area and kitchen, one bedroom, and an overlarge bathroom that could have been remodeled to create another bedroom, but Raymond always believed the landlord wanted a single tenant or a couple, feeling that any family whose best bet was to live above a motor repair shop in the middle of nowhere presented potentially more problems than the rent solved. There was a skylight, an architectural nicety that pleased him deeply. "Girls like skylights," he would say. His living room contained two couches (one wicker, one upholstered), a couple of end tables, a small bench that subbed as a coffee table, and a little stand containing books written by me, my husband, and Fannie Farmer. He had a dark wooden bench that rocked. We saw to it that he had a microwave oven and a gas grill, a blender and a TV, lamps, an air conditioner, dishes, pots and pans, and plenty of clothes. He had a phone and an answering machine. He had a thermometer with a Moxie theme, Moxie being an old-fashioned soft drink that jolted its patron with its vile combination of medicinal flavors. A sign above the hallway leading to the bedroom and bathroom said, ROOMS.

He never married. The few times he had girlfriends he would become obsessed that they were ruining their life. He had a vague notion about what was good about marriage: it can give a guy goals, "like buying dishwashers and automatic garage door openers and all that house crap that keeps women happy."

"My luck I'd end up with the kind of wife, all you ever hear is nag, nag, nag."

Unless he had to be in the valley for doctors' appointments, he had a habit of spending two or three days in Mystic, with our mother, and then returning to Palmer. As he put it, "I spend a couple of days in Connecticut and I get bored, so I go back up to Palmer for a couple of days and I get bored. It works out." We saw to it that he had a car and a credit card for gasoline.

When he had the energy, he would surf the tag sales, collecting various items for a few bucks and later trying to sell them for a few bucks more, at the local auction centers and antique stores. He had a book called *Curios and Collectibles: A Price Guide to the New Antiques* that he would sometimes flip through.

"It's amazing what's valuable. Begin with the *A*'s. You got your Avon bottles, all shapes and sizes. Keep going. Mickey Mouse Club pencil sharpener: fifteen dollars. Little Orphan Annie Shake-Up Ovaltine Mug: twice as much. Those cast-iron dump trucks Michael used to play with: forty, fifty bucks. Want me to keep going? Tiffany-type Coca-Cola hanging fixture, no scratches, no chips? Two thousand easy. Comic books! If I had all those comic books Uncle burned because he said I wasn't studying enough, I'd be on easy street today. The first issue of *Playboy* is a pure gold mine. Old buttons, World's Fair spoons, Shirley Temple anything."

"Junk or Junque?" the book asked on its back cover, a question that intrigued him.

"Usually you want something to be in mint condition: rust-free, not torn and clean if it's paper, no crayon marks if it's a book, shiny if it's supposed to be, still works if it's a toy or a watch. But sometimes you'll run across something that's more valuable because it's all dented and chipped. You think it's covered with shit, but really it's what they call patina."

Once he thought he'd found potential riches in a wire tree with hundreds of bicycle plates that were only slightly rusty. He called it a true resistance piece.

He put it in his car, covered it with old towels to prevent potential wire tree thieves from spotting it, taking it out to show us with an appropriate sense of ceremony. The main problem was that the names on the plates had all been popular for babies born before World War II and were now hopelessly out of date, not yet recycled through to a new generation:

Eugene, Irving, Chester, Ernest.

Nancy, Phyllis, Dorothy, Lorraine.

Sometimes he thought about opening his own booth at a local flea market, between the woman who did charcoal sketches

of people's inner angels and the woman who hand-painted bar-
rettes to coordinate with your boyfriend's tattoo.

No matter how hard we tried to get him into even some sort
of day program so that he would have more structure, he refused,
saying that the next step would be placement in some sort of
halfway house with "rules about everything and group therapy
with psychos."

By the end of Raymond's life, we all had to fight not to see
him as just a series of ailments and diseases: he was manic-
depressive, he was an adult-onset diabetic, a self-medicating alco-
holic, a cancer patient, and a dental nightmare. His days consisted
of awakening at three or four in the morning, arising at five,
heading out for coffee at his favorite donut shop, favorite because a nice waitress said hi and he had not been banned from it
as he had been from so many others, calling my house at 7:45 to
deliver a weather report (we jokingly called him Doppler Ray-
dar), marking time until the first doctor's appointment, getting
lunch, stocking some meat and potatoes for dinner, opening his
first beer at two or three, eating at around five, falling asleep by
six. He had no access to the large consolations that take most of
us outside ourselves—marriage, children, the stock market—or
to the small ones—a cup of tea, a brisk walk, some dumb video.
He had lost the ability to concentrate on much of anything; even
TV was a fuzzy assault of confusing images. Weakened from all
the drugs, the lithium and the insulin and the Haldol, hands that
once fisted in fury now trembled in despair. He had no escape
from the shackles of a tormented self.

The summer before Raymond died, I spent an afternoon outside of time at a college campus in the northern part of Vermont,
a place thick with pine trees and rivers. My task that day was to
talk about writing and memoir to a group of students, mostly

poets, who gathered for a couple of weeks several times a year
as part of a low-residency master's degree program. I told them
about the time I had to write a foliage ditty for a newspaper,
and how I had trouble coming up with something witty and inci-
sive on the spot. When I started out as a journalist, I thought reporting would strike the proper balance between artistry and
profit. At the beginning, there was little of either, and it took the
usual appalling number of years to get to the point where I understood what was compelling to me about reporting, whose Latin
root means to carry back. It was the power to capture what is real,
the music of what happens, and to impound all those details that
defy embellishment—the *Life* magazines hidden beneath the mattress, the wallpaper with the drummer boys, the wire tree with
the outmoded name plates. Every hardworking reporter knows
the glow of coming in from the field having just heard or seen
something riveting: *And the best part is I didn't even make it up.*

The students and I sat in idleness and we opined. What was
the difference between a story you want to tell and one you have
to? The story you choose and the one that chooses you? As someone who had spent her entire professional life listening to the
stories of other people, I had begun to wonder: was it time to
tell my own? What was prompting the recent epidemic of memoirs? Why were so many writers trying to find the pattern in the
morass of this and that which makes up a life and to present it
to the anonymous public? What had turned us into a nation of
magpies, of chattering housewives?

I've always assumed that the impulse to divulge is connected
to the wish to settle scores. Or to set the record straight. "Set rec"
is what the editors called it at the *Miami Herald.* The best part
about those little boxes with revisions in the newspaper is the
implication that except for this one tiny flaw—so and so's medical degree is not from Harvard, it's from Yale—every fact is truth's

official ambassador. Are memoirs simply book-length versions of corrections boxes? Not objective so much as self-serving? Or are they something else, these slender volumes, these mere weekend guests, these evanescent versions of lost time and lost places, something with unexpected force and overlooked heft. I am reminded of those unobtrusive little red peppers in General Tso's chicken at Chinese restaurants and how just a small bite can have such intense reverberations. And thinking of those peppers, I am reminded anew of how memory creates memory. A friend from Ursuline once told me that her husband almost died when a pepper he consumed pierced his internal organs and he began to weaken and to hemorrhage mysteriously. At the time I thought of the story as somehow Irish with its easy sense of doom, as the product of a culture that fosters a high level of suspicion because even the most innocent objects can backfire and do. Betrayal can be swift and fatal. In Ireland, the story is often told of the fine lady who went to tea one afternoon in black '47. On the way she passed a field filled with plump potatoes and took grateful note of their health, only to pass it again later that day and nearly pass out from the stench that had overtaken the entire crop.

But now I view the story of the pepper differently, more figuratively.

Bleeding from within, another memoir writer, Kim Barnes, once said, also happens to people who keep their stories to themselves.

We talked that still summer's day at the workshop about how as a culture we've stopped believing there is anyone in charge. Through the Second World War, there was a commonly held set of beliefs about who we were as a country and where we were headed. But since then, we have been exposed to a long reign of bullies and fools. We've had Joe McCarthy and the cold war; we've had those quiz shows on TV in the fifties. The pope actually fired some lesser saints, on what grounds was never clear, though obviously they must have failed to make some quota or another. We've had Watergate and the lust in Carter's heart. We've had a president who believed that trees cause pollution, another who never inhaled. We've been inundated with priests who molest, ballplayers who extort, and trigger-happy officers of the law. There's a feeling today of being orphaned, adrift, left to one's own resources. Is it possible that the self is the one enduring institution? Funneled through the individual, history at last achieves resonance.

One of the poets had recently undergone a spiritual awakening and become a Buddhist. "If anyone had ever said I'd be part of an organized religion when I reached the age of forty-five, I would have told them they were full of it," she said. With the famed fervor of a recent convert, she went on to describe a training that consisted of passing through what are called the Five Gateways. To pass through one, she had to sit still for eleven hours. It was more than worth it, she said.

"Normal life seemed dull to me. Everything was slow and muffled. It was as if I were wearing a snowsuit all year long. And then," she said, picking up speed, "when I undertook the training, everything, I don't know, it all just seemed to fall into place."

"What is the fifth and final gateway?"

"You have a private meeting with the leader, and he asks you questions for which you are not allowed to prepare."

"Like?"

"Like, 'What is mortality?'"

I pondered for a minute, figuring that a poet would answer a conundrum with an image.

What did she say?

A broken teacup? That's what I would have said. What was W. H. Auden's line? Something about how the crack in the teacup opens a lane to the land of the dead.

"It actually took me a long time to come up with a response, but finally I told him that mortality is the flip side of everything I have ever known."

After that, she was welcomed into the temple with a feast of rice, vegetables, and puffy homemade bread.

The next day, I was back home in the trapped heat of the Connecticut River Valley in western Massachusetts, having volunteered to take my brother to a day of double doctor's appointments, one to check the toe that had been infected on a life-threatening scale when he tripped and ripped open a knob of flesh while answering a phone call from Jacqueline, who merely wished to check on his well-being, and the other to assess the progress of the radiation that was supposed to cure his throat cancer.

We were down to living by the sentiments you see expressed on bumper stickers: *One Day at a Time* and *Easy Does It*. I am reminded of a Roz Chast cartoon from *The New Yorker*, about a store called the House of Low Goals, specializing in tributes for people who have lowered their sights. The storefront contained T-shirts that said "I survived conjunctivitis" and "I can read a bus schedule"; special occasion cakes that trumpeted the good news "Wow! Only six cavities" and "No loitering arrests in one year"; greeting cards such as "I'm so glad you're not an arsonist" and "Congratulations on your EASY CHAIR!" and a trophy that said, simply, "Participant."

That day I brought him flowers, a merry assortment of purples and pinks purchased at one of the many roadside stands that open their doors and thrust their seasonal bounty on passing motorists during the summer months, that kind of stand to which he had always hoped to hitch his star. Looking, I am sure, thrilled with myself, intoxicated with the tableau of my own goodness, I was both taken aback by and filled with grudging admiration for the brutal candor of my brother's response, "What a waste of money."

One of his tried and true topics was how little I knew about money.

"Guess it comes from being loaded," he used to tell our siblings. "Big house, two cars, plenty of furniture. Both her kids got braces when they needed them. She has so much money she can be stupid about it."

He expressed contempt for my choice in groceries, especially lamenting my tendency to purchase what he called "screwy" vinegar with weird berries and sprigs in the bottle, yuppie mustard that wasn't even yellow, and pricey free-range chicken that did not, in his opinion, taste one whit better just because it had been allowed a social life. And as far as my current choice of where to live, in a college town in which citizens recently voted two to one to decriminalize marijuana and the high school was forbidden to put on *West Side Story* because its message is too inflammatory, he said, "Everyone in that town is flaky," and it was clear that I was part of everyone.

That day, I asked him to smoke his cigarette before we set forth because I did not want the odor of tobacco to linger in the car. It was new and I was trying to keep it in mint condition. In addition, one of my children has asthma and the other gags at even the slightest trace of smoke.

"That's it," he said. "I'm not going with you."

I was used to this kind of tantrumlike pronouncement. If you used finesse, it passed as quickly into oblivion as an ash out a car window.

"Listen, have a smoke now and if you really want another one, we'll stop along the way."

I watched while he puffed away, knowing it would be useless to suggest that given his circumstances it might be logical to give up smoking altogether. Arguing with him on some subjects was like arguing with the Vatican, the Mafia, the phone company, the National Collegiate Athletic Association, the Cuban exile community in Miami as well as the Cuban community in Cuba, combined.

We took one of Raymond's customary eccentric routes to Baystate, the convolutions and the detours helping to fill the time. He pointed out the scenic spots. First on the tour was a strip joint known as the Magic Lantern.

"Best in the area," he told me, and I wondered what best meant, under such circumstances. Sometimes he joked about taking his two oldest nephews there, but this was said mostly in the spirit of getting my goat. In fact, he wasn't wild about the place because he had heard they charged seven bucks for a beer.

"Highway robbery," he said, "or Route 20 robbery anyway."

Next, he motioned toward a joint famous for sub sandwiches; farther down the road, he waved a hand at the factory where they make State Line Potato Chips. Raymond recalled the first time he saw the factory, when he was ten or eleven, and that giddy feeling of seeing a landmark in person for the first time.

"Yeah," I agreed. "Seeing it made you feel like you'd gone to Europe and seen the Eiffel Tower."

"A person of the world," he responded, in a musing manner, almost sighing as he spoke.

I told him that I had heard that the house in Granby was up for sale again.

As a topic the house in Granby had complete immunity and was always acceptable.

"Yeah, I guess that publisher who lived there for a while moved to Florida. Did you know that one time he had a party in our backyard and Jane Fonda was there?"

Jane Fonda had tried to make the movie *Stanley and Iris*, which was about being working class and illiterate, in Holyoke, hoping to use the flats and some of the factory sites in Chicopee as a backdrop. I had heard this story many times from Raymond, but I let him tell me once more.

"Don't tell Mother that they picked Chicopee because it looks down and out. You know she can't stand hearing a word against Chicopee. Anyway, they didn't make it here because the vets all demonstrated and said Jane Fonda was a traitor during Vietnam, so that was the end of that."

I knew what was coming next.

"You know what I've always wondered. I've always wondered if that day, you know, when they were having the barbecue or whatever it was at the old house, if she ever went inside. Maybe she used the bathroom Chuck and I fixed up."

It doesn't matter what you think of Jane Fonda and her politics. The woman still has a bladder. "You know," I said, as if I'd never heard this speculation before and had never responded to it, "I bet she did."

"I heard," said Raymond, "it's taking awhile to sell the house because they found lead paint."

Lead paint? My ears perked up; yet another possible culprit, another explanation for Raymond's troubles. Had he swallowed paint chips as a child?

"Yeah, and did you know that Granby now has its own Dunkin' Donuts?"

I had heard: its arrival was construed as a big compliment from corporate America. Finally Granby was enough of a critical mass to merit a franchise operation.

"Too bad it's so hot today," I said. "It would have been nice to take a drive up to Summit House."

I knew this was his favorite spot in the valley; it is the trite but true favorite of just about everyone who lives in the shadow of the Holyoke Mountain Range. The very mention of it stirs up the endorphins, unleashes those feel-good chemicals. A short drive up, or a thirty-minute hike, leads to picnic benches and grills, all in prized spots, some with sweeping views. In the forgiving mist of distance, the nearly collapsing Coolidge Bridge is a confident arc passing over the Connecticut River, reduced to filament from afar. The eyesore skyscraper dormitories at UMass next to the vast fields are finally in the correct scale. They have a hardly noteworthy rightness, like salt and pepper shakers on a table. The diminutive cars move at a measured pace, free of honking and exhaust. There is a memorial on the mountain for some soldiers who crashed into its side while on a training mission during World War II: a rock with a plaque and the rudder from their plane. At the top there is also a stately white house, with a certain pride in its own improbability, its porch filled with benches, one of which is inscribed in honor of a man and a woman by their children on their fortieth wedding anniversary. This is where the couple became engaged. A nearby boulder contains another plaque, which celebrates the commissioning of the land, signed by Governor Saltonstall in 1941, pledging that Skinner Park will be there for the citizens of the commonwealth, to enjoy, big letters now, capitalized too, engraved on metal, "FOREVER."

Here in this panorama is the all of it, the ultimate in razzmatazz: Love, death, beauty, and the promise, from state legislators no less, of eternity.

Every time Raymond visited Skinner State Park, he said, "I feel better now."

Nearly every seat in the waiting room was occupied. "That's what happens when you have an appointment at 1:45," he said, pleased with his sense of authority. "Everyone's late coming back from lunch."

My brother was used to waiting rooms.

If I had told him that the day before I had met a woman who had given herself over to eleven hours of pure waiting for the sake of spiritual insight, he would have put it in the category where he put all my goofiness and that of my friends and acquaintances.

His definition of mortality would differ from the poet's: mortality is what he knew better than anything else.

"The doctor's a broad," he told me. "These days it's amazing how many doctors are broads."

He was hoping to get the doctor to say everything was okay so he could dismiss the visiting nurse who came twice a day to administer antibiotics intravenously. In this we were at odds: our family always felt better about Raymond when he had a concrete physical ailment, because then he got the medical attention he needed, including the simple gestures of a kind touch and a listening ear. When he was mentally ill, he was often abandoned to his own terrifying lack of resources.

"Diabetes sure makes a lot of things into mountains," he said.

"Even a stubbed toe," I agreed.

We sat.

Moments went by laden with silence.

Raymond stirred.

He remembered that he had good news about his friend Joey, who had an under-the-table job directing traffic at the Brimfield Flea Market. Ten dollars an hour under the hot sun: it wasn't what you'd call winning the lottery, but it beat sitting around, smoking, waiting for your toe to get normal. He had known Joey since they were teenagers. Joey had about six D.U.I.s.

"Thanks to those MADD people, you can't drive even if you've only had one pop. Boy, are they out to get you." Another favorite topic.

According to Raymond, Joey kept applying for a Cinderella license, which allows offenders to drive just to work and back, but the state wouldn't let him have one. Sometimes Joey crashed at his place, which was fine. Joey traveled light. His prize possession was a snake flashlight, which his mother gave him one year for Christmas. "It helps you look around the corners of pipes and stuff. It's good for fixing cars." Joey didn't try to grub food or anything. In fact, he had his own pretty big collection of canned goods. In exchange for the free use of Raymond's sofa he didn't mind cooking or doing the dishes. Sometimes Joey's girlfriend dropped by, which usually meant there would be some good cooking.

A few seats down, a man was moaning. A little boy kept trying to get his attention: "Daddy, Daddy."

"Puerto Rican," said my brother, "by the looks of him." The man had a metal protector, secured with white tape, covering his eye. Whenever the child squirmed out of his chair and starting crawling under it, the man would yell at him to get back in his seat or else he would kick his butt from here to you know where.

"Nothing wrong with Puerto Ricans," Raymond said. "Once, when I was bumming around in Springfield, they kept giving me cigarettes without me even asking, just to be nice." And of course he had been to Puerto Rico years and years ago, in another lifetime really. Selling encyclopedias. A nice place. Sunny. Good drinks. Pretty girls.

Outside it was ninety-five degrees. Everyone was wearing shorts and T-shirts and sandals. Everyone except my brother.

He had on his uniform, the blue jeans and the polo shirt, winter and summer. Raymond's most arresting feature was his hazel eyes, not just because they shifted color, but because they seemed to tunnel backward into a private dimension. People often assumed that Raymond was a Vietnam vet, and when they did, he just let them think it. It was at the Veterans' Hospital in Leeds after all where he went to get his shots of Haldol from a nurse he liked named Karen.

"Mr. Melendez," came the voice from the nurse's station, bored and steady. "Please come to the front desk."

Mr. Melendez made his way slowly forward, his arms feeling the air in front of him, like someone practicing to be blind, only in his case it might not have been just practice.

His little kid scooted after him.

"Sit down and wait for me," he yelled. "Here, you can play with my keys while I talk to the doctor."

"That's pretty generous, you know," said my brother. He said he would never let anyone play with his keys. He loved to feel their drag in his pocket and to hear their jangle. Keys were lucky. They meant you had a place to live, or a car, sometimes both.

"What would you like for dinner tonight?" I asked him. "We'll stop and get something on the way home."

A shrug. More silence. The radiation had eaten into his appetite. The doctor had told him to try to fill up on soups, applesauce, and milkshakes.

"I don't know," he said. "I'm indifferent."

It was typical of him to suddenly marshal the precise word. He was often attuned and muffled at the same time.

"Mr. Blais."

At first he appeared not to hear, then he looked up slowly.

Shuffling, he passed through the door being held open by a uniformed nurse and entered the antiseptic maze.

The doctor said his toe was better.

Later, in another office at the same hospital, his cancer doctor looked at Raymond's throat with an instrument not unlike Joey's snake flashlight and then scheduled a more elaborate "look-see" under anesthesia. "Awesome," he said, rocking back on the heels of his comfortable shoes.

My brother had beaten the disease.

"Yeah, it's good news," said Raymond, with a shrug. He had begun a process of disconnection that we all tried not to notice. We teased him that he had nine lives.

If so, after the cancer, he was on his tenth.

His last months were perhaps the most peaceful he had ever known.

He was calm, even reasonable.

Not long before he died, he said, "Mother, do you notice anything about me?"

"Well, I notice a lot, Ray. Is there something in particular?"

"Have you noticed that I never swear anymore?"

It was true: it had dissipated, the verbal rage that used to cause him to strut around the house screaming slurs and other obscenities when he was a teenager, that prompted him to call the Department of Mental Health threatening lawsuits, or to harass a girl in a video store or a waitress at Friendly's, to call 911 repeatedly to report out-of-control aircraft, or to call Sotheby's to see if his alleged antiques were potential auction material. "Sir," said the voice at the other end, dripping with reserve, "whatever it is that they are worth now, they will be worth even more in twenty years, so," adding, totally icy now, "call back then."

Raymond was subdued at the end, oriented to time and place. The calendar at his apartment above the motor shop was on the right month in the right year.

We fooled ourselves into believing that his days were no more numbered than anyone else's.

He had made it through the fall, through Thanksgiving, and Christmas, supplying us with the usual lists, though this time, no longer able to wield a pen, he dictated them to our mother. The day before he died he called me at 7:45 in the morning and we discussed the mild weather for as long a time as it is possible to discuss mild weather. That afternoon, I spoke to my mother, who said she thought he was "failing, to use an old-fashioned word. I hope you'll do something to lift his spirits." His broken state made him less demanding, which made it easier to say no to his requests for company, and I was feeling the usual mantle of guilt after I hung up the phone with my mother. I made a promise to myself, which I can only hope I would have kept, to come up with some distraction: a trip to Nick's Nest in Holyoke, a restaurant that serves franks and beans, popcorn, coffee, and milkshakes and nothing else, like an elderly relation with five basic stories to tell; or maybe to the Quabbin Reservoir, to stare at the water supply and try to see beneath its surface the outline of any of the four towns that were drowned to create it; or perhaps a visit to one of those maple sugar houses in the hills for a pancake breakfast. I would have held my breath against the odor of smoke and sweat embedded in his clothing and done my best to force conversation onto the long bolts of dead air that unfurled in his company.

The next day he headed to Mystic, after a doctor's appointment.

Late that afternoon, my mother served him his favorite meal, steak and potatoes. She left briefly to return a book to the library, which was one block away. When she returned, he had already gone to bed so she didn't get a chance to bid him a good night.

He died in his sleep in early March more or less of old age, two months shy of his fifty-fourth birthday. There was no sign of trauma, no postmortem evidence of fingers and toes curled up in agony, which the mortician told us is a sign of someone trying to fight off pain. As far as I know, the room went white and then it filled with angels.

No matter how thoroughly anticipated death is, or even desired as the only way to alleviate suffering, there is still, when death occurs, a disconcerting sense of a wholesale shifting of the solar system. One time when my children were little and spent Saturday mornings watching cartoons, they saw one in which apparently a great big orb in the sky exploded. They came running into the kitchen.

"We need a new planet!" they shouted, jumping up and down.

"Why?" I asked.

"Because the old one is broken."

Our mother dictated to us her usual elaborate obituary: "A visionary entrepreneur as well as a connoisseur of antiques and an expert on valley lore, he was active in the produce business . . ."

She spoke at length about his talent and his promise, his brilliance and his humor. She said that the obituary should point out that he had valor, and in case anyone was wondering, she was using the word with absolute precision. She had looked it up. *Valor* means more than ordinary courage; it means courage for the battle. Shunned at times, frightening at others, frightened himself more often than not, he fought bad odds day in, day out, yet he kept on keeping on. She said he had been a good boy, a loyal son, and when he was at Mount St. Charles he had sent the most thoughtful letters home. We took it all down, her magnificent tribute, but in the end all he got from the newspaper were a few lines, garbled at that.

A few days later, we emptied out our brother's apartment. Raymond's friend Joey had offered to take over the lease. We left him all the major furniture and the dishes.

"You don't have to," he said. "It all belonged to Ray. Everything except the food." He promised to send my mother a picture he had taken of Raymond by his small artificial Christmas tree. If the picture was any good, Raymond had intended to reproduce it and to send it out (to whom, besides us, we had to wonder) the following year at the holidays.

There was no funeral, just a simple burial at St. Patrick's Cemetery, on the ninth day of the third month, the month of precipitously sad parkas, of impulsive and ill-advised haircuts, the month when normal courtesies are suspended, the month of extremes. Lambs, lions, pussy willows, icicles, spring puddles, blizzards. The calendar should be rewritten, January, February, Bipolar, April, May.

The service would be private.

Dermot came in from Boston.

I suggested that perhaps donations could be made in Raymond's memory to the Survival Center in Amherst or to the Honor Court in Northampton, both of which reach out to people of slender means, but our mother chose instead to suggest that remembrances be offered to the Dominican nuns at the Monastery of the Mother of God on Riverdale Road in Springfield, a cloistered order devoted to a regimen of constant prayer.

I would have allowed friends of the family to attend.

"No," she said, adding the Gaelic, *"Sinn Fein."*

I did not fight city hall.

"And," she said, giving us her infamous glare, blue, icy, piercing, beyond language, "I shouldn't have to say this, but I do. Don't you girls dare wear slacks."

The priest who would normally have presided was away on vacation: we were asked if we minded if a nun was sent in his stead.

Would we mind a nun?

Us?

Sister Edith arrived at the cemetery a few minutes before one o'clock on March 9, 1998. Like everyone else that winter, we blamed the bad weather on El Niño. With her white hair, spirited manner, and doughy, modestly suited body, Sister Edith was a familiar figure, interchangeable with the procession of elderly Irish ladies who have dotted the family landscape over the years. She possessed a master's degree in pastoral counseling. Because she did such a remarkable job of remembering who was who, I decided she must have earned an "A" in the course called Keeping the Names of the Bereaved Straight.

At first, we stood huddled together.

She told us to spread out, to make a circle.

The day was raw, windy, bitter; it was raining ice. Our mother stood as tall as she could against the weather. Her posture put me in mind of the four times she was singled out and called to stand during her high school graduation ceremony. Her friend Kay Mannix had written on the Class Day program: "In your chain of memories consider me a link."

Above her eyes where there had once been eyebrows was just another crease of dotted skin. And not just that thick dark ridge had disappeared. What about time itself? On her face was an expression of pure bewilderment, as if she were trying to answer the question of where Time goes, as if she were flipping through some invisible filing system, observing how just a few minutes ago Christina and Maureen were fighting over each other's Ginny dolls, and Michael wanted a BB gun for his birthday, and Jacqueline and Madeleine were helping to fold Raymond's white shirts to put in that heavy black trunk for Camp Leo. And minutes before that, Raymond was an infant during the war and Lizzie was writing to her in Fort Pierce with instructions on how to knit him a sweater. Earlier still, some very sweet children in the sixth grade at the Valentine School were wishing her luck in her new life as a married woman. And then, she was back in college at Bridgewater, crafting perfectly scripted essays on Tolerance, playing the piano at the nearby prison while that gifted girl with the good voice belted out that entirely inappropriate song about looking down the long lonesome road, and then, even younger, she was back at the house on Belcher Street in Chicopee and was so glad her father had won the mayoral election because then she would get to play the harp at the inaugural ceremony, and then, burrowing further into the past, she was in the fourth grade, at her friend's birthday party doing a silly dance she made up called "The Powder Puff," hoping to get that quiet little boy who kept buying her trinkets to save his pennies and buy a scooter of his own someday, and then there she is, younger still, a toddler, caught in the shade of a linden tree, walking down the street, holding the hands of her parents, bathed in the smiles of neighbors, on the verge of pronouncing her first complete sentence. *I like lilacs.* Someone should scold Time for zooming forth to an unconvincing and altogether intolerable present. Time should take that drug that helps unruly children to settle down.

The ice had turned to rain, and it was coming down sideways.

Sister Edith led us in prayer. How it gets inside your bones, seeps into the sinews and the corpuscles, and hits a person up from time to time. The power derives from its repetitive quality, each prayer recalling every other time the prayer was offered, recalling the way, adorned in hats, we lifted our voices to recite the rote words on that succession of Easter Sundays, or in high school when the girls got to be the altar boys, to recite the sacred Latin words, *"Domine non sum dignus,"* or during those days in late summer, perfect days, cool and blue, with no sign of the devil anywhere when, much to the bafflement of anyone who wasn't Catholic, on August 15 we celebrated the Feast of the Assumption, donning our madras shifts, streaming into church to honor the Virgin for having been the only human ever to be automatically assumed into the Beatific Kingdom, no questions asked.

The service for Raymond lasted no more than ten minutes, concluding with a poem.

Michael stepped forward slightly.

Michael always amazes me. If my sisters and I had childhoods that sometimes operated on less than a quarter tank, his flirted with empty, operating on fumes. Yet he turned into a man of deep convictions with an assortment of passions. He likes cars, computers, RFK, John McCain, nonfiction, dogs, and influencing his niece and his nephews. He recently inspired one of them to start a debate team at his high school. He withholds judgment from just about everyone except petite actresses who say, "You like me. You people really, really like me" when they win an Oscar. He finds the rest of us excessively verbal. "Words, words, words," he once said to me. "You people live in a bubble of words."

Yet he turned out strong and tall and, the sisters' greatest compliment, true blue.

He was the one who spoke for Raymond, to Raymond, at the final moment.

Without hesitation, in a solemn voice that did not falter, he read a poem called "Leaves" by Derek Mahon:

> *The Prisoners of infinite choice have built their house*
> *in a field below the wood,*
> *And are at peace.*
>
> *It is autumn, and dead leaves on their way to the river*
> *Scratch like birds at the windows or tick on the road.*
>
> *Somewhere there is an afterlife of dead leaves.*
> *A stadium filled with an infinite rustling and sighing.*
>
> *Somewhere in the heaven of lost futures,*
> *The lives we might have lived*
> *Have found their own fulfillment.*

We moved in clumps toward the cars that would take everyone back to my house for the reception I had assumed for years would be held there. Our mother was shivering. As we proceeded to leave, my brother's friend, Joey, showed up, driven by his mother. The ritual had taken less time than we expected. Our mother paused in her leave-taking to greet them.

The news that evening was filled was the usual mix of folly and dread. The vice president was implicated in some kind of fundraising hanky-panky. There were no new leads in the death of that little girl in Colorado. A disgruntled former employee killed four people at the headquarters for the state lottery in Connecticut.

Before I went to sleep that night, I examined the contents of a wooden box about the size of a briefcase in which Raymond kept his lifetime accumulation of papers. There was a sales slip from Ames, his favorite department store. Recipes, for baked spaghetti and meatballs, oven-roasted potatoes, and, in our mother's handwriting, meat loaf. He had a paperback copy of the *Train-Watcher's Guide to North American Railroads*. There was a series of receipts for odds and ends that he used to pick up at tag sales and then bring to the Amherst Auction Galleries to resell: a chair and a globe for which he was paid $10, a lamp for $15, a canister set for $5, an "as is" trunk for $5. Refill request forms for various pharmaceutical products, including alcohol prep pads, insulin lisinopril in 5 mg tabs, lithium carbonate in 300 mg capsules to be taken by mouth three times a day. There was no address book, but there were several return addresses ripped off the corner of envelopes. A "separation document" from the United States Air Force confirmed that he had entered the service on April 30, 1962, served a total of twenty days, had completed two years of high school at the time, was not eligible for veteran's benefits, and was given an honorable discharge. The Social Security Administration had contacted him at various times, to inform him that his monthly stipend would be $485 after deductions for Medicare. Sometimes these documents were accompanied by their Spanish and their Khmer translations. His housing subsidy from the government amounted to $328 a month. He was obligated to pay an additional $71 rent out of his Social Security. The box had an odometer disclosure form for his VW Jetta and information about car insurance. There was a card dated December 21, 1989, from an old acquaintance from his encyclopedia days.

There was a newspaper ad, dated 1990, from a store called Bradlee's for a dozen long-stem roses, premium quality, eighteen-inch minimum length, wrapped with greens and baby's breath, arranged in a crystal vase for $19.99.

That night I dreamt that the Summit House had slowly collapsed and slid down the mountainside, plummeting in silence.

At work the next day I received a message from Raymond's oncologist at Baystate: "I'm very sorry to see in one of our reports that Raymond had expired. Would you please be willing to give me a call and tell me what happened?"

The voice of the doctor was soft and respectful, "What happened?" I wanted to call him back and comfort him, to say that this recent report was meaningless. My brother had died long ago. The boy who might have been had gotten lost in the forest one night and never returned.

I wanted to tell him that I have often heard it said that when a plane crashes, it is usually the result of not one glaring mistake so much as a series of seemingly unrelated events. It occurs to me that the same may be true when a personality disintegrates, a mind collapses. Was there a key time in my brother's life when timely intervention might have made a difference? How much was he slowed down by our insistence on interpreting his failings and failures in moral rather than medical terms? What of the failure of medicine to see the mind and body as each other's spokesman? Did the high expectations, those third-generation immigrant dreams of striving, keep him from settling for a downsized, more reasonable existence? What was the price of shame?

A few weeks after Raymond's death, Jacqueline and I visited the courthouse in Springfield in order to settle, and I use the term with all the irony due it, his estate, which consisted of the car with which we supplied him, a few pieces of furniture of little objective value, and less than two thousand dollars in the bank.

"One thousand and seven hundred and eighteen dollars and change," said Jacqueline. "Knowing Ray, he would want us to buy a lottery ticket with this combination."

As we looked for the arrows pointing the way to Probate, we saw a sign that said, DOMESTIC VIOLENCE. TAKE A NUMBER.

Since then, well-meaning friends have asked me more than once whether or not I miss him. The question fills me with incredulity: how can you miss someone who is missing to himself? Yet the memory of him returns to me unbeckoned, his offbeat observations and passionate opinions, often at moments when it might be said that I am wallowing in ease. The children are home, we are eating dinner, the house is friendly with rich colors and treasured objects, a life of chenille and kilims, dinners with napkin rings and bread served in a wrought-silver basket. It is a dreamworld of satisfied people who might be tempted not to reveal their good fortune, people who fret over artificial dilemmas, the more artificial the better, such as how the wrong swatch arrived from Brunschwig & Fils or how Bread and Circus has for some reason run out of fresh capers, a life filled on the surface with what might be called Protestant tragedies, designer woes.

We could pass for my mother's dreaded smuggos and complacos. We are talking about something of little consequence, a neighbor's new minivan, the deplorable conditions of the rain-ravaged soccer fields at Smith and Wesson, the return of the college students from one of their endless breaks with their mattresses teetering off the roofs of their cars. We discuss my daughter's dress for the eighth-grade dance. Long? Short? Black? White? We discuss my son's summer job prospect pumping air into bicycle tires at an establishment called Wheel Happy. We audition ideas for what to do during the next spring vacation. Should we visit our old haunt, Florida, the Fleeing Felon State, where I love the lanolin odor of the air, the creaminess of a tropical night, and take a perverse delight in what we used to call

"Only in Miami" stories, the outlandish events fueled by the peculiar atmosphere consisting of sunlight and garlic and fire-arms? Or will it be back to Italy, where I have supervised students at the University of Massachusetts in the writing portion of a photojournalism class for the past two years? My all-time favorite student proposal for an essay was entitled "Sicily Today: Now and Then."

Into this busy, nearly spoiled talk, my brother will suddenly intrude, and I will recall his face. In Raymond's agony to lead as normal a life as possible, his struggles became as much mine as his, and they belonged to my other brother and our three sisters as well, let alone our mother. Most people I know have a Raymond somewhere in their family. Everyone's Raymond is special; everyone's Raymond is impossible. I have little doubt that in another family in another time his life might not have been so blighted, but I also believe, perhaps because any other belief is intolerable, that despite the flaws of the family he had, some measure of coherence and caring kicked in so that he died in relative peace. In the end he killed neither himself nor any-one else. As success stories go, this may seem grim, but I find I must look at it differently. "Where is it written that families have to be (a) happy or (b) unhappy?" Jacqueline once said, and then answering her own question, "Oh, yeah, it was Tolstoy, sort of. Do you think it ever occurred to him they can be both at once?" My husband always says that we were either the most normal eccentric family in the world, or the most eccentric normal one.

In the end, we did what we could to inject tenderness into a life that often courted its opposite. We were, as Jacqueline says, "good enough."

Northampton State Hospital is closed down, as shuttered as a bad clam after it's been boiled, a series of boarded-up buildings that are sometimes explored by teenagers on a dare or a double dare. The interiors are collapsing in on themselves. The last patient left in the early nineties.

Outside, the gardens that used to be tended by the patients as a form of therapy in the early hopeful days are now given over to the community at large for its radishes and its lettuce.

A field is devoted to youth soccer, and on weekends you can hear fans shouting for a pass or cussing out a bad call. Plans are underway to tear down much of the hospital and rebuild on the property, with a mix of housing for the poor and the not so poor.

Raymond would have shaken his head in wonderment to learn that Northampton State Hospital got star billing as the setting for the movie *The Cider House Rules*, and he would have been even more flabbergasted to learn that a performance artist got money from the state of Massachusetts to stage a kind of public exorcism at the hospital. The artist, Anna Schuleit, first saw the hospital in 1991 while on a field trip from her nearby prep school, and later told a reporter that she had been taken aback by the beauty and the architecture of the facility. "It was created with such care, such amazing attention down to the last detail. It was obvious to me that the people who built the hospital were idealists, that this was going to be a great place—a real contribution to human happiness and fulfillment. And it all went so badly." She found the silence most stunning, "It was like an indrawn breath. It felt like the end of the world."

At first, she could think of no graphic or pictorial way to capture the essence of what she felt about the hospital, but eventually she came up with a plan that would fight the silence. She would make the building sing. She spent several years getting permission from the state to allow a group of technicians to run wires through the abandoned buildings so that for twenty-eight minutes, Bach's *Magnificat* would be played over state-of-the-art loudspeakers in its entirety. The piece is a polyglot of voices, never a mere babble, but in fact a conversation between one movement and the next. The *Magnificat* is about feeling and emotion as much as it is about tempo and pitch and crescendo. It is a mosaic of moods, and as such she believed it would make a perfect set piece to accompany an otherwise silent vigil at a defunct mental hospital.

Articles in the local press quoted naysayers who dismissed her scheme as an ego trip, speculating that no other possible end than Anna Schuleit's self-aggrandisement would be served by the event. Before the musical tribute, a two-day symposium entitled "Beyond Asylum: Transforming Mental Health Care" was held on the campus at nearby Smith College, culminating in statements from former patients about their time at the "haunted house on the hill." They spoke with a sense of subdued outrage, but sometimes ventured toward nostalgia and even outright humor. One woman said, "Yes, there were gang showers and you could go on about that, but we were all women at least." Someone else burst into laughter as she recalled faking seizures for the fun of it. Another patient remembered how there wasn't enough money for towels and the patients were given men's underwear that had been laundered, but was nonetheless tattered and stained, to use as washcloths. The pure absurdity of it was lost on no one, staff and patients alike.

The former patients who spoke that day saw the end of the Northampton State Hospital in large historic terms, writ in boldface across a huge convas. They likened its proposed demolition to the dismantling of the Berlin Wall. When they were finished, the crowd of hundreds walked from the campus up the steep incline to the adjacent grounds of the hospital where they were joined by hundreds more. At noon, all the churches of Northampton rang their bells and everyone in the city was asked to observe a moment of silence in honor of what had been done intentionally, or unintentionally, at the hospital to harm those who had stayed there.

Later, dressed in dark bulky coats and the scarves and hats needed in a New England winter, most of the audience circled the building in a trance while the music resonated through the air. A few people sat by themselves off to the side, in apparent meditation. Some in the crowd exchanged greetings with a nod of the head, or a quick hello, but, as if by common consent, it was understood that no one would ask any one else why he or she had chosen to be there.

Not birds but Bach fought against the gray sky and, in this, the composer's most ambitious and life-affirming work, a glorious chorus, called for renewal, expressing the desire for God's divine mercy on all people. The fallen creation embodied by Northampton State Hospital was transformed, if only for a moment. The snake pit was replaced by a cathedral.

To this day my desk drawers are filled with requests from Raymond for small items that helped guarantee his daily survival, especially grocery lists, with their unceasing emphasis on Dinty Moore canned stew. By the end, we all operated a sort of bucket brigade, trying, not always with perfect success, to see that he received the proper medical attention, and food and clothing. Maureen not only offered him an invitation to her house on every holiday, she even helped with his laundry. "Not that he didn't have twenty hours a day to do it himself," she used to say, laughing, but she also understood that we all trade in symbols and the symbol consoled him. Sweet with the smell of soap, starched and civic-minded, carefully folded clothes are the opposite of abandonment. Whenever he was feeling well enough to express his gratitude, he did. For my children a candy bar or a dollar, free balloons from a bank opening; for all of us, various plants that he would get at one of his vaunted bargains. One time he gave me a dictionary, and since then, I have sometimes wondered: was this a gift with a subtext, implying permission for this endeavor, perhaps even endowing it with his blessing? I can assure you he would have had no truck with such blatant sentimentality. "Now that," he would be likely to say, leaning forward, his face reddening with conviction, "is pure bull."

Chapter
Fourteen

Lucky Ladies

RECENTLY, WE GOT TOGETHER, THE FOUR BLAIS GIRLS, IN CONNECTICUT, where our mother's efforts to pair us have paid off especially with Maureen and Christina, who are neighbors on the same street and teachers in the same school system.

In her work as a kindergarten teacher, Christina spends her time helping others put their feet out the door. Perhaps because the world greeted Christina with a warm bath of approval, she had one foot out the door early, marrying first, owning a house first, producing the first baby, and, eventually, getting the first divorce.

Her marriage lasted almost twenty years.

Christina's husband worked his way up to representing a firm in Finland that manufactured luxury yachts, selling them to men who call beer "brewskies" and who pride themselves on not wearing socks between Memorial Day and Labor Day and who act as if they were the very first people ever to think of marrying someone half their age. Despite their wealth, these men took childish delight in the nautical tradition of making do, of, say, reworking wire coat hangers into sticks for kebobs, or stirring their coffee with the shank of their sunglasses rather than using a spoon. Christina would go to parties in Greenwich, Connecticut, at which all the women wore the same black dress and for which the invitations were calligraphic works of art suitable for framing. After the marriage ended, our mother often pointed out that Christina is her most modern daughter in the sense that she has those blended-family dilemmas that one hears about on daytime TV—and, in that she roller-blades almost every day.

Maureen lives with her husband and her two school-age sons. As a child, she was known to be stubborn, and now she is known as fierce, especially about her job teaching emotionally disturbed children, who are either mired in silence or, just as likely, boisterous. They are like her younger self, easily overlooked, or, like Raymond, likely to live out crippled fates if not for massive intervention. She slaves over her year-end reports, which serve as guidebooks for the fancy shrinks hired by the state to ratify my sister's sensible advice about the best placement for each child.

Jacqueline and I ended up sharing the address of a similar profession. She is now an editor at *USA Today*, and one of her accomplishments was to go one-on-one with the *New York Times* to break its lock on the best-seller lists for books, creating one for the Gannett newspaper chain.

She had no children of her own, but instead became the designated "extra mother," the spare that Anne Tyler talks about in the opening pages of her novel *Dinner at the Homesick Restaurant*. She keeps the scrapbooks for the next generation, saves their emails and their artwork. She treats them to astronaut ice cream from the Smithsonian and enters their relays and diving contests with an enthusiasm that the rest of us often cannot muster.

The children call her Aunt Mom.

And I remain dictatorial as ever, still bearing the burden, perhaps more a delusion than a reality, of being the one to report on the outside world to my sisters, to make pronouncements on fashion, such as, "Black goes with black," or "Taupe is a godsend," or to come up with the complicated recipes, the preparation of which transforms me into a banshee in the kitchen, shouting directions as if they were brave-spirited slogans, "Toast the almonds! Section the grapefruit! Splay the cornichons!" I am the standard bearer, the queen of the brave front, the setter of example, the apostle of good grades, the arbiter of who does what for whom in the family, a low-level Mafiosa doling out the homely chore. All this, when I have long nursed the secret suspicion that my true nature was to be an adventurer, but circumstances replaced my original personality with one that is entirely different. I went from the rebel to that most odious of girl fates, the goody-goody. Born to be footloose and impulsive, I became tethered and domineering; born Jo, I became Meg.

Some clever person once said that in big Irish families the children squabble over everything, including which prefix attaches to their name, and there are three to choose from: *poor*, *that*, or *dear*. In our family, it was usually poor all of us for having lost our father. It was poor Raymond for having so many crosses to bear, and that Raymond for causing so much commotion bearing them. It was poor Jacqueline for having to put up with me, dear Jacqueline for being the kindest, that Jacqueline when she tried too hard and, of course, failed to make everything perfect. It was poor Christina when her marriage ended, dear Christina when she showed any evidence of her overall handiness, that Christina when she appeared to prefer others to her own family. It was poor Maureen for being so quiet, dear Maureen for being almost as kind as Jacqueline, and never that Maureen. It was poor Michael for having the added hardship of a brother who could not be a brother to him the way the girls could be sisters to each other, and dear Michael for being so good to his mother, and that Michael when he set the children up to commit some act of mischief or another. I rarely slowed down enough in my efforts to whip everyone into shape to earn the word dear, I avoid being called poor, and mostly, given my role as Mother Superior, am known, at my worst, as that Madeleine, "one cold cookie."

First things first, on the day of our recent visit.

The world will end if we don't pause to admire Maureen's garden, which she sees as her annual chance to get things right. Dirt, seeds, and colorful expectations all watered at regular intervals. Though the least verbal of the six Blais children, she is a walking lexicon of plant names, genus, phylum, species.

"Mademoiselle has a fine eye for flowers," Jacqueline says to Maureen, echoing Franny's old construction in French class. "Mademoiselle was wise to marry an engineer because now there is someone contributing to the gene pool who knows the difference between a wrench and a screwdriver."

It is common for twins, especially if they share the same crib, to develop their own private language. We are quadruplets, sharing a vocabulary of catchwords and references known only to us, which, when we communicate with each other in our maddeningly low voices, evoke reactions so excessive that others often feel infuriated, left out, stranded on the shore.

For a while now, as an antidote to the burden of all those years with Raymond, we have had a glad-tidings policy in our dealings with each other.

The most minuscule event is greeted with whoops of joy. Jacqueline was recently taken out to lunch by her boss, and she had scallops. Maureen *might* get a new shower door. Christina's son's band has been asked to play at some girl's sweet sixteen party. "Good news," she says. "The Afflicted have a gig."

"Since when," Jacqueline wants to know, "in the history of humankind have the afflicted not had a gig?"

We often think about what our children will do with their lives. They are no longer babies picking flowers off our dresses. We applauded when they sang the Earth Day rap at their crunchy elementary schools. We went on the field trips to the Egyptian section of museums for a scavenger hunt: Find a sarcophagus, find Horus, find an ankh. We sat through *The Mikado* and *The Snow Queen* as well as the usual assortment of swim meets and track events and painful piano recitals in which each note came out encased in concrete. We hosted mud football birthday parties, which are exactly what they sound like. To my children and their friends, John Fitzgerald Kennedy is the good-looking president, the one to whom that famous girl with cleavage, Marilyn Monroe, sang a sultry version of "Happy Birthday" in Madison Square Garden. JFK was for civil rights and for men on the moon, and he had a showdown with Cuba that almost ended the world. The schools that bear his name are called Jail for Kids, an accident of initials that makes every child who makes the joke feel unusually clever.

Feeling shockingly old, we watched as they labored over term papers about the Beatles: *term papers* entitled "Eleanor Rigby as Antihero" and "Assonance in 'Lucy in the Sky with Diamonds.'"

We've seen some of them through acne and first loves. We've supervised projects in which they've created three-dimensional models of cells out of candy, with jawbreakers for the nucleus, trying not to say what we're thinking: *You won't need science. We never did*. We sold tickets to and sat through a community theater production of *Annie* for two weekends in a row. We went

on that awful ride at Disney, the one with the song about how
it's a small world, after all. Two of the children drive already and
are old enough to kill people in a war. The oldest is at Trinity
College in Hartford majoring in English and economics; the next
is off to Wesleyan to play soccer and study French and film.
The others hope to become an English professor, a doctor, a
psychoanalyst with a side business writing children's literature
(or maybe just own a coffee shop on Martha's Vineyard), and
the baby of the bunch would like to grow up to be someone
who invents video games.

We worried, of course, about what would happen to our mother
after Raymond died.

At the beginning, she seemed disoriented, without a foot-
hold. That first summer, she would sometimes sit out in the yard,
turning her face toward the sun, as if to welcome its gentle touch.
We would be gathered, the rest of the children, a couple at a
time, and she would commence her daily dose of listening in on
the conversation of others while pretending not to. She also could
have been a reporter, with her odd conviction that information
is more interesting when obtained in a roundabout way.

Maybe she'd like some butterscotch candies, or some hore-
hound drops, we would say. Some boxed cards from one of the
museums. A trip to Watch Hill for some clear clam chowder.

She would suddenly stir, having heard it all.

"What do you think I am? A trinket monger? An easy mark
for the innocent treat?"

This was the summer in which Clinton had to own up to
having had sex with *that woman*. The DNA in Monica Lewinsky's
dress from the Gap was being examined. At one point the government engaged in a flurry of firepower avenging some international incident against some embassy somewhere as an obvious

distraction from the circus. This oddball moment in American history had the remarkable effect of breaking down all those years of our mother's prudish reserve.

"Oh," she said, bored. "That Clinton. He just doesn't want us to think about his semen."

We were now a family without Major Scenes. The histrionics of the days with Raymond were gone. This latter-day docility was almost as disconcerting.

We knew she had successfully crossed over to the other side of the bridge when she resumed her old laments, the ones that sustain the crankiness that keeps the blood circulating. She recently observed a communication from my son's school about the proper attire for his high school graduation: "Boys should wear suits, or a suit jacket and tie, and girls should wear modest white dresses with slips." She sniffed when she read it: "In my day, you never would have had to specify the modest or the slips, but at least they're trying. At least there are still some scraps of protocol floating around in this very untidy world." In her late eighties, she still smokes, she eats red meat, and she fails to see the sin in a touch of wine in the evening, just a touch.

She still thinks about her own funeral and hopes that in any service to mark her passing, propriety is as important as pomp.

"No guitars. If someone wants to sing, fine, as long as it's in Latin."

Jacqueline pretends to be taking down her requests, scrawling without a pen on an invisible pad.

"No guitars."

"No kiss of peace."

"Banned: the kiss of peace."

"Those handshakes and hugs between strangers, so typical of today's world. No one gives a hoot about formality."

"Hideous."

"As for music, wasn't it St. Augustine who said that when you sing in church, you pray twice? However, I am certain he was not referring to folk songs. What he had in mind was something rich and classical, like 'Ave Maria.'"

"In Latin?"

"Naturally. And, who knows, maybe someone could also sing 'Beautiful Dreamer' or 'The Rose of Tralee.' What's wrong with both?"

"I don't know, Mom. You're not the type for a hootenanny."

"Good point. Jacqueline, when you were little, you used to be so airy-fairy, but now I'd say you have a head on your shoulders. Also, no tributes. I can't stand the idea of my personal affairs being alluded to in public for even a moment."

"We'll pretend we never heard of you."

"Afterwards, a small gathering of the old gang would be fine. What's left of it. You can always serve a decent sherry. Harvey's. Now, I know what you're thinking. This is a funeral. It would be disrespectful to turn it into a picnic. But we're Irish, and technically, after a long life, it can be both."

Finally, for a woman who prides herself on her lack of practicality, she sometimes startles us with odd outbursts of efficiency. "I don't care if I'm cremated. I understand that's more practical and the Church permits it now, but I want a proper burial, and I don't want to be stuck away in the corner of someone's closet."

Don't worry, we assured her, we'll take care of your cremains.

"Cremains? What kind of word is that?"

It's made up, like brunch.

"Brunch? I didn't say a word about brunch."

Zoomie, zoomie, zoomie, zoomie, zoom.

As children in Granby, we used to love to watch *The Wizard of Oz*. It was like *Gone with the Wind*, one of the few movies we got to see more than once during the pre-video age, when the theatrical rerelease of classics was a rare and widely heralded treat.

But we always had to contend with the fresh disappointment that the Wizard was really just a funny little man with smoke and mirrors.

We were coming home one night from seeing the movie in Holyoke, gliding along Route 202 in our mother's hearse-sized Nash Rambler, out of sorts from the empty feeling brought on by the curtain falling and the uneasy truce between the mix of buttery popcorn and Junior Mints in our stomachs. We passed the Green Pine Dairy on our left, the dubious motel on our right, sailed through Five Corners, past Dressel's and the Hilltop Nook.

We jabbed each other with loose elbows, and at one point Michael threatened to open the door of the moving vehicle and jump out if we didn't leave him alone. We had teased him, three simple syllables, a galvanic response: "Toto's dead."

Next came the usual melange of comments whose exact authors are now lost to me.

"I'm so mad at that dumb Wizard."

"He tricked people into thinking he could do more than he could."

"Why couldn't he really be magic?"

"Why couldn't he be someone special?"

At the wheel of the car, our mother resisted the urge to take her eyes off the road.

"Settle down, children."

We kept poking and pulling and kicking.

She lit her second cigarette of the short trip.

"I said settle down. In the end he did what he could. He was a good man. His only real mistake was that he was in over his head."

We amble, my sisters and I, over to the cottage we rent for our mother every summer at Groton Long Point, the place where my uncle owned a house for a time when he was trying to churn out those archetypal experiences of childhood happiness for us: salt air, bracing dips, the freedom to be yourself around the sea. The cottage our mother stays in now is a weather-beaten throwback to the days when cottages really were cottages, with mismatched dishes and sagging wicker chairs and decks of cards buttery from years of overuse and worse-than-mediocre paintings of boats in all kinds of weather. It is a summertime cliché, as predictable as peeling skin, melting ice cream, and hot sand.

While at the cottage, one of us spies an old edition of Trivial Pursuit and starts to riffle through the cards, testing each other with a few sample questions about the fuel capacity of Air Force One and the year in which the League of Nations was formed. The usual blather about wars and treaties, popes and kings, ball games and endgames.

We all agree: they (that amorphous majority called they) should create a Trivial Pursuit just for females. We even come up with possible names for the game. How about Ovarian Oddities or Second Sex Sundries? The questions would be ones that women should be reasonably expected to answer. Quick: What's the difference between baking powder and baking soda? Which is more flattering on most female figures: dirndls or skirts cut on the bias? To the best of your ability imitate the ululation of the women during the Battle of Algiers. How many moons does Jupiter have? Jacqueline's was my favorite: "What lucky lady from Smith College had a guest editorship at *Mademoiselle* magazine during the summer in which the Rosenbergs were electrocuted?"

"Maybe," she says, "the game should just be for our family. What did the teabags that Mom's thrifty friend used to hang on the clothesline resemble? Which tragedy breaks a man, the first or the second? Who are the worst drivers? Recite the last line of *Riders to the Sea*. Did Ronald Reagan ever make a good movie?"

It is hot out and we decide there is no cure for it other than a bold dip in the ocean.

On our walk to Main Beach, we pass small children equipped with string and buckets, wielding rocks in order to smash mussels as bait for crabs. It is a sunny day, but there was a tropical storm a few days before, not a hurricane but its rip-roaring, wind-belching, branch-breaking understudy, in which at least one cottage lost its deck and a large uprooted tree gashed a roof in half. There is an extra layer of stuff on the beach that must have washed overboard from boats during the rains. A dish towel, a single oar, an empty mayonnaise jar. The beach is also, as usual, littered with itself, seaweed and driftwood, smelling of salt and of rotting vegetation. "Free aromatherapy," says Jacqueline. "Do you realize how much this would cost at the mall?"

We head toward the second, less crowded, entrance at Main Beach.

"Do you think Mary Cassatt would want to paint us?" says Jacqueline, less a question than a preposterous wish. The raft out in the distance—a swaying gray square—hosts its usual guests, several perfect teenage bodies, boys and girls, sunning themselves. Despite the best efforts of deep thinkers to find deep meaning, sometimes a raft is just a raft.

"Dream on, Play Jay," we say.

"I've been thinking," she says.

"Uh-oh," I say, unable to resist the old forms, "that must be quite a strain."

I am ignored, most regally.

"Those encyclopedias Raymond used to sell. Well, at least it wasn't Bibles out of a suitcase. Maybe we were all too harsh. Maybe Mom was right: he was ahead of his time."

We have no idea what she's driving at.

"And those wooden spools that he thought would make good candlesticks? There's an element of Martha Stewart to it, of Cute Country Living."

"What do you mean by that?" I ask, impatient.

"You take some useless gewgaw from a defunct factory, paint it an historic Williamsburg color, and sell it for twenty times what you put into it, creating a market for, how does that saying go? You taught it to me, a market for something people don't need and never really knew they wanted."

In the water out by the raft some children are yelling, "Marco! Polo!" Their voices have a disembodied musicality canceled out by the squawks of the ducks.

"And all his collectibles, like the bicycle plates with out-of-date names? Remember them?"

We nod.

"And how about the Moxie thermometer, the old commercial signs with peeling paint, the Pepsi glasses? Well, ever hear of *Antiques Roadshow*?"

Some gulls swoop down, competing for the spillage from a box of Cracker Jacks.

"But this is my favorite. This is the best. This proves my point beyond dispute. Remember the International Book Search?"

"Of course I do," I say. "I'll never forget the letters with twisted syntax from sincere professors from foreign countries putting their faith in his promise to find . . ."

Christina and Maureen join in: "Any book, anywhere, anytime!"

"Think about it," says Jacqueline. "Does that sound familiar? Does that sound like one of those new online companies?" She stops in her tracks, arms akimbo, "Like Alibris.com or what?"

Silence.

"Maddy," says Christina, "why aren't you saying something?"

"I'm quietly agreeing."

"There are some people," says Jacqueline, tossing me a look, "who give their best compliments simply by ceasing to be critical."

"Touché, Jay," say the other two at once.

"Traitors," I mutter. "Crack, crack, dig, dig." I should have treated them more harshly when they were young, like the Oldest Sister I heard of who used to feed her siblings raw hamburger because she liked to pretend to be a lion tamer.

We have thrown our towels on the sand and are at the edge of the water now, poised for first the slap, then the caress.

"One more thing, not about Ray," says Jacqueline. She looks up at the sky, squinting. "Dare I say it? Yes, I do. I dare. If I'm not mistaken, the sky today is the color of . . ."

She pauses.

"Of what?" we ask, smiling, suspecting that the answer will be something that winks at us across the vale of time. We are bonded by blood and by our family language, by all our old slogans and sayings.

"Lapis lazuli." She thrusts two thumbs up.

I stare at her, amazed. "You must have been waiting forty years to use that word in a casual context."

"I have," she says, "and that's too long. How's about a little Tennyson while we're at it?"

All of us begin reciting in unison as we move toward the edge of the beach:

> She left the web, she left the loom,
> She made three paces thro' the room,
> She saw the water lily bloom,
> She saw the helmet and the plume,
> She looked down to Camelot.

Then we propel forward, flinging ourselves into the Long Island Sound, relishing its welcoming embrace, liquid and primitive; such a comfort, such a return. We each swim a few spirited strokes and then, together, we float, and for a sliver of a second, we are light again, light at last, light like long ago.

Epilogue

"NEVER WRITE THE ENDING OF THE STORY," IS THE ADVICE MY MOTHER-in-law the psychoanalyst always gives her patients when they assume the fix is in, when they fool themselves into thinking they have finally figured it all out.

I saw for myself the wisdom of these words when I realized that a book like this is never truly finished, that I am forever coming up with new twigs to add to the nest. And it's not just me, but also the members of my family who keep saying, "You didn't mention the time when . . ." But a memoir, though it records the past, is nearly the opposite of a historical record in any official sense. It is merely one individual's admittedly flawed version.

The question I hear most when people outside the family find out I've written a memoir: "How did they react?"

The answer is simple:

In character.

Jacqueline could not have more helpful, to the point of offering to copy edit the entire proceedings. She did allow that she was pleased to see she got a starring role and that maybe it was long overdue.

Christina had the most misgivings and said that she could happily live with what was in the book already, but she would be just as happy if I refrained from writing one more word about her, her family, and her life.

Maureen said it made her feel wistful that she came across as so quiet, but she felt it was true to her persona, at least as a child. At the same time, she was glad to see that her garden got the salute she feels that it deserves.

Michael said I was wrong about my initial estimate of the price we got for the house at 5 Center Street when it sold in 1975. "Sixty K, not forty." And that I also had the wrong name for the group singing "We Gotta Get Out of This Place." He corrected it to the Animals, and said it showed once again how out of it I was during the heyday of rock 'n' roll. He pointed out, with some glee, that I had misused the conditional tense, not once but twice. What is more delicious than correcting a know-it-all? And he said that he was not certain I had captured just how old-fashioned our mother's childhood had been, how nearly Edwardian, what a leap it must be for her to have lived long enough to see the world transform on the scale it has, to go from antimacassars to spandex, from songs with refrains like "I don't want to play in your yard" to ones about how "if it weren't for date rape, I'd never get laid." As for Raymond, Michael said I failed to point out how in his early twenties he seemed to have aged overnight, and how hard that must have been for him. And, he added, "He knew I loved him because I told him so on the porch at mother's cottage the summer before he died."

My mother's reaction was the most complicated. The words stirred up those old bedeviling feelings of ambivalence. Here was something to be proud of, here was something to keep hidden. She said she was glad to have read the manuscript because now she wouldn't have to read it again. Yet later she surprised me by saying that if there were a movie, she didn't want Katharine Hepburn playing her. I asked her what could possibly be wrong with Katharine Hepburn, Miss High Cheekbones, Miss Intelligent from Connecticut, Miss Here for the Long Haul?

My mother looked at me as if I were slower than the slowest pupil from Ursuline to ever enter her orbit.

Her tone was patient yet final. It reeked with dignity and noblesse oblige.

"Please keep in mind that Katharine Hepburn is older than I am."

Thanks to my mother's long memory and uncanny eye for detail, I was already able to correct many small errors of fact, but some of my mother's other objections I saved until now because I thought they deserved their own spotlight.

The most significant involved Raymond. She said that I had painted a not entirely fair picture. She said there were times when I was off in Miami that Raymond did successfully run several produce stands. "He went to the Farmer's Market in Springfield, very early in the morning, and picked out the best stuff, and he knew how to do it. He became acquainted with several of the old-timers and he learned a lot from them. He was friendly with several Hadley farmers for whom he had an enormous amount of respect. You can put that in. And now you can put this in: they in turn respected him. One of them was the son, or could have been the grandson, of the farmer whom Calvin Coolidge chose to ship fresh corn to the White House. One time one of the farmers loaned Ray a thousand dollars on a handshake because he was in a bind, and Ray paid it back. The farmer trusted him, and you know how those Polish farmers are. They can be pretty flinty. He used to tell me about these things after they happened, and that's how I know about them."

Some of the changes she suggested might seem trifling, but not to her. For instance, she could not believe that on those long-ago trips to New York City, I was so muzzy-headed as to report that we actually ate *dinner* at Horn & Hardart's. "Only lunch or dessert. Dinner was at Stouffer's or the hotel." As far as my description of her as a woman whose tongue could be sharper than the lid on a freshly opened can of tuna, she wrote in the margins, "This isn't *me*. Or is it?"

She also said that my statement about how everything was better in Ireland—the priests, the tea, the trout—was flat-out inaccurate. "No one thinks the priests are better." When I reported my father had left very little insurance, she wrote NOT TRUE: "He left a good estate considering his age, but not big enough for the long years ahead." She urged me at a couple of junctures to "stop knocking Catholicism" and she said that I was wrong to say I prayed to St. Anthony to help locate lost objects. "Catholics *turn* to saints to intercede with their intentions, but they *pray* to the Trinity." And my reference to limbo as the refuge of unbaptized babies and well-intended heathens was outdated. The Church no longer teaches that doctrine.

She agreed that Christina was pretty as a child, but "so were the rest of you. Please change. Do you think I want to be remembered as the mother of three plain girls and one pretty one?"

As for the conversation in which she compared herself to the Kennedy women, she wrote, "I suppose you want to use this but I can't imagine I said this."

I turned to Jacqueline for corroboration.

"Not only did she say it—she said it all the time."

She even rankled at the passing reference to powdered milk. "Don't you remember? We had fresh cold milk. In quart bottles. Delivered daily."

We did, in the fifties. The powdered stuff was the sixties.

Some points, however, are not worth the fight, and I am willing to concede that perhaps my memory of thin blue luke-warm milk served in pitchers with an inevitable sediment cling-ing to the bottom is just a silly fiction. In fact, if anyone asks, I'm going to say what I now believe to be the truth. Not only was every morning of the Blais children's childhood awash with sunlight and optimism, but we also enjoyed *crème fraîche* and ripe strawberries with our Wheaties, even in the dead of winter.

Acknowledgments

As always, first and foremost, I'd like to thank my husband, John Katzenbach.

My agent, Esther Newberg, deserves her reputation as a wise and wonderful woman.

Morgan Entrekin runs a great shop, and Brendan Cahill is a fine editor.

I live in a part of the country that is chockablock with great colleges, and the following people were kind enough to share their resources: Tom Riddell and Holly Davis at Smith College; Lee Edwards, Jay Neugeboren, and Peggy O'Brien at the University of Massachusetts; Susan Snively at Amherst College; Mary Russo at Hampshire College; and Mary Jo Salter at Mt. Holyoke College, who served as poetry consultant. Students, former and current, can often be a source of inspiration, and I'd like to acknowledge Jodi Butler, Carla Costa, Harmony Desmond, Caledonia Kearns, Nan Klingener, Brian Mooney, Patty Norris-Lubold, Aaron Saykin, Shiela Seiler, Brooke Steinberg, and Andrea Ung among many others. I hope the organizers of writers conferences in Aspen, Key West, and Florida International University at Seaside, Florida will accept my gratitude for including me on their faculty from time to time. Certain small portions of this work appeared in somewhat altered form in *The Washington Post*, *The Miami Herald*, and *Newsday* and I would like to thank the editors at those publications for their early encouragement. I would also like to recognize the contributions of Ann Banks, Lynne Barrett, Marjorie Klien, Athelia Knight, Anne O'Brien, Geneva Overholser, Megan Rosenfeld, Julie Stanton, Ted Lawler, and Sharon White.

Finally, as my mother pointed out more than once, my sister Jacqueline deserves a special mention. Here it is.